MACINTOSH HYPERMEDIA

VOLUME I

Reference Guide

MACINTOSH HYPERMEDIA

VOLUME I

Reference Guide

Michael Fraase

Scott, Foresman and Company
Glenview, Illinois London

Library of Congress Cataloging-in-Publication Data
Fraase, Michael.
Macintosh hypermedia/by Michael Fraase.
p. cm.
Includes bibliographical references.
Contents: v. 1. Reference guide.
1. Macintosh (Computer)—Programming. 2. Hypertext systems.
I. Title
QA76.8.M3F73 1989 89-10347
005.265—dc20 CIP

1 2 3 4 5 MUR 94 93 92 91 90 89

ISBN 0-673-38791-7

Printed in the United States of America.

Notice of Liability

The information in this book is distributed on an "As Is" basis, without warranty. Neither the author nor Scott, Foresman and Company shall have any liability to customer or any other person or entity with respect to any liability, loss, or damage caused or alleged to be caused directly or indirectly by the programs contained herein. This includes, but is not limited to, interruption of service, loss of data, loss of business or anticipatory profits, or consequential damages from the use of the programs.

Scott, Foresman professional books are available for bulk sales at quantity discounts. For information, please contact Marketing Manager, Professional Books Group, Scott, Foresman and Company, 1900 East Lake Avenue, Glenview, IL 60025.

TRADEMARK CREDITS

All terms mentioned in this work that are known to be trademarks or service marks are listed below. In addition, terms suspected of being trademarks or service marks have been appropriately capitalized. Use of a term in this work should not be regarded as affecting the validity of any trademark or service mark.

4th Dimension is a trademark of ACIUS.

Acta, Acta Advantage, and HyperDA are trademarks of Symmetry Corporation.

AffiniFile is a trademark of Affinity Microsystems Ltd.

Apple, the Apple Logo, HyperCard, ImageWriter, and LaserWriter are registered trademarks of Apple Computer, Inc.

ArchiText is a trademark of Brainpower, Inc.

Arts & Farces Review, FarceFilm, and the Arts & Farces logo are trademarks of Arts & Farces Video & Information Services.

Augment and Tymshare are trademarks of McDonnell-Douglas Corporation.

CompuServe is a registered trademark of CompuServe Information Services, an H&R Block Company.

GEnie is a trademark of General Electric Information Services, Inc.

GOfer is a trademark of Microlytics, Inc.

Guide, Guidance, and Envelope are trademarks of OWL International, Inc.

HyperGate is a trademark of Eastgate Systems, Inc.

IBM PS/2, OS/2, and Presentation Manager are registered trademarks of International Business Machines Corporation.

Macintosh, Macintosh Plus, Macintosh SE, Macintosh II, HyperTalk, Finder, MultiFinder, and Stackware are trademarks of Apple Computer, Inc.

MacPaint, MacDraw, and MacWrite are registered trademarks of Claris Corporation.

MacRecorder and ScreenRecorder are trademarks of Farallon Computing, Inc.

MicroFilm and μFilm are trademarks of Buck Wheat & Associates, Inc.

Microsoft Word is a trademark of Microsoft Corporation.

Notecards is a trademark of Xerox Corporation.

PageMaker is a trademark of Aldus Corporation.

QuickMail is a trademark of CE Software, Inc.

Dedication

To my wife, Karen . . .

And to Jim Klee, Mike Arons, Henry Moore, and Tiparet Schumrum for insisting that I think . . .

Acknowledgments

I would like to acknowledge contributions from the following. Somewhere along the line they each made a difference:

Jerry Daniels
Amy Davis and the staff of Scott, Foresman and Company
Bill Gladstone
Mary Jane Mara
Holly Rifkind and the staff of Interface Studio
Mark Veljkov

PREFACE

Let's get something straight. Contrary to a closely held belief by many, Apple Computer, Inc., did not invent—nor even discover—hypermedia. In fact, the initial concepts and underlying foundation of hypermedia were firmly in place before either of Apple's cofounders, the Steves Wozniak and Jobs were even a glimmer in either of their respective father's eye. Apple may, however, go down in history as providing the spark that set off the paradigm shift that subsequently launched the widespread acceptance of hypermedia as an effective new communications medium. Ironically, neither Steve will be credited with this next step in Apple's legacy. Although the later Steve, Steve Jobs, and his current endeavor, NeXT, Inc., are known to have some hypermedia tricks up their collective sleeve.

A paradigm shift occurs when, suddenly, a new perspective is gained on an old problem. A solution to a problem unexpectedly, almost painfully, becomes obvious just because someone had the audacity to look at the problem from a different angle.

Paradigm shift, as phenomena as well as nomenclature, is nothing new. My first exposure to the concept was through Marilyn Ferguson's *The Aquarian Conspiracy,*[1] which I used as a textbook when I was practicing to be a college instructor. Ferguson attributes the term to Thomas Kuhn's 1962 book, *The Structure of Scientific Revolutions.*[2] Like I said, nothing new.

Apple has been a participant in the only two personal computer paradigm shifts to date that I'm aware of: first, the introduction and subsequent success of the Apple II; and second, the Macintosh. Both of these products acted as catalysts to drastically change our perception of what a computer is. There were personal computers before the Apple II, and there were predecessors to Macintosh, but none of these provoked a true paradigm shift.

Macintosh changed forever the way we think of computers. Never before had a machine seemed so inviting, so intimate, so nonthreatening, so much *fun.* Many Macintosh owners developed relationships with the computer that could only be called symbiotic. We dressed our Macintoshes up with fancy paint jobs, began referring to it by name (or at least by the generic ''Mac''), and, according to most studies, began to spend an inordinate amount of time with it.

With Apple's introduction of HyperCard in August of 1987, described and subsequently marketed alternatively as a software construction kit and an information manager, the company poised itself for participation in its third paradigm shift. This third paradigm shift—the move from flat, two-dimensional documents to third- and even fourth-dimensional electronic documents—may very well prove to be as important a shift as the introduction and acceptance of the personal computer. As the Apple II and, later, the Macintosh changed the way we thought about what a computer is, HyperCard and other hypermedia products will serve to show us a new way of thinking about what a computer is *for.*

While Apple has been very careful not to use the "h" word in its marketing of HyperCard, it has continually alluded to it between the lines. The product, for instance, was known during its development cycle as "WildCard." Apple discovered that the name was already in use by a New York–based computer peripheral maker who manufactured a hardware device capable of removing copy-protection from some Apple II software. Apple apparently decided not to license the name—as they initially did with the Macintosh itself[3]—for unknown reasons, and magically chose the "h" word as a prefix for their latest software progeny.

This book, while covering HyperCard, will not focus specifically on Apple's product. Additionally, it will cover other Macintosh-specific hypermedia development and production tools, as well as provide a general background and overview of hypertext and Macintosh hypermedia.

A companion to this title, *Development Tools For HyperCard,* will follow quickly on the heels of this book and will deal specifically with HyperCard and the hypermedia development process. It is not my intention to give HyperCard, its development team, or Apple's marketing efforts short shrift; HyperCard is a valuable hypermedia tool. It's just that it's not the only one and will hopefully mature into an even more valuable implement as well as spawn generations of future hypermedia tools that contain the seed of HyperCard. Just as Bill Atkinson's MacPaint was not the final word on Macintosh paint programs, his HyperCard will not be the final word on Macintosh hypermedia. It will, however, forever change the way we view nonlinear thought, writing, and drawing. Let's hear it for the right-brainers.

Hypermedia is a direct descendant of hypertext, a term attributed to Ted Nelson more than 20 years ago to describe nonlinear writing. Today the terms are used almost interchangeably, the exception being that hypermedia includes hypertext, but not vice versa. Where hypertext generally focuses on text and static graphic representations, hypermedia pushes the envelope to include sound and music, animation, and full-motion video, as well as the more familiar text and graphics. The end result is a document—and more importantly, a body of linked, interwoven documents—designed to be displayed and perused on a computer screen, rather than as ink on paper. Or, to borrow another term from Nelson, the document is a series of interconnected materials that are "deeply intertwingled."

OK, so this work is not going to focus specifically on HyperCard. Why, then, is the book specifically about *Macintosh* hypermedia? I use a Macintosh on an average of more than ten hours a day, every day. I know it in the sense that it has become a familiar friend. Its graphical interface—now the object of other computer manufacturer's desires—is currently without parallel for hypermedia. Or at least for hypermedia production that's within reach of the individual. Most of us simply can't afford a UNIX workstation running a highly specialized—make that myopic—hypermedia environment on a network. Many of us, however, can afford a new or used Macintosh Plus and a hard drive. Macintosh hypermedia production tools (the software that lets you create hypermedia documents) are all available for under $500 and the most popular—HyperCard—is either free or less than $50 depending on when you bought your Mac and how good your relationship with your dealer is.

The other major reason why this book focuses specifically on Macintosh hypermedia systems is because of the inherent approachability of the Macintosh. Many among us remain computerphobes. As the Macintosh helped loosen the white-knuckled grip on the driving wheel of those adamantly opposed to using computers on any level, so, too, will hypermedia massage free a few more fingers—and, hopefully, more than a few minds.

Kirkpatrick Sale[4] points out that in terms of translating energy into transportation, there is nothing, neither animal nor machine, that is superior to a human being on a bicycle (0.12 calories per gram per kilometer). As the bicycle was reaching its peak in popularity, along came the Model T to quickly displace it. Sale goes on to point out that the mouse is the least efficient at translating energy into transportation (60 calories per gram per kilometer), barely edging out, ironically, the lemming (42 calories per gram per kilometer).

Consider Macintosh as a bicycle (I won't name any lemmings). In fact, one of the proposed names for Macintosh during its development was, in fact, Bicycle. Efficient. Sleek. Appropriate. If the Macintosh is a bicycle for the mind, then hypermedia can be seen as the pedals—also elegant, efficient, and appropriate. We're still working on sleek.

Perhaps the most interesting phenomenon surrounding Apple and the current state of hypermedia is that at the same time that Apple has pledged to chase after corporate America it releases a tool that specifically empowers the individual. Don't get me wrong. HyperCard is being used extensively in corporate situations, and that will be covered within these pages, but there appears to be something of a dichotomy between what the right and left hands of Apple are doing.

Hypermedia already is having a significant impact on knowledge workers. As we become more and more inundated with information, our skills in sorting that information and creating effective, usable linkages between bits of information will empower us in our jobs as well as in our daily lives. I see some distinct parallels between hypermedia production and video production, not the least of which is the mystification of the medium by the "insiders." Hypermedia is new enough so that no priesthood yet exists, and the Macintosh environment is nonbureaucratic enough to warrant participation on the individual level and to preclude the formation of any such secret order. We're all on the road to find out. And we're all starting at the same level from our individual knowledge bases.

This book will cover a variety of aspects of hypermedia, ranging from its history and underlying concepts—springing as it did from the seminal mind of Vannevar Bush more than 40 years ago—to its social ramifications and current implementations on the Macintosh. I'll also examine the new hardware technologies that impact the creation of hypermedia: CD-ROM and other optical media, as well as the more traditional forms of distribution media in their current and near-future incarnations. I also will take a peek at the future of hypermedia, but at this early stage one of the truly wondrous aspects of the medium is that your crystal ball has the potential of being as clear—or clearer—than mine is.

If you use any form of writing tool in your daily existence, you're familiar—consciously or unconsciously—with the concept of hypertext. If you scribble notes on a napkin at lunch, you use hypertext. If you draw diagrams to represent ideas or make outlines for presentations, you'll be on familiar ground with hypertext. If you see underlying patterns and connections in the work you do, hypermedia could prove to be a very empowering tool for you. If you find yourself, from time to time, daydreaming or thinking in a nonlinear manner, worry not. You have the earmark of a fine hypermediacian.

Michael Fraase
St. Paul, Minnesota
October, 1988

NOTES

[1] Marilyn Ferguson, *The Aquarian Conspiracy* (Los Angeles: J. P. Tarcher, Inc., 1980).

[2] Source not available. Not cited in original work.

[3] The name ''Macintosh'' was originally licensed from McIntosh Labs, a maker of high-end audio equipment.

[4] Kirkpatrick Sale, *Human Scale* (New York: Coward, McCann & Geoghegan, 1980).

TABLE OF CONTENTS

INTRODUCTION

- *Introduction and Overview*
- *The Problem*
- *The Purpose of this Book*
- *Why I Wrote this Book*
- *Introduction to the Concepts of Hypermedia*
- *Conventions Used in this Book*

Introduction and Overview

The concept of hypertext, and its more recent hypermedia branchings, have not changed much since first envisioned by Vannevar Bush in 1945.[5] It has taken this long for both the hardware and software to catch up. Now, with the introduction of the Macintosh hypermedia software tools such as OWL International's Guide and Apple's HyperCard, we have the beginnings of nothing short of a paradigm shift in the way we deal with data, information, and knowledge.

These software tools, however, are only half of the complete hypermedia solution; to be really useful, they require appropriate hardware that is only now beginning to appear. Apple's recent introduction of a CD-ROM drive[6] targeted for the mass market signals the first acknowledgment by a major computer manufacturer of this vast opportunity to reshape the way individuals work with overwhelming amounts of data and information and, in turn, refine that raw data and information into useful knowledge tools.

The availability of appropriate hardware and software solutions for the Macintosh community leaves only a single stumbling block to overcome—a somewhat typical chicken-and-egg dilemma. Few CD-ROM titles will be available, and most will be of questionable quality and innovation, until a terminal mass in unit sales of the CD-ROM drives themselves is reached. Conversely, few CD-ROM drives will be sold until unique and plentiful titles are available. This is at least partially addressed by Apple's entry into the CD-ROM drive market with a reasonably priced unit that is sure to appeal to a broad base of users.

The foreseeable CD-ROM products, however, can at best be termed first generation and as few as two years from now will be seen as terribly obsolete. CD-ROM is a read-only storage medium (it's only half-literate; it can't write), and as Ted Nelson said, "... a read-only medium in this day and age [is] intrinsically oppressive."[7] For this reason, CD-ROM will not play an equal role (relative to the hypermedia software tools) in the work proposed here; it will be surveyed, along with other mass-storage devices as guideposts to future incarnations of more appropriate hardware.

The Problem

As we move from a product-based economy, exemplified by overconsumption of nonrenewable resources, to an economy based largely on intangibles, we will all undergo some serious stress. As we collectively make this shift between the tangible and the intangible, we will be confronted with the regenerative nature of the new intangibles: information, data, and knowledge. We will all be confronted in our daily lives with access to literally mountains of data. Many of us will be at a loss as to how to navigate this unfamiliar territory, although some of us will strive to transform raw data and information into useful knowledge. While it's likely that we all may be offered access to the tools, most of us will not have the navigational skills and deep pockets required to make use of these wondrous implements.

Worst of all, few of us are even aware of the problem, let alone of the possible solutions in the form of navigational aids.

This book will identify the problems we all will face with the influx of data and information and will provide an overview of the hypermedia navigational tools available now as well as those on the near horizon. It also will investigate the transformation process, from raw information to useful knowledge—a renewable-resource-to-renewable/regenerative-resource process rather than the nonrenewable-resource-to-product process of the era we're now leaving.

Perhaps hypermedia is most appropriately perceived as a knowledge trans-escalator. It carries us not only up and down the mountain of information available to us, but transversely as well. A nostalgic rather than futuristic image comes to me as I write this—one of my great-grandfather's study lined with books. He had a small ladder on wheels to navigate the upper reaches of his library, and he could climb up or down pretty well, but he had to climb all the way down the ladder to transverse the library. And the ladder was "hard-wired" to the library shelves; it couldn't be moved to access other libraries. I can't help but think of his reaction to these new information navigators that we have at our fingertips. The potential for the mass customization of information using these knowledge transescalators and the subsequent distillation of that information into knowledge boggles the mind.

The Purpose of this Book

There must be close to 20 HyperCard books on the market as I write this, with more on the way. Yet, no one has adequately addressed the foundation on which this marvelous product is based; nor has anyone discussed in anything other than the most cursory of manners the underlying concepts of hypermedia.

Many people mistakenly believe that hypermedia's roots begin with HyperCard. While HyperCard advanced the concept by putting the power of a rudimentary hypermedia production and browsing system in the hands of everyone, Apple has been remiss in its refusal to recognize significant advances that came before the mid-1980s.

Hypermedia's underlying precept—the interlinking of nonlinear information and information structures—dates back to the mid-1940s. Of course, in the 1940s we didn't have computers, but we did have a state-of-the-art information storage and retrieval device: the microfilm.

Vannevar Bush's ground-breaking noodling that started all of this was embodied in an article, "As We May Think,"[8] published in the August, 1945, issue of *The Atlantic Monthly,* and proposed a device based on the then-state-of-the-art microfilm technology called a "memex." Bush's concept of the memex machine led to Douglas Engelbart's work, culminating in the ideas, further developed by others to create what we now recognize as word processing, outline processing, the mouse, windows, electronic mail, and networks. Engelbart referred to the general body of his work as "The Augmentation of the Human Intellect,"[9] by which he meant the helping of humans to think and work better by giving them more appropriate and better quality tools to work with. The work of both Bush and Engelbart led to Ted Nelson's work, exemplified by *Computer Lib/Dream Machines,*[10] *Literary Machines,*[11] and Project Xanadu.[12] Ted Nelson is credited with introducing the term *hypertext* and continues working on a networked hypermedia system and other knowledge tools. There are many other hypermedia imagineers who have advanced the state of the art of hypermedia, and they also are covered within these pages. They are not mentioned in this introduction because they are not so well known to the hypermedia novice and their contributions are perhaps not so readily recognizable.

Ironically, neither Bush, Engelbart, nor Nelson has produced a viable commercial product. Bellevue, Washington–based OWL International, Inc., successfully marketed the first hypertext system for a microcomputer; their Guide and Envelope products[13] for the Macintosh were followed closely by an IBM PC version of the Guide product. Apple followed two years later with HyperCard,[14] unquestionably the most commercially successful and popular hypermedia system currently available for any microcomputer. Other commercial and noncommercial hypermedia systems have been implemented and they will be covered here as well.

As much as I disliked history and an historical perspective during my formal schooling, I've since come to realize that in order for us to know where we're going—both as individuals and collectively as a society—we must know where we've been. Apple, with its thinly veiled attempts to rewrite history or at least ignore it, is a potentially consequential disservice to the community and we need to recognize those that came before so we can continue to build and move forward.

Why I Wrote this Book

This year marks my tenth year of self-employment. As I pause to look back at my endeavors over the past decade I'm confronted with always having been a little too early on the breaking scene. I began my creative endeavors writing poetry and short stories while in undergraduate school and quickly came to realize that I couldn't *only* write and continue to eat.

I was very fortunate to spend my years of undergraduate and graduate education studying under a handful of very gifted educators and remarkable individuals. I knew, after a brief excursion into it—and surely on some level before—that there was no way that I was going to work within my field of study: humanistic psychology.

While still in graduate school, I began to explore other areas of creative expression that were open to me. At the time (the mid- and late-1970s) independent video production—guerilla television and the video art realm—was beginning to take shape from the miasma of everything that came before: *everything* from the free-speech movement to street theater and beyond. My wife, Karen, and I formed a small independent video production house and pledged to explore the medium in relation to the arts. At that time I also was writing my Master's thesis on the elimination of technology in general, and television in particular, so I felt it was best to have a working knowledge of the beast I was embroiled with.

Before I completed my graduate studies, we got a case of itchy feet and decided we needed to be in a community more conducive to small-scale video production on a cooperative basis. We were living in a small, company-owned college town in the south at the time and had narrowed our choices down to Woodstock, New York, and Minneapolis, Minnesota. Both communities offered a nurturing community for video artists, and we made Minneapolis our choice.

Our fledgling production company, Arts & Farces, bumped along for the next few years, and I had the overwhelming feeling that we were just a little too early and just a little too little. We enjoyed our small successes and lived with the bumps but largely felt we were spinning our wheels.

Infatuated with electronics, I decided that I had to have a character generator to spiff up our productions and avoid the exorbitant studio fees for the titling part of the postproduction process. I looked at everything, quickly got discouraged at the price tags, and naively wandered into a computer dealer and asked if they had anything that could serve my purpose. As it turned out, they had this neat thing that Dick Cavett was advertising at the time, called an Apple II, that I was assured could do all that and more. Of course they didn't bother to tell me that the video output from the Apple was not broadcast quality. I learned that the hard way. Again, too soon and a little too little.[15]

I'll never forget the day I bought the Apple II with a whopping 48K of memory and two—count 'em *two*—143K floppy disk drives. The salesman (they were all men then) asked if I needed any blank disks, and I said that I supposed I did with a sort of glazed look. He asked me how many I needed, and when I found out that they held 143,000 characters *each,* I replied confidently and without hesitation: *One!* I'll never fill all that space. Once again, a little too soon and this time, a lot too little. Now we speak in terms of multiple gigabytes, and like the budget deficit I don't *do* numbers that big.

I began spending more time piddling with the Apple II in concert with the video camera and got my second glimpse of infinity: setting the computer monitor on top of the television monitor and shooting both of them with the video camera (my first glimpse was like everyone else's: the Morton salt box with the picture of the little girl holding the Morton salt box, which in turn held a picture of the little girl . . .). I began experimenting with both mediums and longed to join the two in a tempestuous marriage. During that time I also discovered that I could use the computer to write—and more importantly edit and rewrite—on screen rather than on paper (I didn't buy a printer until two years after I bought the computer and then only for letters with non-computer using correspondents). During that period I also ran into Ted Nelson's *Computer Lib/Dream Machines* and hid it for years, forcing myself to forget about it. I felt I was already riding the wave too far ahead of the crest, and Nelson wasn't even in this dimension let alone the same ocean. I didn't need another distraction.

The Macintosh came out in early 1984, and like everyone else, I had my knickers in a knot after seeing MacPaint. But I was committed to the Apple II, and I knew that given a few weeks, Bill Budge could come up with the same thing on the Apple II and *in color.* He did, but it wasn't the same. By then I was computer-literate and no longer a computerphobe. I dismissed the original (and the second) Macintosh model because it could only handle a ten-page-or-so document—I was looking for an excuse and easily found ten or so. But those graphics and that interface haunted me. I was hooked, I knew it. In 1986, with the introduction of the Macintosh Plus I ran out of excuses and bit the bullet. I changed, and my work changed.

I began reading everything I could find written by this guy, Jerry Daniels. He was dangling even further out than I was, came from a similar hippy-trippy, new-age educational background and was writing about the

Macintosh changing human consciousness. I knew it was happening, but I wasn't about to admit it in public. Daniels was saying it out there in front of God and everybody. Loud even. I also dug out the old Ted Nelson book. I sighed and resigned myself to flying out there on the far edge. But at least I'd have company, and these birds were *really* out there without a net. I assured myself that I'd be safe as long as I stayed just a bit behind these guys.

That same year OWL International released the first hypertext product for a microcomputer, Guide, and it ran on a Macintosh. I remembered the hyper term from reading Nelson and called the company to see if it was the same thing. It was and I ordered a copy on the spot—took a bunch of them to a trade show, demonstrated it and watched in dismay as everyone's eyes glazed.

In January of 1987 I began publishing an electronic magazine, the *Arts & Farces Review,* using the Guide hypertext system. Many of the readers didn't "get" the hypertext concept, but were interested in what I had to say. Many complained that they were always feeling like they were missing something. Interestingly, that remains one of the most difficult hurdles hypermedia must overcome. At any rate I began publishing in the electronic MicroFilm format, using a product designed by Jerry Daniels and published by Buck Wheat and Associates.[16] The MicroFilm product, while not hypermedia, allowed me to publish electronically in a format palatable to most Macintosh users. The singularly most significant thing it did—and continues to do—was to wean the readers from ink on paper. The documents were designed to be read on screen, although they also could be printed out.

In August of 1987, Apple introduced HyperCard at the MacWorld/Boston Expo. I had been fortunate enough to receive prerelease versions from Apple and had two HyperCard products at the expo concurrent with Apple's introduction—both were information and demonstration stacks[17] of products for software companies. Unfortunately, neither product has made it to the market. Sigh. Too soon, *but no longer too little.* And that's the legacy HyperCard promises: empowerment for the individual. We finally managed to get on the horse and ride in the direction it was going. It's exciting, and it's happening now, and nobody is too soon or too little. Come on along.

Introduction to the Concepts of Hypermedia

Like independent video production mentioned previously, hypertext and hypermedia build on a wealth of disciplines that came before them. *Hypertext* was a term coined by Ted Nelson in the mid-1960s to describe the process of creation, storage, and retrieval of nonlinear ideas and information. Nelson attributes the underlying seed of his concept of hypertext to

Vannevar Bush, or, more specifically, to Bush's concept of the ''memex'' proposed in his 1945 *Atlantic Monthly* ''As We May Think'' article.

Bush was working on a ''memex'' system that would allow ''knowledge trails'' to be built through research materials. These trails were pathways connected by links, and Bush's envisioned ''memex'' system would provide a more appropriate way of transmitting and retrieving vast amounts of information. Memex was basically a publishing vehicle that could hold *all* written material and allow *any* user to make ''trails'' in the material.

OK, fine, but what does that mean for me?

Well, let me give you a personal example. While most people view hypertext as an information creation, storage, and retrieval tool, I view hypertext as a ''creative-process-enhancer.''

I recently discovered a creative writing technique known as ''clustering.'' Clustering is the brainchild (as far as I know) of a writing teacher by the name of Gabriele Lusser-Rico. Lusser-Rico, in her book, *Writing the Natural Way,* defines clustering as ''a nonlinear brainstorming process akin to free association. It makes an invisible Design-mind process visible through a nonlinear spilling out of lightning associations that allows patterns to emerge.'' As a nonlinear activity, clustering is well-suited to hypertext.

OK, fine, but what does that mean for me?

Well, consider that report you have to present to your work group next week. You know, the one you ordinarily would begin by developing your ideas in MORE, transferring your outline into Microsoft Word for embellishment, and finally printing out on the LaserWriter for distribution to the group during the meeting.

The very farsighted of you are saying to yourself, ''Ah, but I skip the Microsoft Word and LaserWriter steps and create and display the entire project in MORE, using its slide-show capabilities.''

Consider this: MORE, while a very useful tool, handicaps your creativity by forcing you to work and think hierarchically—albeit without quite so rigid linearity. Also, what do you do in the middle of the meeting when one of the work group members has input that you need to incorporate into your outline? Again, this can be done ''on the fly'' in MORE, but only on a hierarchical and sometimes linear basis.

People don't think linearly. It's not natural. We all think in a nonlinear manner, whether we like to admit it or not. Hypertext and hypermedia allow you to think, design, and display information in a natural, nonlinear manner. Just like we think.

Hypertext generally refers to nonsequential writing. The reader is constantly presented with a series of branches and choices of bits to explore next. The branches and choices are connected via "links" that enable the reader to form "pathways." This branching pathway structure has been contained in systems ranging from the Xerox Palo Alto Research Center "Notecard" system to the Brown University Hypertext system to the Hypertext Abstract Machine at Tektronix to OWL's Guide to Apple's own HyperCard. Hypertext is designed to be read on an interactive computer screen and, in fact, is one of the main components of the mythical (for now, anyway) "paperless office."

Perhaps hypertext can be best thought of as a multidimensional word processor. You enter information into the document as you would with a word processor. But then the fun begins. Say you decide to elaborate on a section. You simply would select the section of text and define the passage of text (or graphic!) as a link to another section of the document; in this case your elaboration. Alternatively, the selected text (or the entire document) can be linked to other text in another document, perhaps even on another computer. As simply as that you can create any number of hyperlinks, comprising a hyperspace, each with different qualities.

Rather than attaching an end note with a graphic of your work group's budget for the next quarter, you can create a hypertext link in the document. This link, when clicked with the mouse (or otherwise activated), displays the group's budget as a pie chart that you imported via the Clipboard from Excel. Or, if need be, it could even open the Excel document and display your graph and underlying data. Additionally, each slice of the pie chart can be linked to further supporting documentation in the form of explanations and embellishments, etc. Like the skin of an onion, the layers of information can be peeled away, without tears, to reveal an intricate labyrinth of information structure.

Nelson takes the original concept of hypertext and extends it one step further and arrives at compound hypertext—where one hypertext "windows" to other materials and is not necessarily limited to computer text and graphics. Think about that one for a minute. "The structure of ideas is never sequential; and indeed, our thought processes are not very sequential either," said Nelson. "True, only a few thoughts at a time pass across the central screen of the mind; but as you consider a thing, your thoughts crisscross it constantly, reviewing first one connection, then another. Each new idea is compared with many parts of the whole picture, or with some mental visualization of the whole picture itself.''[18]

OK, so we have hypertext and compound hypertext. Next comes high-bandwidth hypermedia: things such as hypertext documents connected to digital sound and music recording connected to high-definition video imaging devices. Now remember—this isn't television-flash-'n'-trash-next-century ramblings—this is doable now. Today.

Ted Nelson sounded the political alarms early enough so that there's no excuse for letting the information-distribution mechanisms become constricted. Referring to the hypermedia hybrid he was stringently clear: ''Supposedly when they come out these media will be mass-marketed disks, sold only in a final form, and thus, like phonograph records, delivered by the Information Lords to the Information Peons. This is rather unlike the prevailing thought among computer-text-system people, where everyone's contribution is thought to be valued.''[19]

Interestingly, Nelson's proposed system, Project Xanadu, is designed in such a way as to eliminate the problem of the gatekeepers, the Information Lords. Ted Nelson and his Xanadu design team specifically designed the system to be used by a series of ''normal'' users, thereby eliminating the need for system administrators and operators as we have come to accept the terms. The design group designed, and has begun to implement, the system on the basis of true equality—the design team themselves desiring nothing more than to be normal users as opposed to gatekeepers. ''It is not that our wants are modest, but rather that we want to put an emperor's resources at the fingertips of all users, especially children and scientists and poets.''[20]

Nelson's Xanadu system is a hypertext repository for almost any form of material ranging from ordinary text and pictures to musical notation and recordings to photographs and video material. Furthermore, the system is designed for fast retrieval and delivery of linked documents. According to Nelson, this will provide all of us with the assimilation tools for alternative versions, historical backtracks, and ''arbitrary collaging.''

Best of all, the Xanadu storage and retrieval system will be completely transparent to the user. ''Bit-map graphics will be stored in such a way as to allow panning (graphical scrolling) and zoom (continuously increasing or decreasing magnification) as incremental data deliveries. (How your screen machine will show them is another matter.) Three-dimensional objects, when implemented, may be collaged by users into compound objects, scenes from history, enactments and artwork.''[21]

Obviously, Macintosh with its graphical interface, will have a distinct advantage for use as what Nelson refers to as a "screen machine." Hence this book is Macintosh-specific. There will be other hypermedia systems—both shared and individual—for virtually all computer systems. But Macintosh has the inside-rail position and enough creative, farsighted individuals are involved in Macintosh hypermedia production to keep the envelope stretched to its limits; and the installed base is large enough to ensure the advancement of hypermedia with or without Apple's continued support. Hopefully it will be *with.*

Conventions Used in this Book

Product names are not italicized, nor is the trademark symbol used. Product titles are assumed to be trademarked by their publisher and the names are used here for informational purposes only. No claim is made of ownership of any trademarked products. Products referred to herein are footnoted on the page of their first mention. Full availability information for each product mentioned or covered also is included in Appendix B.

Book, magazine, electronic publication, and journal titles are italicized and are footnoted on first mention. In the case of electronic publications, page number information is not available. Publisher information is included in Appendix B.

Some terms used in this book may be unfamiliar to you. An attempt has been made to provide a thumbnail definition as a footnote on the page where the term is first used. A full glossary is included in Appendix C.

[5] Vannevar Bush, "As We May Think," *The Atlantic Monthly* (August 1945): 101–08.

[6] CD-ROM is an acronym for Compact Disk-Read Only Media and is similar to the compact disk player you may use in your home or office. Apple's CD-ROM, the AppleCD SC™, was announced at the Microsoft CD-ROM Conference in Seattle on March 1, 1988.

[7] Theodor Nelson, *Dream Machines,* rev. ed. (Redmond, Washington: Tempus Books of Microsoft Press, 1987).

[8] Vannevar Bush, "As We May Think," *The Atlantic Monthly* (August 1945): 101–08.

[9] Douglas C. Engelbart, Richard W. Watson, and James C. Norton, "The Augmented Knowledge Workshop," *Proc NCC* (Spring 1973): 9–21.

[10] Theodor Nelson, *Computer Lib/Dream Machines,* rev. ed. (Redmond, Washington: Tempus Books of Microsoft Press, 1987).

[11] Theodor Nelson, *Literary Machines,* rev. ed. (Bellevue, Washington: OWL International, Inc., 1987).

[12] Theodor Nelson, et al. Work in progress.

[13] Guide and Envelope for the Macintosh and Guide for the IBM PC are available from OWL International, Inc., 14218 NE 21st Street, Bellevue, Washington 98007; (206)747-3203.

[14] HyperCard for the Macintosh is available from Apple Computer, Inc., 20525 Mariani Avenue, Cupertino, California 95014.

[15] This isn't so defeatist as it may sound. A small company in Boston, Number Nine Graphics, shortly thereafter marketed a hardware peripheral for the Apple II that enabled it to produce NTSC-standard video signals that, with a little tweaking, were of broadcast quality.

[16] MicroFilm Reader is available as freeware and MicroFilm Compiler is available as a commercial product from Buck Wheat and Associates, 332 Sunderland Court, Lee's Summit, Missouri 64603; (816) 795-0074.

[17] HyperCard documents are called stacks, which is an allusion to the card metaphor employed by the product. Stackware is a trademark of Apple Computer, Inc., used to refer to HyperCard documents.

[18] Theodor Nelson, *Literary Machines,* elect. ed. (Bellevue, Washington: OWL International, Inc., 1987).

[19] Ibid.

[20] Ibid.

[21] Ibid.

HISTORY AND UNDERLYING CONCEPTS

CHAPTER 1

- *Memex: Setting the Stage*
- *"As We May Think" By Vannevar Bush*
- *Commentary on Bush's Memex*
- *Doug Engelbart: Augmenting the Intellect*
- *Ted Nelson: Making It All Work on the Way to Xanadu*

But you who live in dreams are better pleased by sophistical reasonings and frauds of wit in great and uncertain things than by those reasoning which are certain and natural and not so exalted.

Leonardo da Vinci

Ironically, most of the concepts underlying hypertext and hypermedia were proposed by individuals very few of us have heard of. Largely because these farsighted individuals were involved in the business of creating ideas rather than products, they are not remembered. Their ideas, however, will outlive any of our children's children.

Memex: Setting the Stage

Many would rewrite history and would have us believe that hypermedia, as well as its hypertext harbinger, are relatively new developments. And they're right when you look at a time line of man's—or even this society's—history. But they are seriously mistaken when you look at the miniscule slice of the same time line dealing with computers.

Even more serious is the bandying about of the "hyper" moniker in relation to concepts of not even the most remote of relations to the underlying concepts of what we have come to refer to as hypermedia. You'll often hear the term *interactive multimedia* tossed about as synonymous with hypermedia. I think that's a mistake, too—a form of shortsightedness—as multimedia, interactive or otherwise, is itself a form of hypermedia, but to use it as a blanket label is confusing and misleading. Besides, isn't media already a plural form? Those of us who grew up in the 1960s remember full well what multimedia is, and, while the "multimedia experience" helped to expand our collective consciousness, it had little to do with the underlying concepts of hypertext and hypermedia.

So, we have added two very powerful new terms to our high-tech vocabulary in a very short time: hypertext and hypermedia. More than buzzwords and marketing hooks, the history of the discipline (and they are a single discipline) is rich. It's important that we have a firm grasp on that history before we can understand why hypermedia has become so popular—so mainstream—all of a sudden, after having languished in relative obscurity for more than 40 years.

Hypertext, as a concept, dates back to the mid-1940s and as a word to the mid-1960s. An underlying thread runs through the discipline's development from conception to the present. The proponents of hypertext and its younger sibling, hypermedia, have been accurately labeled both visionaries and crackpots—at the same time, sometimes by the same observers. Like a lemon seed on a kitchen counter, the kernel of wisdom that sparked the hyper revolution is easily identified but a bit harder to grasp. Once you think you have it, more likely than not you watch as the kernel squirts out of your grip and comes to rest somewhere else.

Why did it take so long for this concept to reach the state of paradigm shift? And why are things happening so quickly now in relation to hypermedia?

Mainly what has happened in recent years is that our technology finally has begun to catch up with the crackpots, um, I mean visionaries. A very short time ago, affordable computers with the necessary speed coupled with appropriate mass-storage devices (both magnetic and optical) and an easy-to-use graphical interface were unheard of. Now the hardware has arrived, and the first-generation—and in some cases, second-generation—hypermedia software is in the hands of literally millions of knowledge explorers and information developers.

Although the concept of nonlinear writing, reading, and retrieval designed to be read on a computer screen wasn't given a proper name until the 1960s, the underlying concept dates back to the summer of 1945 and one of the most advanced thinkers of that time, Vannevar Bush. The United States was embroiled in World War II and most of the country's efforts, including science and research, were focused on a singular goal: ending the war. In 1941, President Franklin D. Roosevelt named Vannevar Bush to supervise and coordinate all federally funded research through the Office of Scientific Research and Development.

In the summer of 1945, *The Atlantic Monthly* published Bush's seminal article, "As We May Think," a far-reaching piece that is credited—in hindsight, of course—as the impetus for a wealth of computer science concepts, most notably for what we have come to know as hypertext and hypermedia. It is a very chilling effect to read Bush's piece today, with the benefit of having seen many of his crackpot visions come to fruition, albeit in forms further advanced than originally proposed. Bush accurately predicted high-resolution displays, fast information retrieval, and mass storage, all of which were as foreign to him as living on Mars is to us.

One of Bush's central concepts in "As We May Think" was a machine he called the "memex," which sprang directly from his own needs in organizing vast stores of research materials.

One of the most substantial tasks confronting Bush was the continual updating of technical information that was being generated by the scientific community at the close of World War II. He became fascinated with the concept of microfilm, and "As We May Think" was based on his ideas about it. The memex would be capable of holding all the writings generated in the scientific arena, along with cross-reference links and navigational trails. At about the same time, he also proposed the Bush Rapid Selector, a microfilm tool that later came into being as microfilm readers from the Kodak company and others. The key to the Bush Rapid Selector was the various indices on the side of each microfilm strip. Bush's concept of "trails" were marks and sequencing cues that now are called paths or tours in hypermedia parlance.

As World War II was winding down, and the scientists were freed from working on implements of destruction for the war effort and were able to pursue their individual interests, Vannevar Bush began to contemplate the direction and role of science in the future of the society. Bush became more aware of the sheer bulk of the research documents prepared during the war effort and was continually confronted with the difficult process of searching across multiple documents.

In his own words, "The world has arrived at an age of cheap complex devices of great reliability; and something is bound to come of it."[22] Bush was convinced that the answer to his dilemma lay in the technology itself. The then state-of-the-art technology was the microfilm that allowed scientific records to be compressed and stored, and Bush speculated that an entire encyclopedia could be compressed to fit on a single sheet of microfilm and that cheaply reproduced copies would provide access to vast amounts of information.

Vannevar Bush further speculated that there was a discernible difference between repetitive thought and creative thought and that the coming technology—including computers, voice-input devices, and scanners—would significantly enhance the creative-thought process in individuals. Researchers would be freed from mundane repetitive mental tasks and would have more time to spend on projects requiring creative thought.

Bush was well aware that the human mind operates by association and that, by extension, humans would work best by associative properties of thought. In contrast, most forms of data are stored and sorted alphabetically and information is haphazardly found by hunting it from subclass to subclass. Bush speculated that an associative selection process could be mechanized and that such a process, while significantly slower in performance than the human mind, would possess the property of permanence rather than being of a transitory nature as are human associative thought processes. Furthermore, any specific bit of data would be accessible by entering a code, and the document would be displayed on the screen. Margin notes and comments, according to Bush's vision, could be added at any point, and associations could be constructed between two documents and displayed on adjacent screens. The association or ''link''—complete with index—would be made *and stored* at the press of a button. The link easily could be recalled at any time, and a new microfilm, consisting only of the linked pieces of text could be created and distributed separately from the original documents.

Such a system would allow for the creation of customized encyclopedias and other vast repositories of data, designed for a specific task or range of interests. Users easily could access the information via their individual memex machines and amplify the associations with their own notes and comments.

Vannevar Bush's tool for thought, the memex, was never built and his original vision only now is beginning to materialize. Following are his original words written in 1945, as appropriate and as astounding now as they were then.

''As We May Think'' By Vannevar Bush

1945 by Vannevar Bush as originally published by *The Atlantic Monthly* (July 1945). Reprinted with permission.

Of what lasting benefit has been man's use of science and of the new instruments which his research brought into existence? First, they have increased his control of his material environment. They have improved his food, his clothing, his shelter; they have increased his security and released him partly from the bondage of bare existence. They have given him increased knowledge of his own biological processes so that he has had a progressive freedom from disease and an increased span of life. They are illuminating the interactions of his physiological and psychological functions, giving promise of an improved mental health.

Science has provided the swiftest communication between individuals; it has provided a record of ideas and has enabled man to manipulate and to make extracts from that record so that knowledge evolves and endures throughout the life of a race rather than that of an individual.

There is a growing mountain of research. But there is increased evidence that we are being bogged down today as specialization extends. The investigator is staggered by the findings and conclusions of thousands of other workers—conclusions which he cannot find time to grasp, much less to remember, as they appear. Yet specialization becomes increasingly necessary for progress, and the effort to bridge between disciplines is correspondingly superficial.

Professionally, our methods of transmitting and reviewing the results of research are generations old and by now are totally inadequate for their purposes. If the aggregate time spent in writing scholarly works and in reading them could be evaluated, the ratio between these amounts of time might well be startling. Those who conscientiously attempt to keep abreast of current thought, even in restricted fields, by close and continuous reading might well shy away from an examination calculated to show how much of the previous month's efforts could be produced on call. Mendel's concept of the laws of genetics was lost to the world for a generation because his publication did not reach the few who were capable of grasping and extending it; and this sort of catastrophe is undoubtedly being repeated all about us, as truly significant attainments become lost in the mass of the inconsequential.

The difficulty seems to be not so much that we publish unduly in view of the extent and variety of present-day interests, but rather that publication has been extended far beyond our present ability to make real use of the record. The summation of human experience is being expanded at a prodigious rate, and the means we use for threading through the consequent maze to the momentarily important item is the same as was used in the days of square-rigged ships.

But there are signs of a change as new and powerful instrumentalities come into use. Photocells capable of seeing things in a physical sense, advanced photography which can record what is seen or even what is not, thermionic tubes capable of controlling potent forces under the guidance of less power than a mosquito uses to vibrate his wings, cathode ray tubes rendering visible an occurrence so brief that by comparison a microsecond is a long time, relay combinations which will carry out involved sequences of movements more reliably than any human operator and thousands of times as fast—there are plenty of mechanical aids with which to effect a transformation in scientific records.

Two centuries ago Leibnitz invented a calculating machine which embodied most of the essential features of recent keyboard devices, but it could not then come into use. The economics of the situation were against it: the labor involved in constructing it, before the days of mass production, exceeded the labor to be saved by its use, since all it could accomplish could be duplicated by sufficient use of pencil and paper. Moreover, it would have been subject to frequent breakdown, so that it could not have been depended upon; for at that time and long after, complexity and unreliability were synonymous.

Babbage, even with remarkably generous support for his time, could not produce his great arithmetical machine. His idea was sound enough, but construction and maintenance costs were then too heavy. Had a Pharaoh been given detailed and explicit designs of an automobile, and had he understood them completely, it would have taxed the resources of his kingdom to have fashioned the thousands of parts for a single car, and that car would have broken down on the first trip to Giza.

Machines with interchangeable parts can now be constructed with great economy of effort. In spite of much complexity, they perform reliably. Witness the humble typewriter, or the movie camera, or the automobile. Electrical contacts have ceased to stick—note the automatic telephone exchange, which has hundreds of thousands of such contacts, and yet is reliable. A spider web of metal, sealed in a thin glass container, a wire heated to a brilliant glow, in short, the thermionic tube of radio sets, is made by the hundred million, tossed about in packages, plugged into sockets—and it works! Its gossamer parts, the precise location and alignment involved in its construction, would have occupied a master craftsman of the guild for months; now it is built for thirty cents. The world has arrived at an age of cheap complex devices of great reliability; and something is bound to come of it.

The Silver Image

A record, if it is to be useful to science, must be continuously extended, it must be stored, and above all it must be consulted. Today we make the record conventionally by writing and photography, followed by printing; but we also record on film, on wax disks, and on magnetic wires. Even if utterly new recording procedures do not appear, these present ones are certainly in the process of modification and extension.

Certainly progress in photography is not going to stop. Faster material and lenses, more automatic cameras, finer-grained sensitive compounds to allow an extension of the minicamera idea, are all imminent. Let us project this trend ahead to a logical, if not inevitable, outcome. The camera hound of the future wears on his forehead a lump a little larger than a walnut. It takes pictures 3 millimeters square, later to be projected or enlarged, which after all involves only a factor of 10 beyond present practice. The lens is of universal focus, down to any distance accommodated by the unaided eye, simply because it is of short focal length. There is a built-in photocell on the walnut such as we now have on at least one camera, which automatically adjusts exposure for a wide range of illumination. There is film in the walnut for a hundred exposures, and the spring for operating its shutter and shifting its film is wound once and for all when the film clip is inserted. It produces its result in full color. It may well be stereoscopic, and record with two spaced glass eyes, for striking improvements in stereoscopic techniques are just around the corner.

The cord which trips its shutter may extend down a man's sleeve within easy reach of his fingers. A quick squeeze, and the picture is taken. On a pair of ordinary glasses is a square of fine lines near the top of one lens, where it is out of the way of ordinary vision. When an object appears in that square, it is lined up for its picture. As the scientist of the future moves about the laboratory or the field, every time he looks at something worthy of the record, he trips the shutter and in it goes, without even an audible click. Is this all fantastic? The only fantastic thing about it is the idea of making as many pictures as would result from its use.

Will there be dry photography? It is already here in two forms. When Brady made his Civil War pictures, the plate had to be wet at the time of exposure. Now it has to be wet during development instead. In the future, perhaps it need not be wetted at all. There have long been films impregnated with diazo dyes which form a picture without development, so that it is already there as soon as the camera has been operated. An exposure to ammonia gas destroys the unexposed dye, and the picture can then be taken out into the light and examined. The process is now slow, but someone may speed it up, and it has no grain difficulties such as now keep photographic researchers busy. Often it would be advantageous to be able to snap the camera and to look at the picture immediately.

Another process now in use is also slow, and more or less clumsy. For fifty years impregnated papers have been used which turn dark at every point where an electrical contact touches them, by reason of the chemical change thus produced in an iodine compound included in the paper. They have been used to make records, for a pointer moving across them can leave a trail behind. If the electrical potential on the pointer is varied as it moves, the line becomes light or dark in accordance with the potential.

This scheme is now used in facsimile transmission. The pointer draws a set of closely spaced lines across the paper one after another. As it moves, its potential is varied in accordance with a varying current received over wires from a distant station, where these variations are produced by a photocell which is similarly scanning a picture. At every instant the darkness of the line being drawn is made equal to the darkness of the point on the picture being observed by the photocell. Thus, when the whole picture has been covered, a replica appears at the receiving end.

A scene itself can be just as well looked over line-by-line by the photocell in this way as can a photograph of the scene. This whole apparatus constitutes a camera, with the added feature, which can be dispensed with if desired, of making its picture at a distance. It is slow, and the picture is poor in detail. Still, it does give another process of dry photography, in which the picture is finished as soon as it is taken.

It would be a brave man who would predict that such a process will always remain clumsy, slow, and faulty in detail. Television equipment today transmits sixteen reasonably good pictures a second, and it involves only two essential differences from the process described above. For one, the record is made by a moving beam of electrons rather than a moving pointer, for the reason that an electron beam can sweep across the picture very rapidly indeed. The other difference involves merely the use of a screen which glows momentarily when the electrons hit, rather than a chemically treated paper or film which is permanently altered. This speed is necessary in television, for motion pictures rather than stills are the object.

Use chemically treated film in place of the glowing screen, allow the apparatus to transmit one picture only rather than a succession, and use a rapid camera for dry photography. The treated film needs to be far faster in action than present examples, but it probably could be. More serious is the objection that this scheme would involve putting the film inside a vacuum chamber, for electron beams behave normally only in such a rarefied environment. This difficulty could be avoided by allowing the electron beam to play on one side of a partition, and by pressing the film against the other side, if this partition were such as to allow the electrons to go through perpendicular to its surface, and to prevent them from spreading out sideways. Such partitions, in crude form, could certainly be constructed, and they will hardly hold up the general development.

Like dry photography, microphotography still has a long way to go. The basic scheme of reducing the size of the record, and examining it by projection rather than directly, has possibilities too great to be ignored. The combination of optical projection and photographic reduction is already producing some results in microfilm for scholarly purposes, and the potentialities are highly suggestive. Today, with microfilm, reductions by a linear factor of 20 can be employed and still produce full clarity when the material is re-enlarged for examination. The limits are set by the graininess of the film, the excellence of the optical system, and the efficiency of the light sources employed. All of these are rapidly improving.

Assume a linear ratio of 100 for future use. Consider film of the same thickness as paper, although thinner film will certainly be usable. Even under these conditions there would be a total factor of 10,000 between the bulk of the ordinary record in books and its microfilm replica. The "Encyclopedia Britannica" could be reduced to the volume of a matchbox. The library of a million volumes could be compressed into one end of a desk. If the human race has produced since the invention of movable type a total record, in the form of magazines, newspapers, books, tracts, advertising blurbs, correspondence, having a volume corresponding to a billion books, the whole affair, assembled and compressed, could be lugged off in a moving van. Mere compression, of course, is not enough; one needs not only to make and store a record but also be able to consult it, and this aspect of the matter comes later. Even the modern great library is not generally consulted; it is nibbled at by a few.

Compression is important, however, when it comes to costs. The material for the microfilm ''Britannica'' would cost a nickel, and it could be mailed anywhere for a cent. What would it cost to print a million copies? To print a sheet of newspaper, in a large edition, costs a small fraction of a cent. The entire material of the ''Britannica'' in reduced microfilm form would go on a sheet eight and one-half by eleven inches. Once it is available, with the photographic reproduction methods of the future, duplicates in large quantities could probably be turned out for a cent apiece beyond the cost of materials. The preparation of the original copy? That introduces the next aspect of the subject.

Vocoder

To make the record, we now push a pencil or tap a typewriter. Then comes the process of digestion and correction, followed by an intricate process of typesetting, printing, and distribution. To consider the first stage of the procedure, will the author of the future cease writing by hand or typewriter and talk directly to the record? He does so indirectly, by talking to a stenographer or a wax cylinder; but the elements are all present if he wishes to have his talk directly produce a typed record. All he needs to do is to take advantage of existing mechanisms and to alter his language.

At a recent World Fair a machine called a Vocoder was shown. A girl stroked its keys and it emitted recognizable speech. No human vocal cords entered into the procedure at any point; the keys simply combined some electrically produced vibrations and passed these on to a loudspeaker. In the Bell Laboratories there is the converse of this machine, called a Vocoder. The loudspeaker is replaced by a microphone, which picks up sound. Speak to it, and the corresponding keys move. This may be one element of the postulated system.

The other element is found in the stenotype, that somewhat disconcerting device encountered usually at public meetings. A girl strokes its keys languidly and looks about the room and sometimes at the speaker with a disquieting gaze. From it emerges a typed strip which records in a phonetically simplified language a record of what the speaker is supposed to have said. Later this strip is retyped into ordinary language, for in its nascent form it is intelligible only to the initiated. Combine these two elements, let the Vocoder run the stenotype, and the result is a machine which types when talked to.

Our present languages are not especially adapted to this sort of mechanization, it is true. It is strange that the inventors of universal languages have not seized upon the idea of producing one which better fitted the technique for transmitting and recording speech. Mechanization may yet force the issue, especially in the scientific field; whereupon scientific jargon would become still less intelligible to the layman.

One can now picture a future investigator in his laboratory. His hands are free, and he is not anchored. As he moves about and observes, he photographs and comments. Time is automatically recorded to tie the two records together. If he goes into the field, he may be connected by radio to his recorder. As he ponders over his notes in the evening, he again talks his comments into the record. His typed record, as well as his photographs, may both be in miniature, so that he projects them for examination.

Much needs to occur, however, between the collection of data and observations, the extraction of parallel material from the existing record, and the final insertion of new material into the general body of the common record. For mature thought there is no mechanical substitute. But creative thought and essentially repetitive thought are very different things. For the latter there are, and may be, powerful mechanical aids.

Napier's Bones Revisited

Adding a column of figures is a repetitive thought process, and it was long ago properly relegated to the machine. True, the machine is sometimes controlled by a keyboard, and thought of a sort enters in reading the figures and poking the corresponding keys, but even this is avoidable. Machines have been made which will read typed figures by photocells and then depress the corresponding keys; these are combinations of photocells for scanning the type, electric circuits for sorting the consequent variations, and relay circuits for interpreting the result into the action of solenoids to pull the keys down.

All this complication is needed because of the clumsy way in which we have learned to write figures. If we recorded them positionally, simply by the configuration of a set of dots on a card, the automatic reading mechanism would become comparatively simple. In fact, if the dots are holes, we have the punched-card machine long ago produced by Hollorith for the purposes of the census, and now used throughout business. Some types of complex businesses could hardly operate without these machines.

Adding is only one operation. To perform arithmetical computation involves also subtraction, multiplication, and division, and in addition some method for temporary storage of results, removal from storage for further manipulation, and recording of final results by printing. Machines for these purposes are now of two types: keyboard machines for accounting and the like, manually controlled for the insertion of data, and usually automatically controlled as far as the sequence of operations is concerned; and punched-card machines in which separate operations are usually delegated to a series of machines, and the cards then transferred bodily from one to another. Both forms are very useful; but as far as complex computations are concerned, both are still in embryo.

Rapid electrical counting appeared soon after the physicists found it desirable to count cosmic rays. For their own purposes the physicists promptly constructed thermionic-tube equipment capable of counting electrical impulses at the rate of 100,000 a second. The advanced arithmetical machines of the future will be electrical in nature, and they will perform at 100 times present speeds, or more.

Moreover, they will be far more versatile than present commercial machines, so that they may readily be adapted for a wide variety of operations. They will be controlled by a control card or film, they will select their own data and manipulate it in accordance with the instructions thus inserted, they will perform complex arithmetical computations at exceedingly high speed, and they will record results in such form as to be readily available for distribution or for later further manipulation. Such machines will have enormous appetites. One of them will take instructions and data from a whole roomful of people armed with simple keyboard punches, and will deliver sheets of computed results every few minutes. There will always be plenty of things to compute in the detailed affairs of millions of people doing complicated things.

The repetitive processes of thought are not confined, however, to matters of arithmetic and statistics. In fact, every time one combines and records facts in accordance with established logical processes, the creative aspect of thinking is concerned only with the selection of the data and the process to be employed, and the manipulation thereafter is repetitive in nature and hence a fit matter to be relegated to the machines. Not so much has been done along these lines, beyond the bounds of arithmetic, as might be done, primarily because of the economics of the situation. The needs of business, and the extensive market obviously waiting, assured the advent of mass-produced arithmetical machines just as soon as production methods were sufficiently advanced.

With machines for advanced analysis, no such situation existed; for there was and is no extensive market; the users of advanced methods of manipulating data are a very small part of the population. There are, however, machines for solving differential equations—and functional and integral equations, for that matter. There are many special machines, such as the harmonic synthesizer which predicts the tides. There will be many more, appearing certainly first in the hands of the scientist and in small numbers.

If scientific reasoning were limited to the logical processes of arithmetic, we should not get far in our understanding of the physical world. One might as well attempt to grasp the game of poker entirely by the use of the mathematics of probability. The abacus, with its beads strung on parallel wires, led the Arabs to positional numeration and the concept of zero many centuries before the rest of the world; and it was a useful tool—so useful that it still exists.

It is a far cry from the abacus to the modern keyboard accounting machine. It will be an equal step to the arithmetical machine of the future. But even this new machine will not take the scientist where he needs to go. Relief must be secured from laborious detailed manipulation of higher mathematics as well, if the users of it are to free their brains for something more than repetitive detailed transformations in accordance with established rules. A mathematician is not a man who can readily manipulate figures; often he cannot. He is not even a man who can readily perform the transformations of equations by the use of calculus. He is primarily an individual who is skilled in the use of symbolic logic on a high plane, and especially he is a man of intuitive judgment in the choice of the manipulative processes he employs.

All else he should be able to turn over to his mechanic, just as confidently as he turns over the propelling of his car to the intricate mechanism under the hood. Only then will mathematics be practically effective in bringing the growing knowledge of atomistics to the useful solution of the advanced problems of chemistry, metallurgy, and biology. For this reason there will come more machines to handle advanced mathematics for the scientist. Some of them will be sufficiently bizarre to suit the most fastidious connoisseur of the present artifacts of civilization.

The Perpetual Auditor

The scientist, however, is not the only person who manipulates data and examines the world about him by the use of logical processes, although he sometimes preserves this appearance by adopting into the fold anyone who becomes logical, much in the manner in which a British labor leader is elevated to knighthood. Whenever logical processes of thought are employed—that is, whenever thought for a time runs along an accepted groove—there is an opportunity for the machine. Formal logic used to be a keen instrument in the hands of the teacher in his trying of students' souls. It is readily possible to construct a machine which will manipulate premises in accordance with formal logic, simply by the clever use of relay circuits. Put a set of premises into such a device and turn the crank, and it will readily pass out conclusion after conclusion, all in accordance with logical law, and with no more slips than would be expected by a keyboard adding machine.

Logic can become enormously difficult, and it would undoubtedly be well to produce more assurance in its use. The machines for higher analysis have usually been equation solvers. Ideas are beginning to appear for equation transformers, which will rearrange the relationship expressed by an equation in accordance with strict and rather advanced logic. Progress is inhibited by the exceedingly crude way in which mathematicians express their relationships. They employ a symbolism which grew like Topsy and has little consistency; a strange fact in that most logical field.

A new symbolism, probably positional, must apparently precede the reduction of mathematical transformations to machine processes. Then, on beyond the strict logic of the mathematician, lies the application of logic in everyday affairs. We may some day click off arguments on a machine with the same assurance that we now enter sales on a cash register. But the machine of logic will not look like a cash register, even of the streamlined model.

So much for the manipulation of ideas and their insertion into the record. Thus far we seem to be worse off than before—for we can enormously extend the record; yet even in its present bulk we can hardly consult it. This is a much larger matter than merely the extraction of data for the purposes of scientific research; it involves the entire process by which man profits by his inheritance of acquired knowledge. The prime action of use is selection, and here we are halting indeed. There may be millions of fine thoughts, and the account of the experience on which they are based, all encased within stone walls of acceptable architectural form; but if the scholar can get at only one a week by diligent search, his syntheses are not likely to keep up with the current scene.

Selection, in this broad sense, is a stone adze in the hands of a cabinetmaker. Yet, in a narrow sense and in other areas, something has already been done mechanically on selection. The personnel officer of a factory drops a stack of a few thousand employee cards into a selecting machine, sets a code in accordance with an established convention, and produces in a short time a list of all employees who live in Trenton and know Spanish. Even such devices are much too slow when it comes, for example, to matching a set of fingerprints with one of five million on file. Selection devices of this sort will soon be speeded up from their present rate of reviewing data at a few hundred a minute. By the use of photocells and microfilm they will survey items at the rate of a thousand a second, and will print out duplicates of those selected.

This process, however, is simple selection: it proceeds by examining in turn every one of a large set of items, and by picking out those which have certain specified characteristics. There is another form of selection best illustrated by the automatic telephone exchange. You dial a number and the machine selects and connects just one of a million possible stations. It does not run over them all. It pays attention only to a class given by a first digit, then only to a subclass of this given by the second digit, and so on; and thus proceeds rapidly and almost unerringly to the selected station. It requires a few seconds to make the selection, although the process could be speeded up if increased speed were economically warranted.

If necessary, it could be made extremely fast by substituting thermionic-tube switching for mechanical switching, so that the full selection could be made in one one-hundredth of a second. No one would wish to spend the money necessary to make this change in the telephone system, but the general idea is applicable elsewhere.

Take the prosaic problem of the great department store. Every time a charge sale is made, there are a number of things to be done. The inventory needs to be revised, the salesman needs to be given credit for the sale, the general accounts need an entry, and, most important, the customer needs to be charged. A central records device has been developed in which much of this work is done conveniently. The salesman places on a stand the customer's identification card, his own card, and the card taken from the article sold—all punched cards. When he pulls a lever, contacts are made through the holes, machinery at a central point makes the necessary computations and entries, and the proper receipt is printed for the salesman to pass to the customer.

But there may be 10,000 charge customers doing business with the store, and before the full operation can be completed someone has to select the right card and insert it at the central office. Now rapid selection can slide just the proper card into position in an instant or two, and return it afterward. Another difficulty occurs, however. Someone must read a total on the card, so that the machine can add its computed item to it. Conceivably the cards might be of the dry photography type. Existing totals could then be read by photocell, and the new total entered by an electron beam.

The cards may be in miniature, so that they occupy little space. They must move quickly. They need not be transferred far, but merely into position so that the photocell and recorder can operate on them. Positional dots can enter the data. At the end of the month a machine can readily be made to read these and to print an ordinary bill. With tube selection, in which no mechanical parts are involved in the switches, little time need be occupied in bringing the correct card into use—a second should suffice for the entire operation. The whole record on the card may be made by magnetic dots on a steel sheet if desired, instead of dots to be observed optically, following the scheme by which Poulsen long ago put speech on a magnetic wire. This method has the advantage of simplicity and ease of erasure. By using photography, however, one can arrange to project the record in enlarged form, and at a distance by using the process common in television equipment.

One can consider rapid selection of this form and distance projection for other purposes. To be able to key one sheet of a million before an operator in a second or two, with the possibility of then adding notes thereto, is suggestive in many ways. It might even be of use in libraries, but that is another story. At any rate, there are now some interesting combinations possible. One might, for example, speak to a microphone, in the manner described in connection with the speech-controlled typewriter, and thus make his selections. It would certainly beat the usual file clerk.

Memex

The real heart of the matter of selection, however, goes deeper than a lag in the adoption of mechanisms by libraries, or a lack of development of devices for their use. Our ineptitude in getting at the record is largely caused by the artificiality of systems of indexing. When data of any sort are placed in storage, they are filed alphabetically or numerically, and information is found (when it is) by tracing it down from subclass to subclass. It can be in only one place, unless duplicates are used; one has to have rules as to which path will locate it, and the rules are cumbersome. Having found one item, moreover, one has to emerge from the system and re-enter on a new path.

The human mind does not work that way. It operates by association. With one item in its grasp, it snaps instantly to the next that is suggested by the association of thoughts, in accordance with some intricate web of trails carried by the cells of the brain. It has other characteristics, of course; trails that are not frequently followed are prone to fade, items are not fully permanent, memory is transitory. Yet the speed of action, the intricacy of trails, the detail of mental pictures, is awe-inspiring beyond all else in nature.

Man cannot hope fully to duplicate this mental process artificially, but he certainly ought to be able to learn from it. In minor ways he may even improve, for his records have relative permanency. The first idea, however, to be drawn from the analogy concerns selection. Selection by association, rather than by indexing, may yet be mechanized. One cannot hope thus to equal the speed and flexibility with which the mind follows an associative trail, but it should be possible to beat the mind decisively in regard to the permanence and clarity of the items resurrected from storage.

Consider a future device for individual use, which is a sort of mechanized private file and library. It needs a name, and, to coin one at random, "memex" will do. A memex is a device in which an individual stores his books, records, and communications, and which is mechanized so that it may be consulted with exceeding speed and flexibility. It is an enlarged intimate supplement to his memory.

It consists of a desk, and while it can presumably be operated from a distance, it is primarily the piece of furniture at which he works. On the top are slanting translucent screens, on which material can be projected for convenient reading. There is a keyboard, and sets of buttons and levers.

In one end is the stored material. The matter of bulk is well taken care of by improved microfilm. Only a small part of the interior of the memex is devoted to storage, the rest to mechanism. Yet if the user inserted 5000 pages of material a day it would take him hundreds of years to fill the repository, so he can be profligate and enter material freely.

Most of the memex contents are purchased on microfilm ready for insertion. Books of all sorts, pictures, current periodicals, newspapers, are thus obtained and dropped into place. Business correspondence takes the same path. And there is provision for direct entry. On the top of the memex is a transparent platen. On this are placed longhand notes, photographs, memoranda, all sorts of things. When one is in place, the depression of a lever causes it to be photographed onto the next blank space in a section of the memex film, dry photography being employed.

There is, of course, provision for consultation of the record by the usual scheme of indexing. If the user wishes to consult a certain book, he taps its code on the keyboard, and the title page of the book promptly appears before him, projected onto one of his viewing positions. Frequently used codes are mnemonic, so that he seldom consults his code book; but when he does, a single tap of a key projects it for his use. Moreover, he has supplemental levers. On deflecting one of these levers to the right he runs through the book before him, each paper in turn being projected at a speed which just allows a recognizing glance at each. If he deflects it further to the right, he steps through the book 10 pages at a time; still further at 100 pages at a time. Deflection to the left gives him the same control backwards.

A special button transfers him immediately to the first page of the index. Any given book of his library can thus be called up and consulted with far greater facility than if it were taken from a shelf. As he has several projection positions, he can leave one item in position while he calls up another. He can add marginal notes and comments, taking advantage of one possible type of dry photography, and it could even be arranged so that he can do this by a stylus scheme, such as is now employed in the telautograph seen in railroad waiting rooms, just as though he had the physical page before him.

All this is conventional, except for the projection forward of present-day mechanisms and gadgetry. It affords an immediate step, however, to associative indexing, the basic idea of which is a provision whereby any item may be caused at will to select immediately and automatically another. This is the essential feature of the memex. The process of tying two items together is the important thing.

When the user is building a trail, he names it, inserts the name in his code book, and taps it out on his keyboard. Before him are the two items to be joined, projected onto adjacent viewing positions. At the bottom of each there are a number of blank code spaces, and a pointer is set to indicate one of these on each item. The user taps a single key, and the items are permanently joined. In each code space appears the code word. Out of view, but also in the code space, is inserted a set of dots for photocell viewing; and on each item these dots by their positions designate the index number of the other item.

Thereafter, at any time, when one of these items is in view, the other can be instantly recalled merely by tapping a button below the corresponding code space. Moreover, when numerous items have been thus joined together to form a trail, they can be reviewed in turn, rapidly or slowly, by deflecting a lever like that used for turning the pages of a book. It is exactly as though the physical items had been gathered together from widely separated sources and bound together to form a new book. It is more than this, for any item can be joined into numerous trails.

The owner of the memex, let us say, is interested in the origin and properties of the bow and arrow. Specifically he is studying why the short Turkish bow was apparently superior to the English long bow in the skirmishes of the Crusades. He has dozens of possibly pertinent books and articles in his memex. First he runs through an encyclopedia, finds an interesting but sketchy article, leaves it projected. Next, in a history, he finds another pertinent item, and ties the two together. Thus he goes, building a trail of many items. Occasionally he inserts a comment of his own, either linking it into the main trail or joining it by a side trail to a particular item. When it becomes evident that the elastic properties of available materials had a great deal to do with the bow, he branches off on a side trail which takes him through textbooks on elasticity and tables of physical constants. He inserts a page of longhand analysis of his own. Thus he builds a trail of his interest through the maze of materials available to him.

And his trails do not fade. Several years later, his talk with a friend turns to the queer ways in which a people resist innovations, even of vital interest. He has an example, in the fact that the out ranged Europeans still failed to adopt the Turkish bow. In fact, he has a trail on it. A touch brings up the code book. Tapping a few keys projects the head of the trail. A lever runs through it at will, stopping at interesting items, going off on side excursions. It is an interesting trail, pertinent to the discussion. So he sets a reproducer in action, photographs the whole trail out, and passes it to his friend for insertion in his own memex, there to be linked into the more general trail.

Pushing the Limits

Wholly new forms of encyclopedias will appear, ready-made with a mesh of associative trails running through them, ready to be dropped into the memex and there amplified. The lawyer has at his touch the associated opinions and decisions of his whole experience and of the experience of friends and authorities. The patent attorney has on call the millions of issued patents, with familiar trails to every point of his client's interest.

The physician, puzzled by a patient's reactions, strikes the trail established in studying an earlier similar case, and runs rapidly through analogous case histories, with side references to the classics for the pertinent anatomy and histology. The chemist, struggling with the synthesis of an organic compound, has all the chemical literature before him in his laboratory, with trails following the analogies of compounds, the side trails to their physical and chemical behavior.

The historian, with a vast chronological account of a people, parallels it with a skip trail which stops only on the salient items, and can follow at any time contemporary trails which lead him all over civilization at a particular epoch. There is a new profession of trail blazers, those who find delight in the task of establishing useful trails through the enormous mass of the common record. The inheritance from the master becomes not only his additions to the world's record, but for his disciples the entire scaffolding by which they were erected.

Thus science may implement the ways in which man produces, stores, and consults the record of the race. It might be striking to outline the instrumentalities of the future more spectacularly, rather than to stick closely to methods and elements now known and undergoing rapid development, as has been done here. Technical difficulties of all sorts have been ignored, certainly, but also ignored are means as yet unknown which may come any day to accelerate technical progress as violently as did the advent of the thermionic tube. In order that the picture may not be too commonplace, by reason of sticking to present-day patterns, it may be well to mention one such possibility, not to prophesy but merely to suggest, for prophecy based on extension of the known has substance, while prophecy founded on the unknown is only a doubly involved guess.

All our steps in creating or absorbing material of the record proceed through one of the senses —the tactile when we touch keys, the oral when we speak or listen, the visual when we read. Is it not possible that some day the path may be established more directly?

We know that when the eye sees, all the consequent information is transmitted to the brain by means of electrical vibrations in the channel of the optic nerve. This is an exact analogy with the electrical vibrations which occur in the cable of the television set: they convey the picture from the photocells which see it to the radio transmitter from which it is broadcast. We know further that if we can approach that cable with the proper instruments, we do not need to touch it; we can pick up those vibrations by electrical induction and thus discover and reproduce the scene which is being transmitted, just as a telephone wire may be tapped for its message.

The impulses which flow in the arm nerves of a typist convey to her fingers the translated information which reaches her eye or ear, in order that the fingers may be caused to strike the proper keys. Might not these currents be intercepted, either in the original form in which the information is conveyed to the brain, or in the marvelously metamorphosed form in which they then proceed to the hand?

By bone conduction we already introduce sounds into the nerve channels of the deaf in order that they may hear. Is it not possible that we may learn to introduce them without the present cumbersomeness of first transforming electrical vibrations to mechanical ones, which the human mechanism promptly transforms back into the electrical form? With a couple of electrodes on the skull the encephalograph now produces pen-and-ink traces which bear some relation to the electrical phenomena going on in the brain itself. True, the record is unintelligible, except as it points out certain gross misfunctioning of the cerebral mechanism; but who would now place bounds on where such a thing may lead?

In the outside world, all forms of intelligence, whether of sound or sight, have been reduced to the form of varying currents in an electric circuit in order that they may be transmitted. Inside the human frame exactly the same sort of process occurs. Must we always transform to mechanical movements in order to proceed from one electrical phenomenon to another? It is a suggestive thought, but it hardly warrants prediction without losing touch with reality and immediateness.

Presumably man's spirit should be elevated if he can better review his shady past and analyze more completely and objectively his present problems. He has built a civilization so complex that he needs to mechanize his records more fully if he is to push his experiment to its logical conclusion and not merely become bogged down part way there by overtaxing his limited memory. His excursions may be more enjoyable if he can reacquire the privilege of forgetting the manifold things he does not need to have immediately at hand, with some assurance that he can find them again if they prove important.

The applications of science have built man a well-supplied house, and are teaching him to live healthily therein. They have enabled him to throw masses of people against one other with cruel weapons. They may yet allow him truly to encompass the great record and to grow in the wisdom of race experience. He may perish in conflict before he learns to wield that record for his true good. Yet, in the application of science to the needs and desires of man, it would seem to be a singularly unfortunate stage at which to terminate the process, or to lose hope as to the outcome.

Commentary on Bush's Memex

While Bush's envisioned microfilm application—the memex—was never quite realized (microfilm technology *still* hasn't advanced that far), the underlying concept of his vision remains intact and very much alive in hypermedia. The idea of associative thought and information indexed and readily accessible has been made possible through the evolution of the personal computer. Commercially available hypermedia products, especially those that are used with the Macintosh that are based on these ideas, currently enjoy a widespread reception.

The underlying concept of associative links and navigational trails, originally proposed by Vannevar Bush, remains intact and forms the basis for hypertext and hypermedia. Only the media itself has changed; electronic storage and display implements are used rather than the microfilm technology.

One of the most daunting obstacles to the widespread acceptance of hypermedia as a communications medium has been the high cost of mass storage.

When I purchased my first computer, I sincerely felt that I would never have need for more than 143K (the standard disk format of the Apple II) at one time and that, oh, I might need more eventually, but I could always just buy another disk. As of this writing I have in excess of 170 megabytes of data storage on-line and I spend every Sunday evening clearing space for the next week's additions. The cost of appropriate mass storage (about 40 MBytes is a minimal configuration for an individual hyperspace) has begun to fall drastically and various vendors provide options within the reach of the individual. Optical storage systems also are becoming available at almost mass-market prices and with their capacity of easily handling in excess of 550 MBytes of material (550 million characters), the mass-storage horizon looks very bright indeed.

The near-term future also looks rosy as advancements in magneto-optical storage devices (capable of holding as much data as a CD-ROM, but gifted with much faster access speeds and the ability to both read and write) are occurring on an almost daily basis.

With the mass-storage obstacle finally being scaled, the sophistication level of the graphic displays and telecommunications abilities of personal computers continues to rise at a breathtaking level. By no means is Macintosh the last word in any of these areas, but it is the first, and most indications are that Apple will continue to advance the Macintosh technology as demand warrants.

In addition to the technological tools, individuals are becoming hyperliterate at a blinding pace as users are learning to build their own reference links, navigational trails, and indices through vast amounts of data with ease and precision. As more sophisticated hypermedia-user environments are developed that are even more intuitive and powerful, the medium will become attractive to an even wider audience. These more sophisticated environments will require, conversely, a lesser degree of sophistication on the part of the user and will, therefore, become more widespread.

Bush foresaw that memex users would correspond with each other by mailing microfilms back and forth—a precursor to today's implementation of electronic mail. As telecommunications hardware (modems, for now, in the case of personal computers) and software become more and more advanced and less and less intimidating, its acceptance level also is assured of growing in a geometric fashion. Already we can transmit data between personal computers—over ordinary telephone wires—eight times faster today than was possible a year ago. On the very near horizon are developments that promise to preclude the need for what we now recognize as a modem, and we will collectively be wired into a network connecting with other networks across the globe.

The immediacy of information and its attendant links and indexes is the true bequest of hypermedia; as the marriage of computers and telephones is consummated, both aspects will grow at an astonishing rate. As individuals develop their own links and trails through vast stores of information and begin to share their links with other individuals, the associative power of the community's knowledge base begins to grow exponentially and we will be gifted with a sort of mass-customization of the community's collective intellect.

Doug Engelbart: Augmenting the Intellect

Douglas C. Engelbart, the first of the second-generation hypervisionaries to follow in Vannevar Bush's footsteps, realized straight away that while hypermedia was going to revolutionize our access to information, some sort of framework was needed to structure the capabilities we were going to be confronted with. His concept of the "augmentation of the human intellect" sprang from those concerns and has provided the framework for not only the budding hypermedia discipline, but most of the personal computer industry as well.

Regarded largely by his contemporaries as a very well-intentioned crackpot (sound familiar, yet?), Engelbart eventually received Department of Defense funding in the 1960s through the Advanced Research Projects Agency (ARPA). Ideas that were birthed at Engelbart's Augmentation Research Laboratory at the Stanford Research Institute (SRI) include the mouse, windows, electronic mail, and computer conferencing. Engelbart's augmentation system for the knowledge worker, however, remains to be implemented in a manner he considers to be acceptable.

If Vannevar Bush was the cerebral intellectual of the underlying concepts of hypermedia, Doug Engelbart was the task master, the visionary who got his hands dirty and got the job on track. Engelbart read Bush's "As We May Think" piece while he was a radar technician in the Philippines during World War II. The ideas proposed by Bush festered until Engelbart was 25, living in the California of the 1950s, and decided to address in some manner the fact that the most pressing problems facing society were growing faster than the tools we used to solve them. Engelbart envisioned a tool that would give a small work group of people, working together, a better chance at solving problems that were becoming ever more complex.

Engelbart fully understood that what was needed was not a new way to expand knowledge, but new ways of discovering where to look for specific answers—

answers that were already in cold storage somewhere. He also perceived a great need for better communication tools between the individuals working together on complicated problems. Although Engelbart's augmentation system and attendant tools remain "in process," the underlying framework came to him in a flash:

When I first heard about computers, I understood from my radar experience during the war that if these machines can show you information on printouts, they could show that information on a screen. When I saw the connection between a television-like screen, an information processor, and a medium for representing symbols to a person it all tumbled together in about half an hour. I went home and sketched a system in which computers would draw symbols on the screen and I could steer through different information spaces with knobs and levers and look at words and data and graphics in different ways. I imagined ways you could expand it to a theater-like environment where you could sit with colleagues and exchange information on many levels simultaneously. God! Think of how that would let you cut loose in solving problems![23]

The notion of hypertext as bits of documents linked to other bits of information that were easily retrievable by a nonexpert was only part of a bigger picture in the mind of Doug Engelbart. Engelbart first proposed his system in a 29-page paper in 1962, "A Conceptual Framework for the Augmentation of Man's Intellect."[24]

Six years later, in 1968, a working system was up and running under Engelbart's specification. The system, called NLS (for oN Line System) included such advanced features as electronic mail, computer conferencing, multiple windows on a screen, and a mouse. NLS was designed to allow anyone to read material written by anyone else and make comments and other documents from any terminal connected to the system. The system, in basically its original form, still is offered today as Augment by McDonnell-Douglas and is used mostly by the Air Force, although it is accessible via Tymshare, albeit at rates a bit rich for individuals ($18 per hour as of late 1988). Douglas Engelbart has gone on to form the Bootstrap Institute in Palo Alto, California, with seed money provided by an anonymous benefactor from within the computer industry.

Augment, as the first hypermedia system to actually succeed, includes features such as cross-referenced links between documents and provides the user with the ability to expand or contract the information at the user's request, thus tailoring the information flow to the individual user's needs. The amount of information available is further customizable via "viewing filters" that allow the user to specify the level of detail under which a particular document is viewed.

Concepts from both Augment and NLS comprised what was loosely referred to as the "Knowledge Workshop" envisioned by Doug Engelbart. Within the Workshop, any user could log onto the system via any connected display terminal. Once he or she was logged into the Workshop, all owned files as well as any files that were shared among a group of users would immediately become accessible. Files could be read. New files could be created. Shared files could be annotated. In addition, messages that were not connected to any document could be sent—immediately—to other Workshop users. Documents were easily transferred to other members simply by "releasing" them. No paper changed hands, and the transaction was perceptually immediate. Documents could be released to others for their comments and annotations, and the Workshop user would have common access to other members' documents that were specified as a "shared" document.

If all of this sounds vaguely familiar to the modern Macintosh user connected to a local area network, it should. The basic concept of file servers is identical. One of the new buzzwords in the Macintosh community is "groupware." As you can see, that, too, is borrowed from Engelbart's very seminal work.

What separates Engelbart's "Knowledge Workshop" vision from current work group practice is the absence of paper and its attendant paper handling. Paper is eliminated at all levels. If you wrote—especially if you wrote a lot—this meant the end to lost notes that had been scribbled several days earlier on napkins, matchbooks, or other scraps of paper. Within the Workshop, all of one's writings were available immediately, right *there*. Cross-references, footnotes, sidebars, and annotations were instant and painless. The Workshop promised an end to the time-consuming paper chase, looking for that scrap of paper containing last night's brilliant thoughts that just *has* to be here *somewhere*.

Figure 1.1 illustrates a hypothetical implementation of the Knowledge Workshop display as it would likely appear using modern Macintosh conventions and software currently available. The smaller window at the top of the screen (two windows in the case of Engelbart's original specification) would display your commands and a reminder of your query, while the two larger windows below would display the first occurrence of the text requested by the user and the linked occurrences.

Another feature embodied within the Knowledge Workshop was the ability for two people to work in a collaborative manner on the same document or set of documents. Two individuals, connected via a telephone link, could work together on a common document: Changes made by one person on his or her screen were immediately reflected on the other person's screen. No longer were geographically dispersed workmates subjected to the time

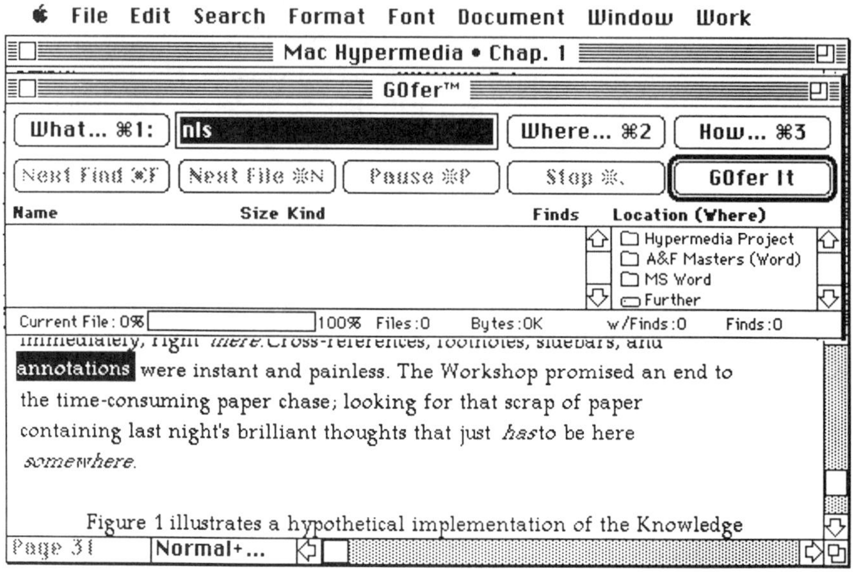

● *Figure 1.1 An illustration of Douglas Engelbart's Knowledge Workshop as mock-implemented on a Macintosh using Microsoft Word and GOfer.*

delays of revision-by-mail. All revisions could take place in real time, or at least in a reasonable facsimile.

NLS and the Knowledge Workshop used a command language rather than the graphical interface familiar to Macintosh users. Although the language was fairly straightforward and the commands themselves were mnemonic (I for insert, M for move, D for delete, etc.), the user was expected to memorize the commands and enter them into the system in the exactly correct sequence. While such a system may have been acceptable to computer scientists, it is too much to ask of the ''real'' people Engelbart hoped to attract to the system. The system did, however, use the mouse as a pointing device to inform the system where the user is pointing on the screen.

Engelbart defined augmentation—the term and concept—as ''increasing the capability of a man to approach a complex problem situation, gain comprehension to suit his particular needs, and to derive solutions to problems. Increased capability in this respect is taken to mean a mixture of the following: that comprehension can be gained more quickly; that better comprehension can be gained; that a useful degree of comprehension can be gained where previously the situation was too complex; that solutions can be produced more quickly; that better solutions can be produced; that solutions can be found where previously the human could find none.''[25] Not only was Engelbart's intention to define and create new tools, but to define new ways of *working* with these new tools.

An appropriate example of augmentation, as per Doug Engelbart, and especially relevant to this forum, is the concept of writing. Before human beings knew how to write they could only transmit ideas by telling each other. This oral tradition today survives in some cultures and even as parts of our own culture, specifically the folklorists of the southeastern parts of the United States. Once humans learned how to write, they could communicate their ideas among themselves and could have a permanent storage archive of their writings. Writing enabled the culture to become more informed by the sheer mathematics of the writer reaching more than one audience at a time. Computer screens take the tradition one step further: No longer confined to the printed word, ideas contained as light elements on a display screen promise to reach even vaster audiences and vastly enhance our individual "reachability" in both directions.

Central to Doug Engelbart's concept of augmentation of intellect was a redefinition of what we recognize as a concept. For Engelbart, a concept was something that, like thinking itself, evolved, and outmoded concepts could be readily replaced by other concepts. In addition, he felt that human thought processes and what he called "concept structures" could not only be monitored and studied, but amplified as well. To quote from his original paper: "We view a concept to be a tool that can be grasped and used by the mental mechanisms, that can be composed, interpreted, and used by the natural mental substances and processes. The grasping and processing done by these mechanisms can often be accomplished more easily if the concept is explicitly represented by a symbol."[26]

This realization—that the human is aided in grasping concepts if the concept is represented by a symbol—led directly to the concept of a hand-held tool used as a pointing device for manipulating representative symbols on a computer screen: what we recognize today as the mouse and similar input devices. Engelbart went on to explain that a concept structure most often evolved on a cultural basis, either on a widespread or individual basis and that it was also, although with less frequency, something that could be "designed or modified." In addition, through appropriate modifications, these structures would improve the individual's ability to understand the most complex problems confronting him or her and subsequently reach more insightful solutions to these most pressing problems.

The "conceptual framework" on which Engelbart based his work was in itself designed to be a specific plan for his own augmentation research and he found that the basic principles applied to both the individual and the societal levels of experience. Engelbart proposed that by designing appropriate hypermedia systems that would work in accord with human thought processes—i.e., systems that worked the way people worked—a synergism would result. Fully aware that the human mind is capable of only small steps, and that each successive step relies on and builds on previous steps, Engelbart felt that the resulting synergy was not capable of producing any larger steps, only more surefooted ones.

Engelbart referred to the extension of human capabilities within his system as "augmentation means." He further divided the augmentation means into a group of four basic classes: artifacts, language, methodology, and training.

- The artifact class of augmentation means referred to the human capability of manipulation of symbols and physical objects to make themselves more comfortable.
- The language class addressed the manner in which the human mind organizes his or her worldview into the concepts that his or her mind uses to create a model of the world and the symbols that are attached to those concepts in the thinking process.
- Methodology spoke directly to the procedures employed by the individual in any problem-solving exercise.
- The training class of Engelbart's augmentation means was the conditioning needed to make the other three augmentation means work effectively.

Based on his concept of augmentation means, Engelbart further observed that the augmentation means served to break up large, complex problems into more manageable chunks, allowing the individual to approach the problem as a series of small steps. He called the structure of the small steps "process hierarchies." Although he recognized that each small step—each subprocess—was in itself a process, Engelbart also realized that the human being never uses a "completely unique process every time he performs a new task."[27] We don't reinvent the wheel each time we are confronted with a new problem; we build on what we already know, using what we already know. To Engelbart, it was clear that there is a finite number of "tools" with which to fashion new solutions but that the finiteness of the number of tools in no way bore on the solutions to complex problems that could be arrived at. As one of my heroes from the 1960s, Mr. Natural, proposed, we have to use the right tool for the job. Even with a finite number of tools at our collective disposal, few of us ever become proficient with more than a handful of them; we continue to reuse tools that have worked in the past when confronted with new problems. The downside of this is that many of us tend to look at every problem as a nail if the only tool we're proficient with is a hammer. Engelbart envisioned a way to surpass that "tool-bias" limitation.

The key to Engelbart's vision of bypassing our built-in tool and process biases was what amounted to screen-based text editing: what we now know as word processing. In an era when it cost hundreds of thousands of 1960s' dollars to produce a computer capable of on-screen text editing, Engelbart was correctly predicting that such appliances would become commonplace.

One of the main elements of hypermedia is that the user and author are both free of linear-thought process constraints: The new medium enables—even helps empower—us to think in a natural, nonlinear manner. Problem solving generally is experienced as a flash of insight as opposed to a series of plodding, linearly linked thoughts. Doug Engelbart had a firm grasp on this concept as well, stating, "The course of action which must respond to new comprehension, new insights, and new intuitive flashes of possible explanations or solutions is not an orderly process. Existing means of composing and working with symbol structures penalize disorderly processes heavily. It is part of the real promise . . . that the human can have the freedom and power of disorderly processes."[28]

Ted Nelson tells a wonderful story about Doug Engelbart's notion of the augmentation of the human intellect. Engelbart was having a very difficult time explaining his concepts to nontechnoids and came up with a wonderful illustration of augmentation. He tied a pencil to a brick and asked one of the observers to write with it. Because his augmentation system existed only in his brain tissue and he had no physical system to show off, he nonetheless was satisfied with reaching the observer with a demonstration of disaugmentation of the intellect, disaugmentation being what happened when tools for thinking with were worse instead of better.[29]

Ted Nelson: Making It All Work on the Way to Xanadu

The third figure in the hypermedia historical triumvirate is a madman extraordinaire and one of the most brilliant minds of our time. How do you describe someone who carries around an encyclopedic knowledge base between his ears and simultaneously manages to maintain the spark of creativity? What are we to think of an individual who, when after almost 30 years of intense work finally receives adequate funding for his publicly accessible hypermedia repository, scribbles notes on his arm in purple marker during a press conference? How much stock should we put in the ideas of a computer visionary who generally refuses to use a computer? Sounds like my kind of guy. The caricatures are of Ted Nelson: the individual generally credited with coining the term *hypertext* and popularizing the concept by making it real to anyone who cared to immerse himself or herself in Nelson's vast stores of rambling knowledge.

Nelson, influenced by Vannevar Bush, first used the term *hypertext* in the mid-1960s to describe a form of nonsequential writing. Most of his written works, most notably *Computer Lib/Dream Machines* and *Literary Machines,* have served to influence the current generation of hypermedia pioneers more than any other texts. If Bush was seen as a forward-thinker, Nelson has to be perceived as not of this planet.

His project of almost 30 years is Xanadu, a global information repository and network he refers to as the "magic place of literary memory." Based on his concept of "universal hypertext," Xanadu will consist of many thousands of nodes throughout the world, some of which will exist as fast-food franchiselike establishments Nelson refers to as "Silverstands." When Xanadu becomes a reality—as it most assuredly will now that implementation funding has been acquired—many thousands of users will have simultaneous access to mountains of information, through which they will be able to create their own knowledge trails and endless document revisions. Of course, Nelson himself acknowledges that the name "Xanadu" is based on Coleridge's unfinished poem, so there are no guarantees.

In the late 1960s, Nelson worked with Andries van Dam and a group of undergraduate students at Brown University to create the Hypertext Editing System, one of the first hypertext systems. The initial project was funded by IBM and was used for the Apollo space missions by National Aeronautics and Space Administration (NASA). The system, almost predictably, was not a commercial success and by 1970 Nelson was on to other projects. Andries van Dam and his students went on to create FRESS (an acronym for File Retrieval Editing SyStem) at Brown.[30]

Hypertext by the Book of Nelson

Ted Nelson, when referring to hypertext, means nonsequential writing, and by extension, nonsequential information retrieval and perusal. "Well, by 'hypertext' I mean nonsequential writing—text that branches and allows choices to the reader, best read at an interactive screen. As popularly conceived, this is a series of text chunks connected by links which offer the reader different pathways."[31] We also can extend the definition of hypertext to cover hypermedia by simply adding animation, sound, and full-motion video to the recipe. Nelson paints the hypertext concept with a very broad brush, initially using the layout of a magazine that employs sidebars and illustrations as a form of hypertext.[32]

Quick to point out that hypertext could include sequential text within its realm, Nelson also referred to hypertext as "the most general form of writing," for it was not limited by sequence and other external structures and conventions. Hypertext also would render a more enjoyable experience for the reader in that the reader would be able to choose a pathway to his or her own liking, rather than the strict one provided by the author in more pedestrian forms of communication. "Unrestricted by sequence, in hypertext we may create new forms of writing which better reflect the structure of what we are writing about, and readers, choosing a pathway, may follow their interests or current line of thought in a way heretofore considered impossible."[33]

Most writing is sequential, according to Nelson, because it grew out of speech making (as opposed to speaking) and because books are easier to read in a sequential manner. In the same breath he assures us, however, that the structure of ideas is not sequential, using a jumble of coat hangers as an apt illustration of the interconnectedness of our ideas. He also credits the concept of the footnote as a break from the sequential, but dismisses it because it cannot be extended. When explaining the hypertext concept to people, Nelson states that relatively few people grasp the concept right away. Most think it's too technical or too philosophical. What they don't understand is that writers write better if they don't have to do it in a sequential manner and that readers read better if *they* don't have to read sequentially. Nonsequential reading allows readers to form impressions and bounce around trying different tacks until they find the one that's the most interesting or germane to their immediate task at hand. Hypertext allows for a totally arbitrary information structure, a structure that opens doors rather than slamming the doors shut.

Ted Nelson took pride in the power of words and was very much aware of the "spin" his word for his general concept would have once he named it. He admits looking for a loaded word like Bucky Fuller's "dymaxion" which, according to Nelson, "condensed his philosophy of high-payoff engineering."[34] After quite a few miscues ("linktext," "jumptext," "nonsequential text," etc.), Nelson knew he had the *right* word with hypertext. Later, he would reflect on the *rightness* of his hypernomenclature: " 'Hyper' to most scientists and mathematicians means *extended* and *generalized,* as in hyperspace, hyperdimensional, hypercube, hypersphere, and even hyperchess. . . . Thus hyper*text* would clearly be the extended, generalized form of writing."[35] Nelson maintained a deaf ear to how the social scientists would react to his "hyper" moniker, including the protests of his father-in-law who was a child psychologist. He addressed this by explaining that his own quest for an understanding of interconnection had always led to chaos and that it was possible, even likely, that the two aspects of hyperness are two sides of the same coin—"deeply intertwingled" in Nelson Speak—and that disorder could be transformed into understanding by accurately mapping the interconnections.

Nelson foresaw that once we were liberated from the pestilent confines of the printed page, our writing would be helped to flow in a naturally interconnected manner. Additionally, a body of text could be authored without regard to a target market or "average" reader. Any level of detail could be achieved without concern for violating the supposed rules of general interest. Documents would be modeled after an onion rather than after a potato. Layers of detail could be peeled back and the reader could immerse himself or herself deeper and deeper into the writer's work instead of the most cursory of treatments. Again, Nelson waxes eloquent: "I wanted everyone to see that we were going to the extended, generalized form of writing: no longer held to convenient sizes by printing and marketing considerations, no longer restricted to a single expository stream, no longer breaking the true interconnections of a subject to make a sequence (like branches snapped into sticks and put into a row)."[36]

There are three immediate incentives for and related benefits of using hypertext: the allowance for preferences, motivation, and lower costs. Nelson correctly perceived that—especially in nonfiction works—readers have different preferences. In this book, for example, some of you may wish to read this section before reading anything else including the preface and introduction, while someone else may prefer to skip this section entirely. On the question of motivation, a reader is much more likely to grasp a subject if given the opportunity to explore freely rather than being "herded" through a text in a strict, predefined sequence. Finally, hypertext costs less to produce and distribute, therefore allowing the publication of more marginal works.

Nelson also was initially very careful to point out explicitly that computers had no essential involvement with the concept of hypertext, but that computers would most certainly be involved with the execution and development. Fully aware that hypertext would be perceived as "drastic and threatening" to the mainstream of society, Nelson took great pains to illustrate that the concept was fundamental to the vast corpus of civilization's literature. Claiming that hypertext's inherent nature of generality was a central theme recurring in our literature, Nelson bemoaned the fact that various computer systems were largely incompatible in a world of print where books and magazines were "at least unified and compatible." He pointed out in an appropriately acerbic tone that one didn't have to start a computer or initialize disks in order to open a magazine.

The generality inherent in hypertext, however, promised to tip the scales of the compatibility and ease-of-use issue by providing a sense of mass-customization in the universe of letters, a drastic and revolutionary idea indeed. "Customary writing chooses one expository sequence from among the possible myriad," he explained, "hypertext allows many, all available to the reader."[37]

Nelson foresaw that hypertext would make writing easier, not more difficult. He noted that in sequential writing, the author must decide on the sequence which, in itself, was an unnecessary task of significant proportion. The hypertext author would be freed of the concern of sequence, and would be enabled to devote more time to the "interconnective structure" of the material. The writer's flexibility would be enhanced greatly as sequential concerns give way to the simpler task of connecting text in a "searchable maze."

Central to almost all of Ted Nelson's work is the sense of pluralism and egalitarianism. Perhaps best exemplified by one of his own line drawings, reproduced here as *Figure 1.2*, on page 34, all of Nelson's concepts and ideas seem to rotate around the notion of freedom and openness and the relations of many to many. Nelson feels very strongly that contributions from *all* users are important and form the basis of any information repository and that new pluralistic writing styles will develop as many authors add to a singular body of writing.

Patently understated, Nelson's reasons for an egalitarian hypertext writing and reading system thread throughout his work: "In hypertext systems, there is a good reason to make the tools and access privileges of all users the same: the reader's tool can be the same as the author's tool. Thus hypertext may be intrinsically an egalitarian medium. (Provided, especially, that preexisting materials may be freely edited and incorporated in new objects without damaging the old.)"[38]

Based on his insistence on the appropriateness and value of pluralistic documents, one of the main stumbling blocks for the Xanadu system as a workable solution for everyone remains the compatibility issue between types of computers, or, rather, the incompatibility between the various kinds of computers. "The initiatives and contributions of many people are assumed to be worthwhile. But there is at present no way to gather, and save, and publish, the many documents and scraps that people are writing on screens and sharing through an immense variety of incompatible systems."[39]

Interestingly, as much as Ted Nelson saw computers, especially personal computers, as appropriate hypermedia tools, he continually decried the

• *Figure 1.2 Pluralism, one of the cornerstones of Ted Nelson's hypertext publishing concepts.*

concept of "computer literacy" as detrimental in that the issues taught to the noncomputer-literate are veiled in layers of unnecessary complication. Very eloquently he stated, "Nearly everything has to be fitted into oppressive and inane hierarchical structure and coded into other people's conceptual frameworks, often seeming rigid and highly inappropriate to the user's own concerns."[40] Nelson also took a firm stand against the traditional structure of the computer "file," voicing a strong distaste for the "tyranny of the file" as illustrated by the file's detachment from relationships and history that subsequently results in more confusion, not less.

A particularly common target of Ted Nelson's venom was the early form of computer-aided instruction (CAI) that began to develop in the early 1960s. Nelson saw this as an attempted paternalism on the part of the schools at best and fascism at worst. "Though the student was implicitly at some position in a branching text complex, he or she would have no way to see it whole, no way to choose," wrote Nelson in 1988, "the student's only option was to *answer questions,* and these answers would implicitly make the next choice in a manner unseen."[41] This concept rested on the attempt to control and restrict users, where Nelson saw the promise inherent in freeing people to pursue their own interests, cross-references, and linkages. Always the pluralist, Nelson was adamant, "This was not the tradition of literature. This was not the tradition of free speech. It was the tradition of the most oppressive aspects of the bureaucratic educational system, dandied up to look scientific."[42]

From this distaste for oppression, Ted Nelson, the visionary, became something of Ted Nelson, the Protector of Our Rights. At the same time that he was singing the high praises of the hypermedia future, he also was sounding the warning bells of being ever-aware of possible encroachments on our freedom of speech.

Nelson's broad-based goal, then, was a form of pluralistically general hypermedia, although he readily recognized that as the bandwidth of the component media grew, so did the potential for confusing disorder. Video, animation, and sound, while drastically increasing the bandwidth of the medium, also raised the potential for disaster and greater incompatibility was symptomatic of the situation. His proposed solution was elegantly simple: "To unify and organize in the right way, so as to clarify and simplify our computer and working lives, and indeed to bring literature, science, art, and civilization to new heights of understanding, through hypertext."[43] Nelson clearly perceived hypertext, and subsequently hypermedia, as a "framework of reunification" rather than just another obscure structure and duly noted Doug Engelbart's initial concept that hypertext should be one piece, not haphazardly scattered about with bits here, there, and everywhere.

By proposing two styles of the organization of material within a hypertext document, Ted Nelson also demonstrated that hypertext would be much more useful for the reader than the more standard sequential forms of reading. He illustrated this succinctly by pointing out that when we read a work of nonfiction, we generally hop around from section to section to get the most information relevant to our current needs in the shortest possible amount of time.

Nelson referred to that style of hypertext organization that concerned itself with its possible effect on the reader—manifesting itself in a series of interlinked "planned presentations" the reader would navigate—as the "presentation and effect" style. At the core of a "presentation and effect" style of hypertext, the sequences would be designed for their look and feel and how they communicate their ideas to the reader.

The alternate hypertext style, which Nelson referred to as "lines of structure," simply represented the organizational pattern of the subject matter. The effect on the reader of the material—in the lines of structure style—

while taken into consideration, was not a major factor and was easier to implement for the author, "since the author is only concerned with analyzing and representing what the structure really is, and the reader is exploring the structure as he or she explores the text."[44]

Ted Nelson also was fully cognizant of the problem with reader orientation in a hypertext document. In my first attempt at electronically publishing hypertext documents for a general readership on a regular basis, one of the strongest complaints I heard from the majority of users was that it was too easy to get lost and too hard to determine what hadn't already been read.

Nelson points out that in traditional paper publications the reader is given "incidental cues" as to his or her location in the material: "the thickness of a book, the recalled position of a paragraph on the left or right page, and whether it was at the bottom or the top."[45] He went on to propose that new cues must be developed that are equivalent to the cues we subconsciously employ when reading the more traditional forms of the printed word. Although initially he didn't offer any ready-made solutions, several viable alternatives have managed to surface in the interim years between Nelson's original proposal and commercial hypermedia systems.

Firmly believing that hypertext—with its inherent ability to present complex ideas companioned by their interconnections in the same documents—would advance the state of writing and learning, Nelson was fully aware of the potential of hypertext to address complex problems, which was Engelbart's original supposition. Furthermore, Nelson envisioned taking hypertext a step further, to include the interconnections of many authors: "Hypertext can represent all the interconnections an author can think of; and compound hypertext can represent all the interconnections many authors can think of. . . ."[46]

Nelson referred to the interconnections of many authors as "compound hypertext" and began exploring the problem of revision-tracking as early as 1960. Referring to such arrangements of the interconnections of the multiple authors of a compound hypertext as problems of "intercomparison," Ted Nelson correctly perceived a need on the part of the reader to be able to compare two alternative document structures on the same screen, side by side. At that point, Nelson set out to address the need of intercomparison and his work to that end is lumped together under the group heading of "thinkertoys." The impetus for this work was clear: "Such intercomparison systems, I still believe, will become a vital aspect of our working lives—once they are easy to use."[47] Such devices and implementations are only now beginning to become available. Perhaps that's why some of the best minds in the Macintosh community continue to work on video-display technology.

The Xanadu system, the embodiment of most of Ted Nelson's work, was originally conceived as a solution to a very real problem while Nelson was a student at Harvard. He needed a note-keeping program that would serve as a repository for his thoughts. Xanadu, however, quickly grew in scope to encompass idea creation, thought organization, backtracking, alternative versions, automatic cross-references, text manipulation, and a complete electronic publishing system, including an automatic royalty-logging mechanism. Whew!

At the eye of the Xanadu hurricane is the concept that every document in the Xanadu repository has links to what it was drawn from and to those documents which draw on it. The linkages are electronic forms of footnotes except that the Xanadu flavor puts any would-be footnote into a separate window where it is readily accessible.

Nelson described a unique storage system for Xanadu, which he called "xanalogical storage," that was based on a single repository that was shared across the system itself and at the same time organized in a myriad of different ways. Once again, the mass-customization of knowledge is at the base of most of Nelson's concept. Originally designed as a vast dumping and storage ground for textual information, the Xanadu concept grew to encompass all interactive media as well and began to be seen more along the lines of a heritage preserve accessible to all community members. Because the knowledge base comprising Xanadu is a single shared pool, the contained materials can be continually rearranged to meet the needs of varied individuals without losing any of the prior organization structures. Sounding like a huge software program, in actuality, Xanadu is relatively small and relies on the cooperative processing power of all the nodes making up the network. Such an architecture further allows the system to be run by various individuals, under many localized ownerships, rather than being subjected to the potential of tyrannical rule by a single body.

Ted Nelson sees the current state of networking and electronic publishing as being in a state of small, mutually resentful bodies hopelessly embroiled: one against all others. He believes that a universal hypertext network would change that, supplying stored text and graphics on demand (again, mass-customization) from anywhere to anywhere else. Such a situation would, according to Nelson, render information "an elemental commodity, like water, telephone service, radio, and television."[48] Furthermore, Nelson holds that such a development would change the basic structure of information and would at last represent the true structure of information "with all its intrinsic complexity and controversy, and provide a universal archival standard worthy of our heritage and freedom and pluralism."[49]

Types of Hypertext à la Ted Nelson

Chunk-style hypertext is best exemplified by the way we currently use footnotes and endnotes, additional text at the end of a section that illuminates a passage of text. Implemented as a footnote reference mark or symbol, when activated it would expand to display another chunk of text.

Collateral hypertext involves complex annotations and links created between two sections of text. It would include parallel text implemented in a manner similar to Nelson's original parallel text specification.

Nelson's original specification for displaying parallel text, the Parallel Textface, was designed to complement the Xanadu system and, in fact, some of the research for the Parallel Textface actually *became* the Xanadu system. At that point, the Parallel Textface became a "front-end function" in Nelson's words. The Parallel Textface presents two portions of text, side by side, which are each windows on a larger body of text, with the windows scrolling together or separately, as appropriate. The window boundaries would be user-configurable by using a light pen to resize each screen element's "pip" or handle. Pretty fascinating stuff for being ten years prior to the birth of Macintosh. As one window scrolled to show more of the underlying text, the other window, if dependent on the text displayed on the first window, also would scroll to maintain the visible link between the two text bodies. If there are no associated links, the dependent window simply stops scrolling.

Another Nelson proposal was the Qframe, similar to the windowing system we are familiar with on the Macintosh. The Qframe is a windowing environment for the creation, retrieval, and display of hypertext. All of the current windowing systems, including the Qframe and Macintosh, are based on Engelbart's NLS system and got their boot into the real world from Xerox's research at its Palo Alto Research Center (PARC) and, more specifically, PARC's venture into the Smalltalk programming environment. In most windowing systems, relations to material in other windows are not displayed. Each window is displayed in and of itself with no connections to anything else, and therefore, no context. Qframes, on the other hand, overtly display all the interconnections between the various views on a body of text provided by the window convention. Each Qframe, however, maintains its independence from the others.

Nelson came up with the name Qframe because the frame of each window would contain information in the form of visual "cues" as to the contents and interconnections of the window. Immediate information concerning each Qframe's interconnections and relations would be available at a glance. Qframes could be of either a hierarchical or hereditorial nature. A hierarchical Qframe would in effect serve as a browser to other connected windows, while a Qframe displaying heredity would show the interconnections themselves. Qframes also could be compressed so that more windows would be viewable on the screen at the same time.

Another Ted Nelson vision, the Walking Net, is a networked hypermedia system that is navigable through the use of a "walk-through" metaphor with branches, intersections, forked paths, and the like. The Walking Net is envisioned to be extremely simple to learn by users with the lowest levels of expertise. The user would be presented with a single one-dimensional choice at any given time, rather than being confronted with the myriad of choices inherent in any Xanadu information branch.

Stretchtext is a method of hypertext that enables the user to expand or stretch a small section of text into a much larger body that, in turn, expands into an even larger body of text. The metaphor employed is one of going successively deeper into a subject.

In the best case, chunk hypertext, collateral hypertext, and stretch hypertext would be combined in function to form a basic workable hypertext system, but would fall short of Nelson's grand dream—universal hypertext—that would include *everything* on a given subject matter.

Conceived as a solution to the incompatibilities plaguing users of different computer systems, Ted Nelson's concept of a universal hypertext was envisioned as the formation of an electronic literature that would set aside all the concerns of incompatible equipment and data structures. Where hypertext could be created and used by individuals, the call for greater data spaces useful by everyone, everywhere, all at once is addressed by the universal hypertext principle. In Nelson's words, "that is the vision of universal hypertext: a world in which everything that is published becomes electronically available, in an ever-growing interconnected whole."[50]

The principle of a universal hypertext refers most directly to a new publishing system, and therefore travels back full circle to Ted Nelson's Xanadu project. Once again, the concept is best thought of as the mass-customization of information. The key principle is that because everyone has access to everything, there is little need to have copies of much of anything in your physical possession. Another Nelson concept, "fragmentary publishing," springs from this principle of everything everywhere all at once and nowhere in particular. It would be absurd to have to request a full copy of a title consisting of hundreds of thousands of words when all that is needed is to follow a link to the work's third chapter. Mass-customization on a grand scale!

Even with a universal hypertext, however, Nelson continues to voice concern over the control issues: Who makes the links and who governs what kinds of links will be allowed? Nelson proposes that a universal hypertext is not synonymous with an open hypertext; an open hypertext is one in which anyone may contribute anything and establish his or her own connections. A universal hypertext would form a sort of hybrid, a system that is both open and universal.

So who gets to contribute? According to Nelson, "Some believe that participants must have special qualifications, that only certain persons anointed in some way are truly worthy of contributing; that information should be monopolized and that only some should be allowed to write and publish: that information should be a monopoly resource. They see the world of literature as something that has to be carefully controlled."[51] Nelson attributes such reasoning under a variety of misperceptions, generally centering on questions of professionalism. "But these are essentially styles of information monopoly, the assumption that Information Lords will decide what is to be available, and that the Information Peons (the rest of us) will have to accept what's dished out."[52] Under any circumstances such a position is indefensible and not to be tolerated.

Nelson goes on to identify a variation on the information monopoly theme, that only authoritative versions should be allowed. Access should be available and granted only to approved information versions for the sake of stability and consistency. Nelson's position is that *all* the works in *all* the disciplines should be available as well as *all the comments made on them*. Each work, each viewpoint, would be available as it was originally created—and clearly labeled as such—and no comments or corrections would be made on the virgin original. The links to other referenced material would be available to anyone who wanted them, but all the original works would remain intact.

Where the original material would be locked, free from modification (including correction), the links to other materials would be wide open. Anyone could link anything to anything else and anyone would be able to follow anyone else's connections—*in any direction*. "This means not just the ability to follow connections in the direction they were originally made, but to follow them backwards as well."[53] Why would this be important? Individuals would want to know the origins of many documents as well as related or auxiliary documents. In order to see comments made on one's own work, you would have to be able to trace the current document backward; it would give the corpus of massive works a sense of time and place.

The key issue here for Nelson, once again, is pluralism in the form of openness and freedom: "What I have been trying to communicate here is a sense of manifest destiny: we must recognize that the hypertext future is destined to be open, vast, free, and without restriction; with all participants and all links on a formally equal footing; in which intellectual property will not be an encumbrance but (like other property rights) a simple precondition, handled by a simple mechanism for automatic royalty payments and acknowledgment of origins. All this will bring a vast, new, practical, and intellectual freedom: What I call open hypertext publishing."[54]

As an example of the benefits of a universal and open hypertext system, Nelson explains that permissions to republish material (such as those that were required from various individuals for this book) would not need to be requested. Material could be republished simply by including the underlying work in the new document. The material itself would not be physically included in the new document, but, rather, a reference would be formed and linked to the original material.

An additional, perhaps more significant benefit would be the virtual elimination—by definition—of misquotes and taking things out of the original context. And royalties to the original author would be guaranteed by being automatically paid through a mechanism built into the system. A blanket inclusion and cross-reference permission would be implicit, by prior contractual agreement, before any individual work was allowed to be published on the system. Private documents would be allowed on the same system and could contain links to public documents, but the reverse case would not be allowed. Obviously, private documents would not be eligible for as broad a royalty arrangement.

Users requesting parts of public documents for inclusion in their new documents would not need to be aware of which documents the fragments came from, although the information would be readily obtainable. The only element the author requesting inclusion would be required to know would be the links used to access the document containing the fragments to be included.

The result would be an on-line electronic publishing system of vast proportions, easily transversed and accessible by minimally computer-literate individuals. Such a system would, over a relatively short period of time, serve to significantly enhance our collective body of literature. The most significant benefit to an open and universal hypertext system would be the seamless handling of the problem of multiple versions that, according to Nelson, requires a significantly advanced level of hypertext consciousness than we now generally enjoy.

Thinkertoys and Super Virtualities

Ted Nelson, along with Doug Engelbart and Vannevar Bush before him, perceived our planet's greatest problems as involving "thinking and the visualization of complexity."[55] Similar in scope to Engelbart's concept of ''augmentation of intellect,'' thinkertoys are more specific: a computer system designed to help ''envision complex alternatives.''[56]

The crux of any thinkertoy is the ability of the device to allow things of varying levels of complexity to be intercompared and subsequently intercomprehended via their interconnections. Nelson gives very specific instances in which such devices would prove beneficial, ranging from alternative designs and theories to successive drafts of text documents to discrepancies in courtroom testimony. The underlying concept of the thinkertoy is that although the interconnections between vastly different problems appear to be vastly different, in actuality, they are more similar than dissimilar.

Significant differences between types of problems remain, however, leading Nelson to propose the most general of approaches to problem-solving including a technique he referred to as ''collateration,'' which is the ''linking of materials into 'collateral structures.' ''[57] (Nelson had previously referred to collateral structures as ''zippered lists.'')[58, 59] Structures would be collateral if there are specific links between them, although the specific sequences of the connections may be different. ''Collateration, then,'' according to Nelson, ''is the creation of such multiple and viewable links *between any two data structures,* in principle.''[60]

To Nelson, the guiding principal of any computer system, regardless of its intended function, but extremely important in the case of a thinkertoy, is that any such system must be inherently, even disquietingly, easy to use. ''If it is desirable that computer systems for *simple-minded* purposes be easy to use,'' he said, ''it is *absolutely necessary* that computer systems for *complicated purposes* be simple to use.''[61] Patently obvious, yes, but exceptionally difficult to implement: Therein lies what many consider to be Ted Nelson's greatest acumen. Power and apparent simplicity are not mutually exclusive in the eyes of Ted Nelson and he always has aimed at (and consistently achieved) the demystification of the various hypermedia technologies.

Nelson aims for simplicity to such an extent as to admonish systems that are more complicated than what he calls a ''ten-minute system'' (a system that can be learned by a novice and put to useful application in less than ten minutes) as almost useless. ''I believe that interaction with computers can be at least ten times easier,'' Nelson states, ''ten times more powerful, ten times more vivid; and that these are issues not of hardware but of virtuality design,'' he concludes.[62]

In order for us to take the step toward the super virtualities, interactive systems with a level of power and simplicity that the original Macintosh only flirted with, however, we are going to have to let go of paper as an ''ideal and as a security blanket,'' and realize that ''screen systems, without paper, will and must be the home of the mind in the future.''[63] This is not a gushing statement to be taken lightly in a print publication, to be sure. Nelson points out several recent developments as enabling super virtualities, such as OWL International's Guide hypertext system that is available for both Macintosh and the IBM PC, his own Zig-Zag hypertext system for individuals, Alan Kay's Dynabook (a very powerful book-size computer that is easily affordable but alas, nonexistent), and Apple's HyperCard software construction kit.

Hypertext and Idea Transfer

Hypermedia is, before and above anything else, a method of communication. Tantamount to any communication medium is the underlying concept of idea transferal. Hypermedia is a more appropriate communication medium for many endeavors, although it is not a communications panacea.

Ideas may be presented in any number of ways that are virtually unlimited for the articulate communicator: animations, various texts, graphics, sound, even with the face of the typography. Underlying the cosmetics of idea transfer—just as in the case of information systems—are the only guiding rules: simplicity and clarity.

Nelson also points out the value of a ''socially neutral'' information transfer, using as an example maps and some texts. I would hasten to take issue with the supposed neutrality of any communications medium. Like objectivity, there isn't much, and what little there is can be indistinguishable from what isn't, especially when such variables as time and place enter into the equation. We're better off, generally, not to expect it and to be wary when we think we've found a neutral communications medium. Nelson argues that the best hypertext system would contain both socially neutral and socially active elements. I argue that this violates his own precept of no ruling body being in control of the medium. Who is to say what is neutral and what is active? A better position would be to consider everything as socially active.

The central problem, according to Nelson, is the widely held misperception of the writing process. Most nonwriters feel that the process of writing is to construct and subsequently fill in an outline. Nelson points to a National Safety Council pamphlet on how to survive a hotel fire as indicative of this general misperception. The pamphlet consists of ''seventeen fine-print 'step-by-step' instructions [that] transcends imbecility. . . .''[64]

Three procedures involved in the writing process sometimes occur simultaneously, according to Nelson. The first is what he refers to as the provisional development of ideas and points wherein the author forms his or her organizing ideas and relationships. The second procedure is sorting the points arrived at during the first process (yes, this can happen simultaneously with the first procedure). The final step is connecting the sequences using such mechanisms as cross-references.

Nelson called the structure of the organizing principles "arches" and defined them specifically as "final ironies, things to be led up to, themes, plots, concepts, principles, expository structures, organizing titles, overconcepts."[65] Nelson goes on to reveal that between the points used to elucidate the arches are transitions and that the main problem in writing as a method of idea transfer is that "overall structures you choose (systems of arches) may not link well to the points that have to be included among them; and that transitions between points don't work out the way you want them to."[66] There are times when the points just don't connect the "right way" or times when the transitions seem overly weak.

With the notion of idea transfer, especially if we take as a given the "activeness" rather than "neutrality" of the media itself, comes the possibility—even likelihood—of misrepresentation. Nelson bemoans the decline of diagrammatics (the ability to read and create charts and diagrams) in our society. He also goes on to illustrate the misrepresentation problem inherent in the concept of idea transfer using the broadcast journalism tactic of displaying an oversized arrow—either up or down—to represent the stock market's activity for the day. No level of quantification is given in the visual cue; the market is either up or down, and we have no way of determining the size of the fluctuation. This problem is addressed exceptionally well in Edward Tufte's *The Visual Display of Quantitative Information*.[67]

Beyond Idea Transfer: Fantics

Ted Nelson's formulated linguistics are seen by many as camouflage covering the weakness inherent in his ideas. Nothing could be further from the truth, although I'm sure Nelson would not take exception to being called a vaudevillian. Nelson as vaudevillian is best exemplified by his concept of fantics. In Nelson Speak, fantics is simply the showmanship of ideas. "I derive 'fantics' from the Greek words 'phainein' (show) and its derivative 'phantastein' (present to the eye or mind)."[68] Well, that's what he says, but I am not going to be convinced that he didn't get it by combining fanatic antics. Some of the other words Nelson says he could have used for the concept were "teachotechnics," "showmanshipnogogy," "intelletronics," "thoughtomation," and "mediatronics." Like I said, he is a vaudevillian.

In describing the underlying motives for the importance Nelson lies at the doorstep of the showmanship of ideas, he is quite explicit: "But I think it's all show business. Penny arcades are the model for interactive computer systems, not classrooms or libraries or imaginary robot playmates.''[69]

Call it what you will, but Nelson's concept of fanatic antics to get ideas expressed and comprehended is right on the money. Contrary to closely held beliefs throughout most sectors of our society, the new media—and hypermedia in particular—will not require more and more technical specialization, but less.

All computers contain an inherent ''learning curve,'' that period of time required to learn how to use the system in question. New approaches to any problem have a learning curve attached to them: automatic teller machines, new cars, food processors, and computers. The beauty of the original Macintosh was its downsized learning curve. Anyone could be creating something useful on the machine in less than a half hour. Macintosh formed a new paradigm for powerful computing machinery. Software designed to run on Macintosh helped solidify this paradigm, and cries of ''once you master any Macintosh program you have a great head start on most others'' were heard throughout the land. How did this come to be? Aside from excellent design and the notion of ''evangelizing'' the product, it had to do with fanatic antics. People were actually enjoying working with computers—for the first time ever. So it's not for nil that Nelson tells us, ''I think that when the *real* media of the future arrive, the smallest child will know it right away (and perhaps first).''[70]

Fanatic? You bet. With words such as ''responsive computer display systems can, should, and will restructure and light up the mental life of mankind,'' what would *you* call it?

Antics? Please. This is the man with the purple marker notes on his arms during a press conference, remember?

If the problems barricading the acceptance of hypermedia are not technical, what are they? ''The fundamental issues are *not technical.* To understand this is basically a matter of *media consciousness,* not technical knowledge.''[71] Central to this concept are four Nelsonisms surrounding the understanding and personalization of media.

''Anything can be said in any medium.'' The techniques used to impart the idea are unpredictable, however, and cause most of the problems we associate with the myopia of most visual media.

''Transposability.'' Related directly to the first Nelsonism, transposability speaks directly to the interrelatedness of all media. You can get your idea across in any number of ways, but generally one or more media are "better" or at least more appropriate for your task at hand.

"Big and small approaches." Big ideas can be communicated any number of ways, and, generally, the smaller the approach the more effective the communication. There is always a more powerful way to transfer an idea, and the way to do so is not by massaging the content of the idea but by massaging the information structure used to transmit the idea.

"The word-picture continuum." Writing and drawing—or, more specifically, diagramming—are a continuum, and where words are slow, graphic representation is lightning fast. Where graphics are generally inarticulate, words are fluent.

OK, fine, but what good are fantics in the real world? Well, consider that our intent is, first and foremost, to communicate an idea to either an individual or group of individuals. With that as our intent, then, we can say that fantics is concerned with vaudevillian showmanship as a presentation skill as well as specific techniques of presentation and the media themselves. From those three concerns we can distill that the basis for our endeavor is the design of the presentation system on both a conceptual and technical level.

In order to fully understand the concept and potential impact of fantics, according to Ted Nelson, we must understand that in the past, information structures, as the transporters of ideas, "sprang naturally from the nature of things." This is no longer true, however, and "*we must acknowledge that we are* ***inventing*** *presentational techniques in the new media* and not merely transporting or transposing particular things into them because they seem right. *The psychological constructs of man-machine systems may turn out to be largely arbitrary.*[72]

Nobody knows and you can't find out. You can, however, get in on the ground floor, roll your sleeves up, and put on your exploration shoes.

Thankfully, the human mind can draw unity out of vastly diverse concepts and ideas. This is one of the things we do best. Even more important, according to Nelson, is the fact that our *perceptions* also can be unified—he cites the example of our being able to "feel" with our fingernails even though we "know" our fingernails have no sensory nerves. "This principle of mental unification is what makes things come together, both literally and figuratively, in a fantic field."[73]

The best we can do as hypermedia authors and information developers is to help our readers/viewers make this "mental unification" in any way that we can. The most appropriate and powerful way to do this is through the use of an interface and control mechanisms that *appear* to be simplistic. To date, the best work on human interface issues remains Apple's *Human Interface Guidelines: The Apple Desktop Interface*.[74] Interface design issues are among the most important aspects of hypermedia production and will be covered only briefly in this volume. A more in-depth treatment is offered in *HyperCard Development Tools,* a companion to this work by the same author.

Hypermedia production entails many interface issues that must be addressed. Most center around control and navigation devices within the document itself and include, more specifically, text editing, searching, and retrieval issues; how the viewer/reader navigates from section to section without getting lost; how the viewer/reader backtracks to and through material that already has been browsed; and so on.

As important a consideration as the control devices themselves are the "real world" replicas chosen to represent the task at hand: Which guiding metaphor is employed and how do the other smaller supporting metaphors relate to the guiding metaphors. The guiding metaphor—the big picture—generally appears "all at once" and is usually arrived at first with the supporting metaphors (dials, buttons, slide controls, levers, knobs, and so on) following.

According to Nelson and most design experts, clarity and apparent simplicity is the easiest way to help the user from making mistakes, which, after the idea transfer, is our primary goal. A mistakefree implementation of an appropriate metaphor in the form of the user interface will keep the reader/viewer/contributor interested and at the same time won't intimidate him or her. Instead it will invite, mostly by using techniques such as tension and compression to draw the user in.

For example, consider the original design metaphor for one of the first HyperCard stackware products, Mac TV.[75] The opening screen consisted solely of a black background with a simple "on" button in a corner. I have yet to see a user who could resist clicking the button.

"Clear and simple systems are easier to learn, harder to forget, less likely to be screwed up by the user, and thus are more economical—getting more done for the resources put in."[76] The key to obtaining apparent simplicity in the interface and control mechanisms of a system lies in the generality of the thought behind the design. To the degree that the designer utilized generalized thought, the more simple the system will appear to the user.

The complete body of control devices, in addition to requiring painstaking thought concerning their individual design, also form a synergy that also must be addressed appropriately. This synergy resides mostly in the relationships and connections between the various screen elements. Again, this is best accomplished by thinking about the problem in the most general way possible. A single button out of place or of an inappropriate type could potentially affect the approachability and apparent simplicity of the entire interface. Nelson states the problem quite eloquently: "So the problem is to devise techniques which have elucidating value but do not cut connections or ties or other relationships you want to save."[77]

One of the most appropriate control devices available to the hypermedia designer is the map. A navigational map, readily available at all times, displaying where the reader is and where he or she can go (and ideally where he or she already has been) serves to orient the user and to provide a constant reassurance. Of course, in the future, we are likely to be able to call up a software "agent" that will be able to make an educated guess about where we would most likely wish to go based on where we are now, where we have been, and what the agent recognizes as our interests, but the concept of software agents is still a bit in the future. Even for us.

So there you have it. The history and underlying concepts of hypermedia in a nutshell. And now we can ask the $64 question with a gleam in our eye and a knowing wink: "What did Vannevar Bush, Preston Tucker, Doug Engelbart, and Ted Nelson all have in common?" May I have the envelope, please. They were all crackpots. They were all right. And all their ideas will last forever.

NOTES

[22] Vannevar Bush, "As We May Think," *The Atlantic Monthly* (July 1945).

[23] Douglas C. Engelbart, "A Conceptual Framework for the Augmentation of Man's Intellect," edited and annotated by Howard Rheingold, *HyperAge* (May–June, 1988): 12–16.

[24] Douglas C. Engelbart, "A Conceptual Framework for the Augmentation of Man's Intellect," *Vistas in Information Handling*, Volume 1, ed. Paul Howerton. (Washington, D.C.: Spartan Books, 1962).

[25] Ibid.

[26] Ibid.

[27] Ibid.

[28] Ibid.

[29] Theodor Nelson, *Dream Machines,* rev. ed. (Redmond, Washington: Tempus Books of Microsoft Press, 1987), 16.

[30] Andries van Dam is currently on the board of directors of Context, Inc., of Portland, Oregon, a hypertext development company, and has no official connection with Brown University's current hypertext system, Intermedia, which will be covered in a later chapter.

[31] Theodor Nelson, *Literary Machines,* electronic ed. (Bellevue, Washington: OWL International, Inc., 1987).

[32] Ibid.

[33] Ibid.

[34] Theodor Nelson, "To Strike the Lightning," *HyperAge* (February–March, 1988): 5–6.

[35] Ibid.

[36] Ibid.

[37] Theodor Nelson, *Literary Machines,* elect. ed. (Bellevue, Washington: OWL International, Inc., 1987).

[38] Theodor Nelson, *Dream Machines,* rev. ed. (Redmond, Washington: Tempus Books of Microsoft Press, 1987).

[39] Ibid.

[40] Ibid.

[41] Theodor Nelson, "To Strike the Lightning," *HyperAge* (February–March, 1988): 5–6.

[42] Ibid.

[43] Ibid.

[44] Ibid.

[45] Ibid.

[46] Ibid.

[47] Ibid.

[48] Ibid.

[49] Ibid.

[50]Theodor Nelson, "The Call of the Ocean: Hypertext Universal and Open," *Hyper-Age* (May–June, 1988): 5–7.

[51] Ibid.

[52] Ibid.

[53] Ibid.

[54] Ibid.

[55] Theodor Nelson, *Dream Machines,* rev. ed. (Redmond, Washington: Tempus Books of Microsoft Press, 1987).

[56] Ibid.

[57] Ibid.

[58] Theodor Nelson, "The Hypertext," *Proc. World Documentation Federation,* 1965.

[59] Theodor Nelson, "A File Structure for the Complex, the Changing, and the Indeterminate," *Proc. Association for Computing Machinery,* 1965.

[60]Theodor Nelson, *Dream Machines,* rev. ed. (Redmond, Washington: Tempus Books of Microsoft Press, 1987).

[61] Ibid.

[62] Ibid.

[63] Ibid.

[64] Ibid.

[65] Ibid.

[66] Ibid.

[67] Edward Tufte, *The Visual Display of Quantitative Information* (New York: Graphics Press, 1983).

[68] Theodor Nelson, *Dream Machines,* rev. ed. (Redmond, Washington: Tempus Books of Microsoft Press, 1987).

[69] Ibid.

[70] Ibid.

[71] Ibid.

[72] Ibid.

[73] Ibid.

[74] Apple Computer, Inc., *Human Interface Guidelines: The Apple Desktop Interface* (Reading, Massachusetts: Addison-Wesley Publishing Company, Inc., 1987).

[75] Designed and implemented by Jerry Daniels and Mary Jane Mara for *MACazine* (August 1987).

[76] Theodor Nelson, *Dream Machines,* rev. ed. (Redmond, Washington: Tempus Books of Microsoft Press, 1987).

[77] Ibid.

CURRENT MACINTOSH HYPERMEDIA IMPLEMENTATIONS

CHAPTER 2

- *Nonsequential Writing Tools*
- *Text Archiving and Retrieval Tools*
- *Noncommercial Hypermedia Applications*
- *Commercial Macintosh Hypermedia Products*
- *Other Pending Hypermedia Developments*
- *Conclusion and Recommendations*

Aside from OWL International's Guide for the PC, few significant hypermedia products are commercially available for any personal computer other than Apple's Macintosh. This is likely to change in the near future, but we will forever look back on OWL International's initial release of Guide for the Macintosh and Apple's subsequent release of HyperCard and the AppleCD SC CD-ROM Drive as the roots of hypermedia systems on the personal computer.

Of course, if we take a strict definition of hypermedia from the book of Ted Nelson as nonsequential writing, many ancillary products would fit into the definition other than the two that spring most readily to mind: OWL's Guide and Apple's HyperCard. Included in this broad category would be outline processors, text archiving and retrieval utilities, and freeform data bases, as well as what we've come to recognize as hypertext and hypermedia production tools. We will take a look at a diverse cross-section of these products from the aspect of applicability to hypermedia development.

Nonsequential Writing Tools

While not truly hypermedia tools in and of themselves, these products are useful in the production of nonsequential writing, Ted Nelson's underlying precept for hypertext. Most of the products covered in this section are outliners or derivatives of that genre of software. They are useful in designing and maintaining the overall information content of a hypertext or hypermedia project, and because this is, after all, the Macintosh, graphic support in addition to the text-handling capabilities is a given.

The hypermedia development process begins on the same level as virtually all other creative endeavors. Contrary to the romantic notion that the muse suddenly appears and the hypermedia project jumps up and writes itself down, this process is painstaking,with a distinct beginning, middle, and end.

The nonsequential writing tools covered in this section are appropriate for the ''beginning'' and ''middle'' parts of the hypermedia development process. During the beginning part of the process, information is gathered and sifted. While some hypertext tools in themselves are useful during this stage, I've generally found it easier to use a tool outside of the development platform itself for the initial hunting and gathering ''dumping grounds'' stage of development. They also have proven invaluable as a staging area for the renegade idea that appears while working on something else: the electronic equivalent of the matchbook or napkin we use in restaurants and the other odd scraps of paper many of us tend to accumulate as we go through the day.

During the ''middle'' parts of the process, these nonsequential writing tools are useful for initially cross-referencing and grouping the topics to be covered by the hypermedia endeavor and later for actual placement into the hypermedia system.

I hasten to point out, however, that in my own development process, if the end product is to be distributed in the Guide format, I bypass the nonsequential writing tools covered in this section and follow the same process within the Guide application itself. Guide is unique in the hypermedia development tools because it is completely self-contained. Most of you, however, will be using HyperCard as your hypermedia development platform and you will find that the nonsequential writing tools covered here are indisposable.

Symantec's MORE

MORE, the most powerful of the outline processors for the Macintosh began life as a less-powerful product, ThinkTank. The original and subsequent publishers—Living Videotext and Symantec, respectively—attribute its development as a direct response to user requests for enhancements to ThinkTank. MORE, which experienced a series of timely updates, was one of the first products to support the color capabilities of the Macintosh II when it was first introduced.

For the user interested in hypermedia, MORE is likely most useful as a structured idea repository in the preproduction process. Structured as a paper emulator, the product also is useful for those applications that require printing the information contained in the document.

We all learned how to develop outlines in our early schooling years. The hierarchy of ideas and the subsequent ''fleshing-out'' process is something everyone involved with any communications medium is aware of. MORE helps to automate the process and also can be used as a presentation tool, for it easily produces bullet charts and tree charts.

MORE offers the hypermedia devotee a full palette of idea formation tools. Ideas are easily cross-referenced through the ''clone headline'' command that dynamically links headlines. Once linked, changes made in one clone are immediately updated in the linked clone. In this manner, MORE can be employed as a form of rudimentary collateral hypertext. The dynamic links are most useful when information appearing in more than one place is updated. While multiple clones can be made, the only restraint to the cloning process in MORE is that a headline clone cannot be moved lower in the document's hierarchy than another clone of the same headline.

Topics can be grouped and rearranged en masse using MORE's ''mark and gather'' feature. The mark and gather commands allow material throughout the document to be cross-referenced so that information can be gathered

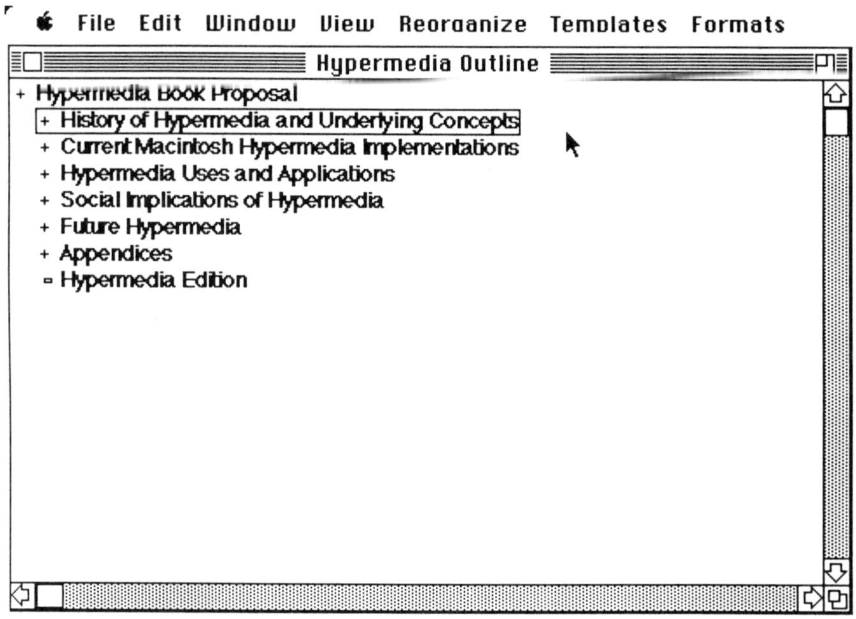

● *Figure 2.1* *Symantec's MORE Outliner in compressed format.*

based on a variety of criteria. Once the information is grouped together via the gather command, it can be rearranged into a single subtopic.

Included in MORE is a document editor that allows for virtually an unlimited amount of text, and as many as six document windows may be open at the same time. Additionally, the product is capable of saving documents in a variety of formats, including plain ASCII text and a variety of IBM formats. Idea topics may be moved extremely easily up and down the hierarchical structure simply by clicking on a headline or subheading and dragging it to the desired position. The headings also are easily collapsible and expandable, allowing for varying degrees of information display as shown in *Figure 2.2*.

MORE V1.1

Requires: 512K of RAM; external floppy disk drive or hard disk drive; MultiFinder-compatible.

Retail Price: $295.00

Street Price: $235.00

Contact: Symantec Corp.
10201 Torre Avenue
Cupertino, CA 95014
(408) 253-9600

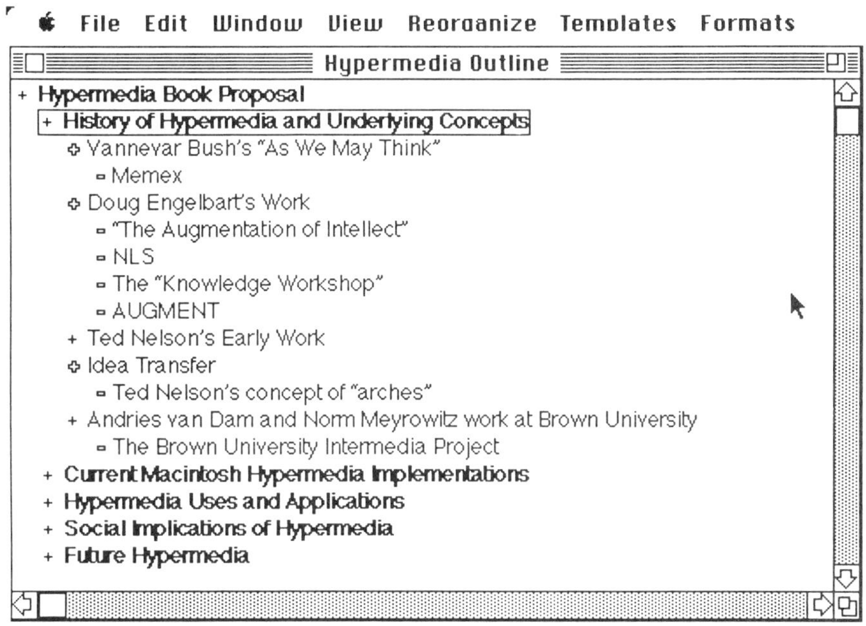

● *Figure 2.2 The same MORE outline as in Figure 2.1, partially expanded.*

Symmetry's Acta

Symmetry Corp.'s Acta can best be thought of as a smaller sibling to Symantec's MORE. Implemented as a desk accessory, this outliner is available from within any application that supports desk accessories. Not as feature-rich as its big brother, MORE, Acta, for example, has no built-in presentation features to speak of, and yet I find myself using it on a regular basis.

Initially I was wary of the product largely because of its guiding metaphor of referring to headlines and subtopics as aunts, mothers, and daughters. While my background is in psychology, I am not much for Freudian familiarity. This all sounded just a bit too incestuous to me. My attitude changed drastically when I mentioned this fact to the program's author, David Dunham, who graciously sent me a copy for review. I haven't been able to get along without it since.

Acta would be accurately perceived as a trade-off. While not packing the punch of the significantly more powerful MORE, Acta also does not carry a heavyweight price tag. And because it's a desk accessory, it's always available, making it useful for applications the designer never thought of, including a Scrapbook replacement complete with an index and a super notepad.

For the hypermedia producer, the most significant feature that is lacking is the ability for ideas to be cross-referenced. Remember, however, that this is, after all, an outliner in a desk accessory and its constant availability goes a long way to balance the scales.

As we've come to expect in an outliner, all the basic features are included in Acta. Outlines can be expanded and contracted easily to offer varying depths of information display, and idea topics can be moved simply by clicking and dragging to the desired location in the information hierarchy as shown in *Figure 2.3*. Multiple windows are supported and filters are provided for various file formats, including the standard Scrapbook format, MORE, Microsoft Works, MacWrite, WriteNow, and rich text format. The rich text format is interesting for it can be used to transfer the information contained in the outline to virtually any system by providing exacting structure and style definitions, including font, size, and style information in the form of parenthetical notes containing information regarding the structure and style of the document.

I use Acta mostly as an intellectual dumping grounds, placing random notes in a series of hierarchical idea structures for use later in various projects. It's great for those flashes of insight that come when you are in the middle of working on something else.

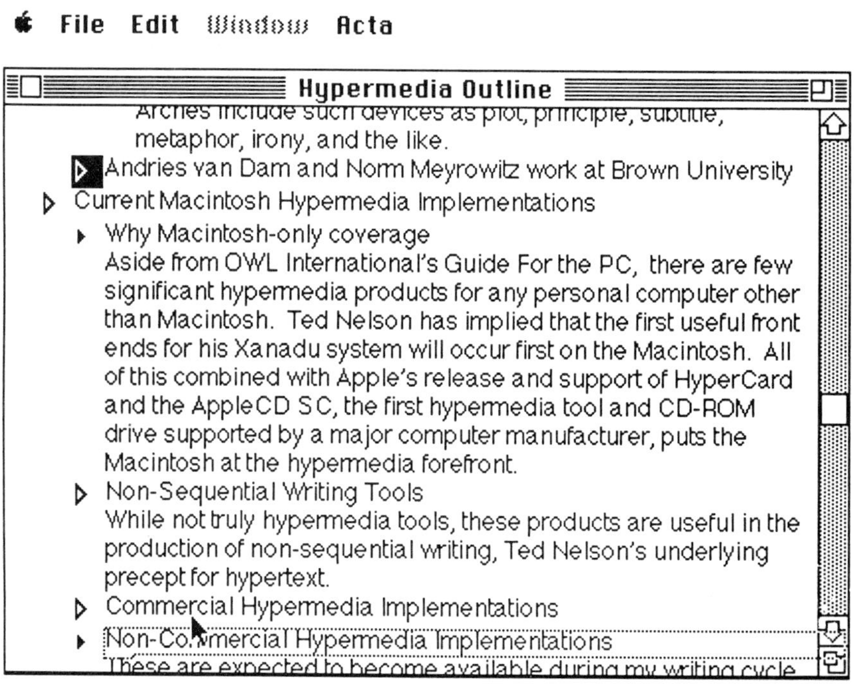

● *Figure 2.3 Symmetry's Acta used to reorganize an outline.*

Acta V2.0

Requires: 512K of RAM; external floppy disk drive or hard disk drive; MultiFinder-tolerant.

Retail Price: $59.95
Street Price: $48.00
Contact: Symmetry Corp.
761 East University Drive
Mesa, AZ 85203
(602) 844-2199

Typical of the way things happen in the Macintosh community, both MORE and Acta were scheduled for major updates, MORE II and Acta Advantage, respectively, just before the final version of this manuscript was submitted to the publisher. Both updates are expected to offer significant feature enhancements, and it would be well worth the time involved to investigate them.

Affinity Microsystems' AffiniFile

AffiniFile is a unique cross-referencing data base in desk accessory format with support for both bit-map and PICT format graphic images. Perhaps it could be best thought of as a Scrapbook replacement with index and cross-referencing abilities. Although limited to a single subtopic for each main heading, the product is much more useful than it might appear at first glance. Beginning hypermedia producers may feel constrained by this apparent limitation, but I feel that AffiniFile is useful for just this reason: It forces the user to think of his or her project in small, interrelated pieces rather than in fathomless pits of archaic bits of information. Remember, we're talking about the dumping-grounds stage here. The deep levels of interconnection are performed within the hypermedia development application.

AffiniFile allows information to be stored as a series of cross-referenced topics and subtopics, each with attached notes. A single graphic also may be attached to any topic or subtopic. *Figure 2.4* shows a topic with a variety of subtopics, several cross-references, and a graphic illustration (in the bottom right corner).

Topics are listed alphabetically, with no provision for maintaining any other sort of information hierarchy. This is, at first, a limitation, but easy enough to work around given AffiniFile's cross-referencing capabilities.

AffiniFile's cross-references are stored under a "See also. . ." compartment and the window is updated constantly based on which topic is highlighted in the Topics Index window. Topics also may be linked via the AffiniFile convention of the "Alias Link," which allows the same information to be stored under a variety of different topic names. The alias links

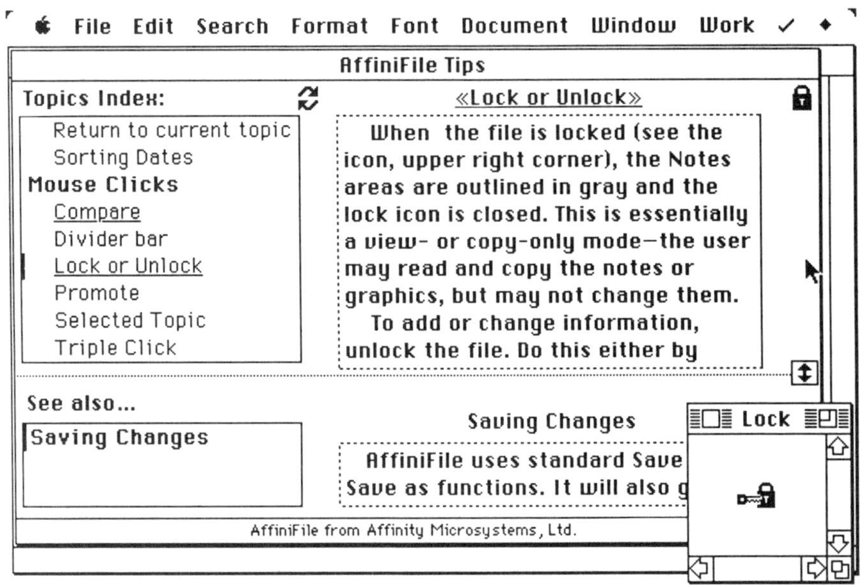

● *Figure 2.4 Affinity Microsystems' AffiniFile with an associated cross-reference and open graphic.*

are dynamic for information changed in any linked topic is updated immediately in all of the aliases.

When a topic is selected that contains an alias link, its name is displayed over the Notes window surrounded by $_9$international quotation marks$_0$; selecting the Alias Link menu item calls up a list of the links associated with the selected topic as displayed in *Figure 2.5*. To establish the alias link the user need only select a topic and choose Alias Link from the menu.

The alias link also may be broken at any time through the Alias Link Dialog shown in *Figure 2.6*. When the link is broken, the linked topics become independent of the other topics rather than being deleted.

AffiniFile is capable of importing and exporting both standard ASCII text files as well as fully formatted MORE documents. The product also has a very useful merge function that allows either all or selected topics from two AffiniFile documents to be merged into a new AffiniFile document.

AffiniFile V1.1
Requires: 512K of RAM; external floppy disk drive or hard disk drive; MultiFinder-tolerant.

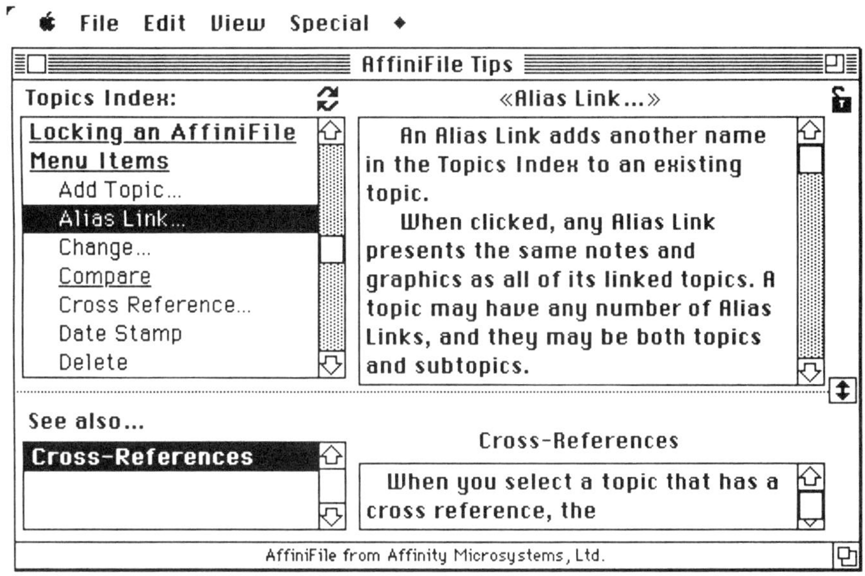

• *Figure 2.5 AffiniFile showing an Alias Link.*

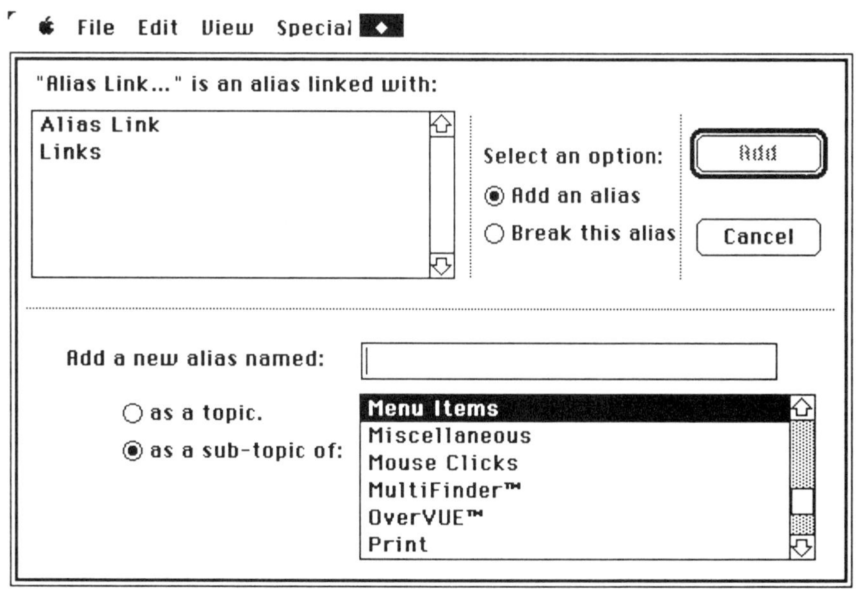

• *Figure 2.6 AffiniFile's Alias Link Dialog.*

Retail Price: $79.95
Street Price: $65.00
Contact: Affinity Microsystems Ltd.
1050 Walnut Street
Suite 425
Boulder, CO 80302
(303) 442-4840

Text Archiving and Retrieval Tools

Brainpower's ArchiText

It seems to me that there is an undue Chinese influence on the high-technology community and especially among Macintosh aficionados. Every year is the "year of" something. With just a brief glimpse over our shoulder, we can see the Year of Integrated Software, the Year of the Macintosh Office, and the Year of the LAN. 1988, and probably all the years through 1995 are sure to be the Year of Hypermedia. If things go really well, the 1990s could be the HyperDecade.

Virtually every product released sports some claim of hyperness. It's inevitable, I suppose, as all the marginal bean counters scurry to cash in on the hyper craze. (I wonder if it could simultaneously be the Year of the Rat?)

With all the nonsense and marketing fluff, sometimes useful products (hyper or not) tend to slip through the cracks, especially if they're manufactured by smaller outfits without big names and million-dollar MacWorld Expo budgets.

ArchiText from Brainpower, Calabasas, California, is just such a product. Billed as a text management and presentation package, Brainpower's collateral materials from the company and the back cover of the manual carry the "H" word prominently displayed in all headlines. The good news is that use of the "H" word in this case is indeed warranted. Using Ted Nelson's definition of hypertext as nonsequential writing, ArchiText fits the bill.

As a hypertext system, ArchiText is quite adequate and even offers several significant advantages over other systems, such as the inclusion of a read-only viewer that may be distributed freely and a graphics "mapping" facility. The mapping capabilities of the product address one of the most damning criticisms of hypermedia systems: finding one's way around complex documents.

An ArchiText document generally consists of "nodes" and "maps." Nodes are subdocuments contained within the main document and can contain text and/or graphics, as shown in *Figure 2.7.* Maps are graphic representations

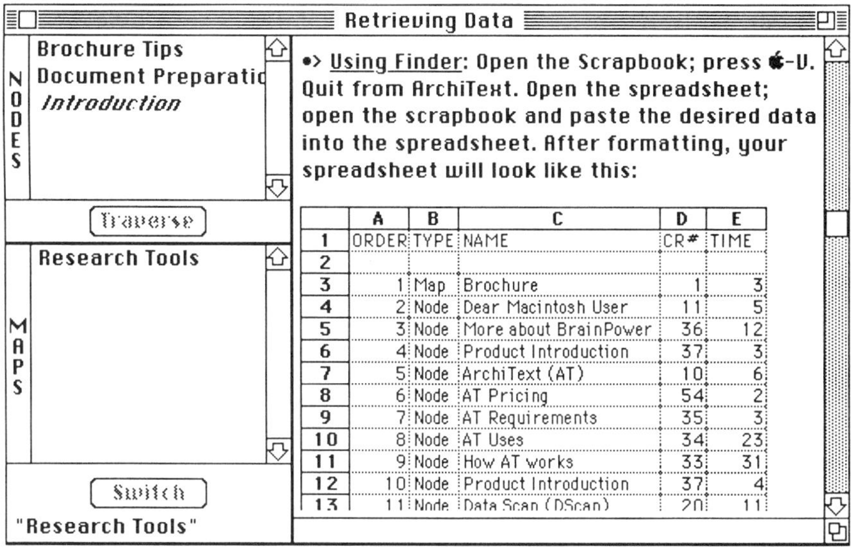

● *Figure 2.7* *ArchiText information nodes can contain text and graphics.*

of the nodes and are used to establish the links between the information contained in various nodes. An example of an ArchiText data Map is shown in *Figure 2.8.* Graphics must be imported via the Clipboard and text may be entered via the keyboard or imported as straight ASCII text files.

An ArchiText node is a singular unit of information containing either text or graphic or a combination of the two. As shown in *Figure 2.7,* nodes are maintained in the Node section (the upper left window panel) of the Node Window. The Node Window itself is divided into three sections: the Node Editing Pane, where text and graphics are entered (text may be imported and graphic material must be pasted in via the Clipboard); the Destination Nodes Pane, located on the upper left, contains the Destination Nodes List and the Traverse button; the lower left pane is the Related Maps Pane, which contains the Related Maps List and the Switch button.

The Traverse button is used to move between nodes that are linked, and a navigational shortcut is available: The user simply double-clicks on the desired node to move, which performs the same action as using the Traverse button. Obviously, links must be created before they can be traversed.

The Switch button is used to establish a selected map as the Driver Map. The Driver Map determines which nodes are contained in the Destination Nodes List and therefore which nodes can be traversed. Any map in the active node window's Related Maps list can be made the Driver Map simply by selecting it and clicking the Switch button. Alternatively, any map can be made

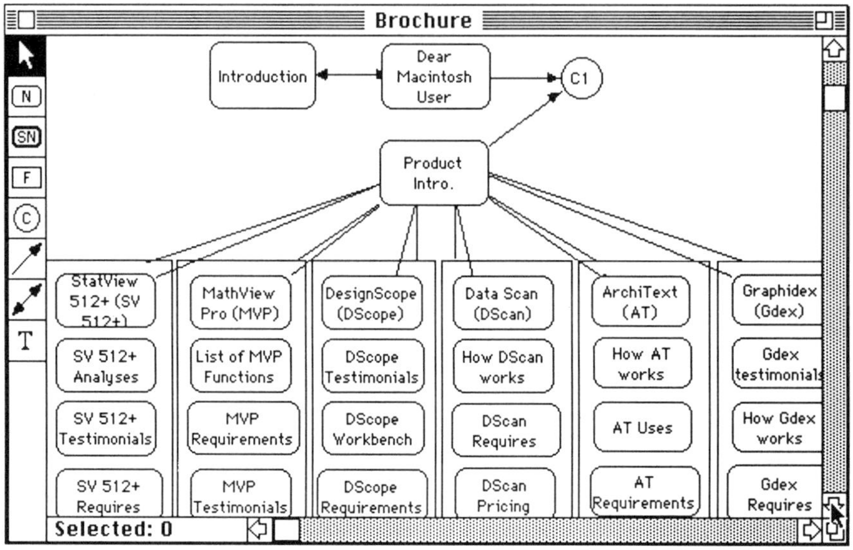

• *Figure 2.8 An ArchiText Map with Linked Nodes.*

a Driver Map by opening the map and choosing the Make Driver command from the Maps menu. The current Driver Map may be changed at any time by performing either option. The current Driver Map is listed in the Node/Map Directory window.

A map, within the ArchiText nomenclature, is a set of relationships between nodes (a unit of information) in a document. The set of relationships are displayed graphically as a data map, hence its name. Multiple maps for the same nodes are permissible and would be used to express different relationships between the same information.

MAP windows, as shown in *Figure 2.8,* consist of two panes, both of which are resizable by using the boundary line separating them. The right pane of the map window contains the Map Toolbox with the implements used to link the various elements contained in the Map Editing Area (also a segment of the right pane). The left pane is the Node On-Call List that lists all existing nodes that may be included in the current map.

An ArchiText map consists of interrelated objects. These objects may be nodes (a unit of information), frames (a series of grouped nodes bound by a surrounding frame), or links (the interconnection between nodes that may be either one-way or bidirectional). The links and connections between various nodes are created by simply selecting the appropriate link or connector tool from the Map Toolbox and physically drawing the interrelation between the desired nodes.

In addition to its hyperness, ArchiText also shines as a text archiving and retrieval system. It has a complete searching facility, including Boolean searches, with the option of creating automatic links based on the results of a search. ArchiText's robust search dialog is illustrated in *Figure 2.9*. The product is capable of searching for words, word combinations, full paragraphs, and even complete node text blocks, using a variety of search criteria.

One limitation is that a search may be conducted only in an active map, although the results of a search are represented in a graphic manner. Search "hits" are shown as highlighted elements in the node name list and carry a specific prefix based on the type of find: ¶ if the found text resides as a paragraph, § if found in a sentence, and ∞ if the result of the search was found in a node.

A Find command is accessible in the Nodes menu that allows a search to be performed for any text with the search constrained to a single node. Alternatively, the Search command in the Maps menu allows an entire document to be searched (although a map consisting of all the nodes within the document must first be created).

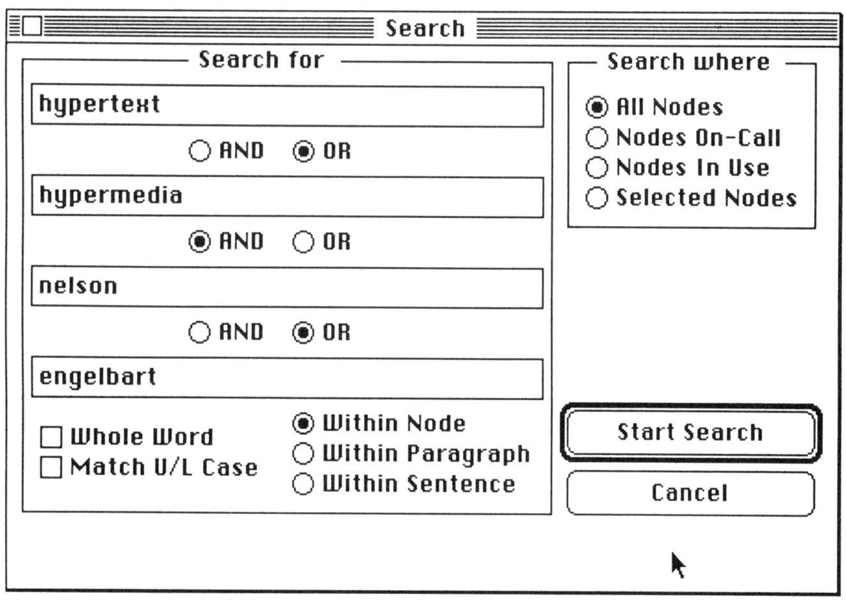

• ***Figure 2.9*** *The ArchiText Search Dialog.*

A search is initiated by selecting Search in the Maps menu, which brings up the search dialog shown in *Figure 2.9*. The "Search for" portion of the window controls the specific text ArchiText will attempt to find. The user enters the specific search for information in the four data entry boxes provided along with specifying the type of search desired by selecting the desired Boolean logic button between each data entry box.

The term *Boolean* will be encountered from time to time in the rest of this book, especially in relation to text-retrieval software, and I'll take a couple of paragraphs here to explain the concept to those who may be unfamiliar with it.

The search mechanisms of most software and word processors in particular are limited to a basic search for a string of characters. The search yields the first occurrence of the specified string of characters and provides options for continuing or canceling the search. For example, I used the search mechanism in Microsoft Word to search for the "Boolean" string of characters to make sure that this is the first section I made reference to it in preparing this book's manuscript.

The biggest drawback when using a search mechanism such as this to retrieve information from, and find relationships between, large bodies of text is that the yield is so large and usually quite irrelevant. If we were to perform a text string search of this manuscript for "hypertext," for instance, we would be overwhelmed by the yield of the search because we would most likely be attempting to find a reference to hypertext in *relation* to something else.

Most retrieval software builds on the character-string approach by allowing the user to build relations into the search using the connectives "and," "or," and "not."

The basis for this connective searching is Boolean algebra, named after George Boole, a nineteenth-century mathematician. Boolean algebra uses algebraic notation to express logical relationships by using the logical connectives mentioned previously.

As efficient as the Boolean search may sound, it is not. The predominant reason is the creative ways in which we use language. We generally refer to the same events, persons, and objects in any number of ways that are not predictable. Boolean algebra relies on the predictable and is completely lost with the unpredictable. The Boolean search has no way of knowing that when you say "hypertext" you also mean "hypermedia" and vice versa. Moreover, the mechanism has no way of ascertaining who "he" is even though it's obvious from the context of the paragraph. Several possible replacements for Boolean searches are currently under development and will be covered in the chapter on future hypermedia.

Using a Boolean search in ArchiText to look for the text contained in the first data entry box *and* the text contained in the second box, the user would select the **AND** button by clicking on it. This action would result in a search for *both* text elements in the two data entry boxes.

To search for the text element contained in the first data entry box *or* the text contained in the second box, the user would select the **OR** button that would produce a search for *either* text elements in the two data entry boxes.

For example, to search a document for occurrences of *both* "hypertext" *and* "Ted Nelson," the user would enter **HYPERTEXT AND TED NELSON**. Similarly, if the instances of *either* hypertext *or* Ted Nelson were desired, **HYPERTEXT OR TED NELSON** would be entered.

It's important to note that the *order* of items in the data entry boxes is significant. Consider the difference in the yield of a search containing **HYPERTEXT OR HYPERMEDIA AND TED NELSON** as opposed to the search of **TED NELSON AND HYPERMEDIA OR HYPERTEXT.** In the former, ArchiText would first find all occurrences of either hypertext or hypermedia and then check those to find Ted Nelson. In the latter, ArchiText would search first for all instances of Ted Nelson and hypermedia and then add all the text blocks that contain hypertext.

The search could be further expanded or narrowed by selecting one of the "Within Node," "Within Paragraph," or "Within Sentence" options. This group of options controls the size of the text block to be searched. The search criteria are further refined by the remaining two options, "Whole Word" and "Match U/L Case." A whole word search results in the location of entire words, rather than partial words. For example, a whole word search of "SMITH" would find "SMITH" but not "SMITHEREEN" or "SMITHSONIAN." The "match case" option is provided to specify whether the search is case-sensitive or not. Again using the "SMITH" search with this option turned off would find "SMITH," "Smith," "smith," and "sMITh."

The "Search Where" portion of ArchiText's search dialog box is used to specify options controlling which nodes are searched during the process. By selecting "All Nodes," all the nodes in the document would be searched. Specifying "Nodes On-Call" would request that only those nodes contained in the Node On-Call list (those nodes not displayed as a node object on the map) be searched. A "Nodes In Use" selection would specify that all nodes in use by the map be used in the search. The "Selected Nodes" option would yield a search wherein only nodes selected (highlighted) in the Node On-Call List would be included.

Any number of nodes may be combined into a new node by either searching or by physically selecting the nodes to be combined with the mouse. The node combination action implemented in tandem with the search command places the amount of text specified by the Node, Paragraph, or Sentence option in the new node. For example, if you have selected the Paragraph mode of search, only paragraphs containing the found text would be copied to the newly created node. If you had selected the sentence mode, only sentences would be copied; and with the node option selected, the entire node would be copied to the newly created node.

The node combination action is initiated by choosing the Combine Nodes command from the Maps menu at the end of a search sequence. A dialog box will appear prompting for a name for the new node. The combination sequence will take place automatically.

Individual nodes can be combined into a new node manually by holding down the Command key and clicking on the nodes in the order desired. Once they are added to a map they may be used to create a new node by choosing the Combine Nodes command from the Maps menu and naming the newly created node.

ArchiText also provides an automatic node linking feature for nodes on any Map. This task is straightforward and is initiated by simply activating the map on which the automatic node linking is to be performed and choosing the AutoLink command from the Maps menu. Initiation of the command brings up the AutoLink dialog shown in *Figure 2.10*, a graphic dialog with nine possible options.

ArchiText is the only hypertext system currently available that allows the author to control the manner in which the document is used. Restrictions may be placed on what material is accessible to the user and a user's progress also may be tracked throughout the document. Brainpower, the developer and publisher of the ArchiText system, provides an ArchiText Viewer application that may be freely distributed along with the document, which is another first in the Macintosh community and is very much appreciated. The ArchiText Viewer is a read-only version of the ArchiText system; with it, a user may open but may not modify an ArchiText document, thus guaranteeing the data integrity of the ArchiText document.

Viewer access to an ArchiText document is author-controlled, as shown in *Figure 2.11;* the creator of the document can set various attributes controlling how the document may be viewed and used, which links are visible,

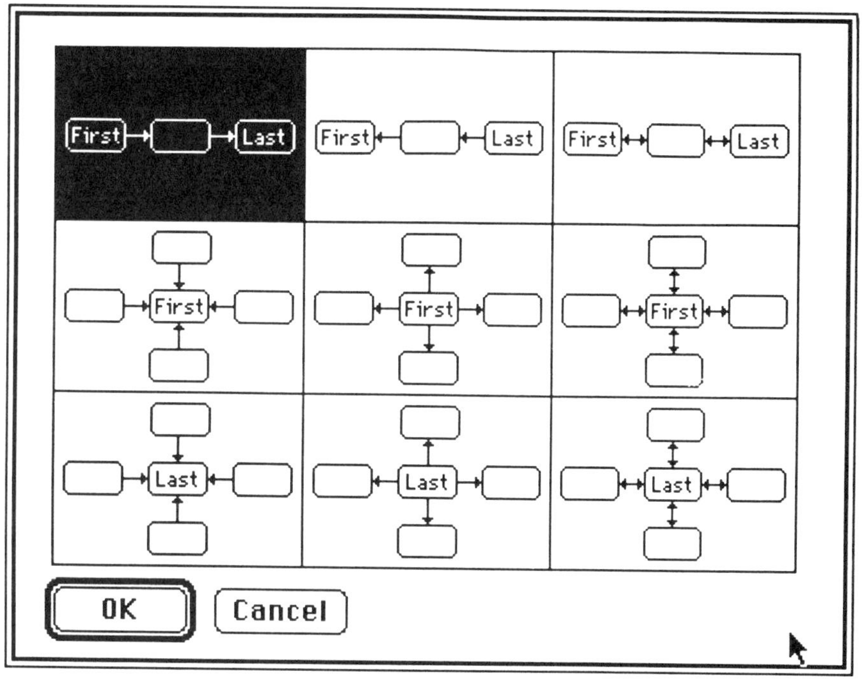

• *Figure 2.10* *The ArchiText AutoLink Options Dialog.*

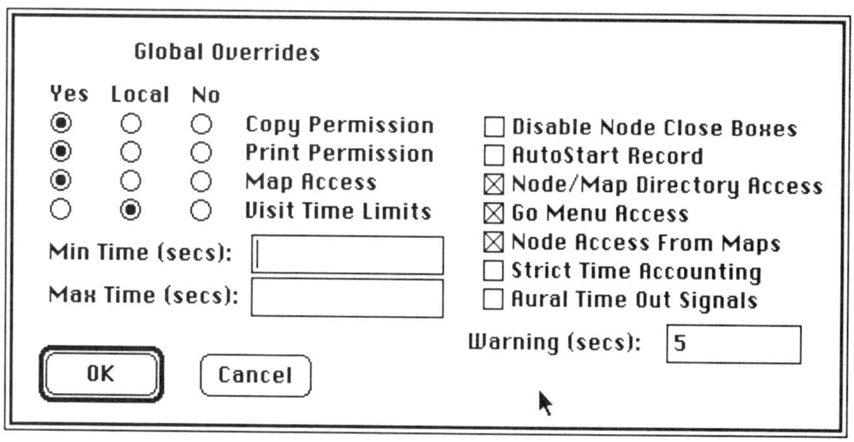

• *Figure 2.11* *The ArchiText Viewer Options Dialog.*

which maps are visible, whether or not information may be copied to the Clipboard or printed, and how much time may be spent in each node. Full reporting capabilities also exist for tracking a viewer's use of the document, making the system ideal for usability testing of on-line documentation and the like.

Viewer options in ArchiText may be set globally (affecting the entire document) or locally (affecting individual nodes and maps) and the selected settings are saved with the document itself in a manner that is completely transparent to the user. The Individual options are covered in the following paragraphs.

- Copy Permission governs whether the user can copy nodes and maps to the Clipboard.
- Print Permission controls whether the user can output nodes and maps to the printer.
- The Map Access option determines whether the user can open maps.
- The Visit Time Limits setting governs the amount of time a user may spend viewing any particular node. A minimum time may be specified that prevents the user from traversing the document any further until the minimum amount of time has passed. A maximum time, if specified, automatically closes a node and proceeds to the next node when the maximum time setting has elapsed.
- The Disable Node Close Box option controls whether the close box on a given node is activated and available for use by the viewer.
- AutoStart Record, when selected, automatically begins when a user opens a document and writes a report of the actions taken by the user during the session to a disk file.
- Node/Map Directory Access governs whether the user has access to the Node/Map Directory window.
- The Go Menu Access setting determines whether the user has access to the commands under the Go menu.
- Node Access From Maps determines if the user can open nodes from a map window by double-clicking on the node name.
- The Strict Time Accounting setting governs how idle time is accounted for in a viewer record. If enabled, this setting accounts for all time spent, including desk accessory access and other application access under MultiFinder. If disabled, only the time spent while a node or map window is active is accounted for.

- Aural Time Out Signals, when activated, causes the Macintosh to beep twice when the user has exceeded the maximum time limit in a node set by the Visit Time Limits setting. A warning signal will be given the specified number of seconds before the time limit expires if specified in the dialog.

In addition to offering extensive control to the author over access privileges to his or her document by others, ArchiText also offers a unique tracking mechanism for recording user movements within any ArchiText document. A facility is implemented whereby the author may optionally enable a feature to record all user activity and save it as a file on disk. Viewer records are stored within the ArchiText document and are accessible to the author via a directory similar to the Node/Map Directory.

A Viewer Record may be initiated and ended manually with the appropriate commands in the Viewer menu or the author may enable the AutoStart Record feature. The data in the Viewer Record is secure because once the record has been entered, it may not be modified in any way except to either delete it or rename it.

The Record consists of a series of rows and columns with each row signifying a separate instance of a node or map window being active from within the document. The eight columns provide the following information:

- The Order field contains the order in which the nodes and maps were activated.
- The N/M field indicates whether a node or map was active.
- The Name field contains the name of the node or map that was activated by the user.
- The ID field is the internal identifier for the node or map that was activated.
- The Min(s) field contains the minimum time limit in seconds that was in effect during the time that the node or map was active.
- The Max(s) field contains the maximum time limit in seconds that was in effect during the time that the node or map was active.
- The Visit(s) field shows the actual time in seconds that the user spent in the node or map.
- The PExit? field is a yes or no that signifies whether the user traversed to the node in question via a Priority Link. Priority links are set via the Preferences dialog and are preselected in all Destination Node Lists.

- At the bottom of each Report is a summary for the entire Viewer Record, which contains the total number of nodes and maps activated, the total time spent, and the total number of visits.

Brainpower's ArchiText is useful in a variety of applications, ranging from research employing the product's text analysis and archiving tools to usability testing using the viewer tracking feature. I'm currently using the product as a central dumping station for research materials for multiple book projects and as a text repository for keeping track of, referencing, and cross-linking my dreams for future reference.

As powerful as ArchiText is, it has some shortcomings. The lack of even the most rudimentary drawing tools is a hindrance, and I still haven't gotten the hang of the grid controls for the mapping functions. It would be nice if graphics could be imported and placed in their native format rather than imported via the Clipboard. Also text should be importable as native documents from standard word processors; currently only ASCII text can be imported (although individual text style attributes are supported within the application itself). Finally, the text selection action—double-clicking on a word to select it, and so on—common to most Macintosh applications is nonstandard as implemented in ArchiText and needs improvement.

Perhaps ArchiText's greatest contribution to the Macintosh milieu is that it has pointed to the need for interprocess communications. The concept of ArchiText should be built into the operating system and each save dialog in any application would have something like an ArchiText button. Of course, by then we'll no longer be constrained by the Mac's modalness—there won't be a word-processing mode or a telecommunications mode or a spreadsheet mode or a graphics mode; there will only be Macintosh and it will be smart enough to know what you want to do with various types of information.

Even with its shortcomings and design flaws, ArchiText will prove very useful for those who need a text archiving and retrieval utility with some elements of hypermedia. The product's viewer tracking procedures are unique, if somewhat Orwellian, and may prove useful for market researchers and perhaps even interface designers concerned with information management and presentation. As a free-form text holding tank with multiple cross-referencing capabilities and fairly advanced text analysis and searching routines, ArchiText is a welcome addition to my software library and has earned its place among those applications I keep installed on my hard disk for use on a regular basis.

ArchiText V1.02
Requires: Macintosh Plus or greater; 642K under MultiFinder.
Retail price: $349.95 (Demonstration disk available for $10.00)

Street price: $300.00

Contact: Brainpower, Inc.
24009 Ventura Boulevard
Suite 250
Calabasas, CA 91302
(800) 345-0591
(818) 884-6911

Virginia Systems' SONAR

SONAR, from Virginia Systems Software Services, was one of the first text-retrieval products available for the Macintosh. Text-retrieval software, common for years on "big" computers, is used to search for specific information contained in different files. Its main use is for individuals requiring information that must be gathered from a variety of long files, such as a lawyer searching case depositions for related information. Personal computer industry analysts expect the text-retrieval market for personal computers to grow in excess of 60 percent each year through 1992 and the installed base of users to grow to more than 280,000.

Where the search facilities of word processors and other applications allow a search to take place only within a single document, text-retrieval software is capable of searching multitudes of documents from a variety of applications. SONAR is capable of searching plain ASCII text, MacWrite, Microsoft Word, MORE, WriteNow, Trapeze, ReadySetGo, and Microsoft Works formatted files in their native formats.

SONAR requires a Macintosh with a minimum of one megabyte of memory and even then it is limited to searching documents of less than 200 pages each. With an additional megabyte available, SONAR can process documents of up to 500 pages in length. Process is the key word here, because before SONAR can perform any sort of text retrieval or analysis, each document must be processed. The document processing is a tedious procedure that also requires a good bit of disk real estate, including the size of each original document for the SONAR file and another healthy chunk for the internal index file used. Additionally, if changes are made to the document, it must be reprocessed before any changes are updated in the SONAR file.

Once the documents have been processed, the retrieval mechanism is fairly straightforward. Nonrelational searches are performed by simply entering or highlighting the desired target word or words within the text and selecting the Search command. SONAR reports to the screen the number of occurrences of the word group in all searched documents and lists, via the Occurrence Analysis option from the Display menu, documents containing the targeted word or word group. The paragraph containing the first occurrence of the targeted word is displayed on screen, as shown in *Figure 2.12,* and options are provided for Next Occurrence, Previous Occurrence, Next Document, and Previous Document. This allows the found text to be displayed in context.

The retrieved bits of text can be saved to a disk file by using the Append command from the Edit menu. Comments and annotations also may be added to the retrieved text before initiating the Append command. The text from multiple Append commands is also saved on the Clipboard in an accumulated fashion: New text is appended to the end rather than overwriting what was already there.

SONAR's strongest feature is its ability to search various files for related information and interrelationships between data. Options are included for proximity searches, wild cards, and full Boolean searching. The Boolean search dialog from SONAR is shown in *Figure 2.13.* The results of such a search are illustrated in *Figure 2.14.*

Additionally, an initiated search in progress can be interrupted to go on a tangential search; an interactive search process can be implemented in this manner and is much more useful than it appears at first glance. For instance,

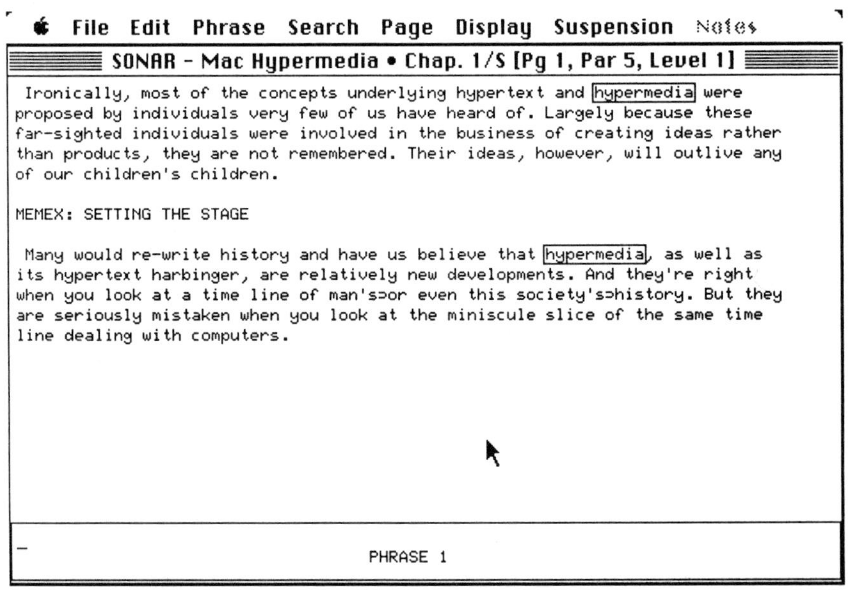

• ***Figure 2.12*** *Results of a nonrelational search for "HYPERMEDIA" in SONAR.*

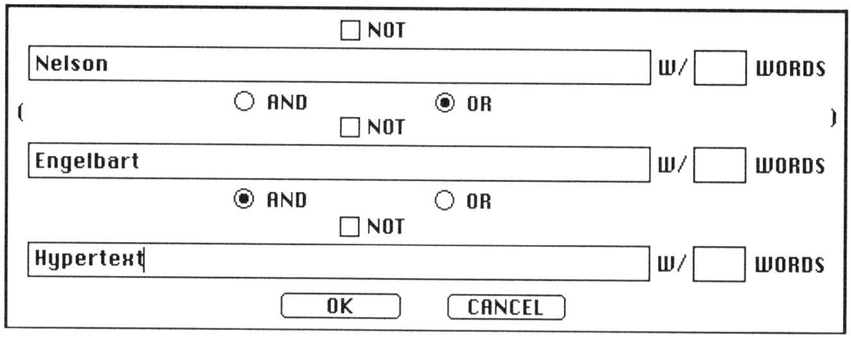

● *Figure 2-13 The SONAR Relational Search Dialog.*

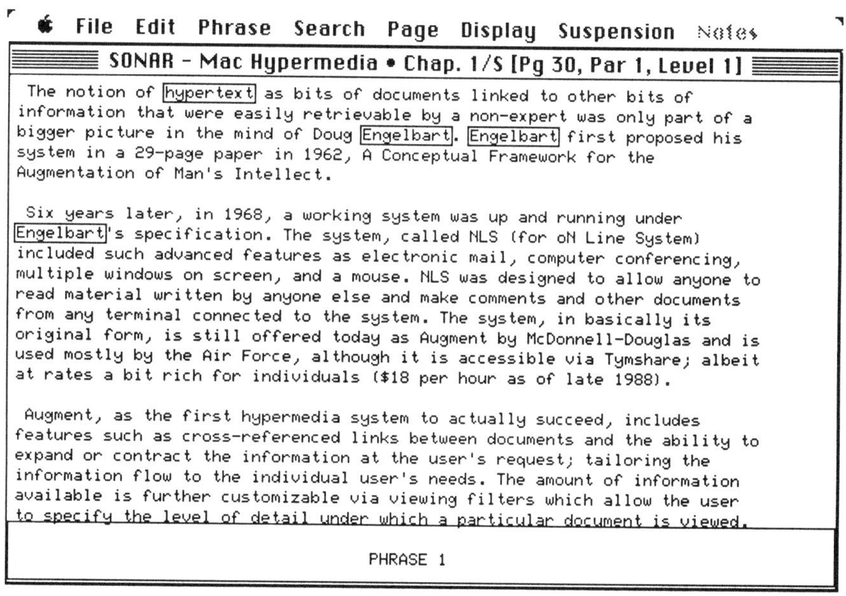

● *Figure 2.14 Results of a relational search in SONAR.*

consider that you had initiated a search for HYPERTEXT **AND** TED NELSON and halfway through the search decided that you also should add Doug Engelbart to the search criteria. You would simply interrupt the search and add ENGELBART to the criteria. At the end of that search you could go back and pick up where the original search left off and continue with your initial search.

Another useful feature of SONAR is its ability to index any document or range of documents of a supported file type. Key words may be specified in a text document or the index may, alternatively, consist of all words with a frequency of less than the limit specified.

When I first began using SONAR I was very excited at the speed of its retrieval process and its level of relationship searching once the documents were indexed. I grew frustrated and dismayed, however, with the time and storage-space requirements of the indexing process and have subsequently ceased using the product. I found that more times than not I needed to retrieve information from documents that had either not been indexed or had subsequently been revised, rendering the index inaccurate.

SONAR V4.6

Requires: Macintosh Plus or greater.
Retail price: $295.00
Street price: $236.00
Contact: Virginia Systems Software Services
5509 West Bay Court
Midlothian, VA 23113
(804) 739-3200

Microlytics' GOfer

GOfer is the newest of the Macintosh text-retrieval software packages covered here and will without doubt popularize the importance and need for text retrieval in a variety of disciplines. The product is implemented as a desk accessory and where other software programs of this nature suffer from some, shall we say, liberal interpretations of the Macintosh user interface, GOfer has the most transparent user interface for a text-retrieval package currently available.

As illustrated in *Figure 2.15,* GOfer operations, whether simple or relational, consist of defining three basic steps: search for **What, Where** to search, and **How** to conduct the search. The user has complete control over what to do with the information yielded by the search, which is also shown. The results of a typical nonrelational search are shown in *Figure 2.16.*

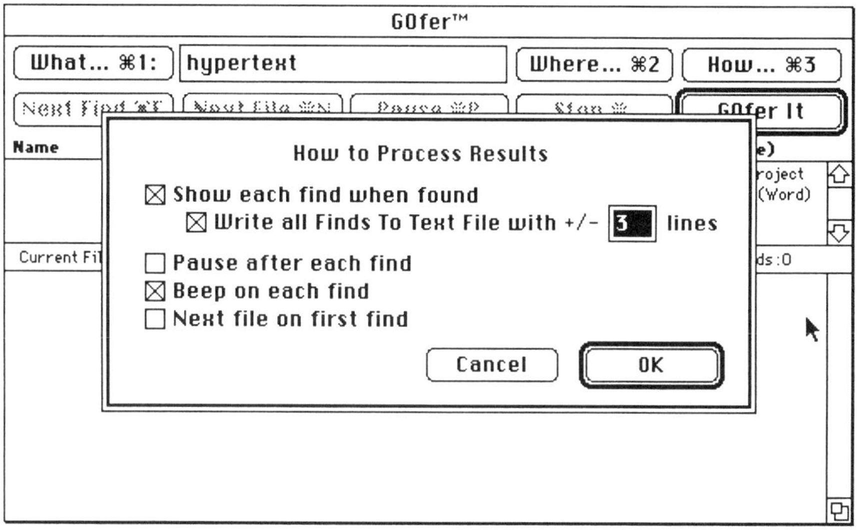

• *Figure 2.15 GOfer's nonrelational search setup and Process Results Dialog.*

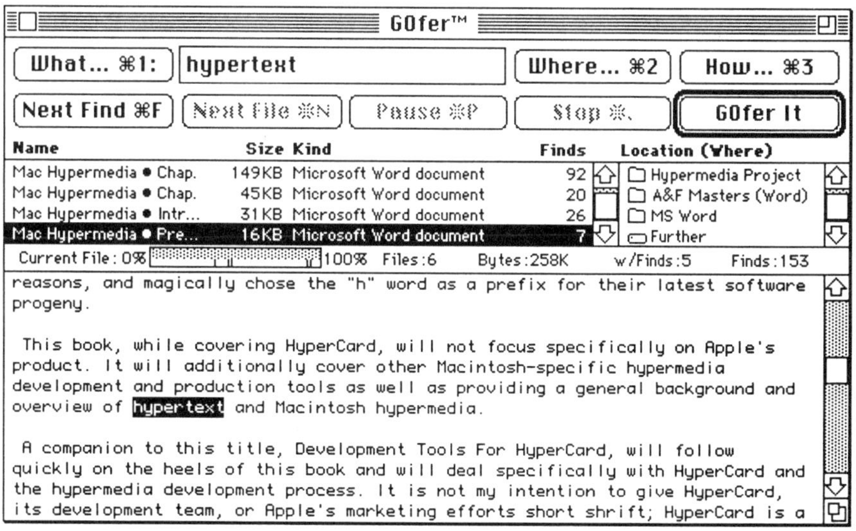

• *Figure 2.16 Results of a nonrelational search in GOfer.*

The beauty of GOfer is in its simplicity. No indexing or processing of files is required, and the product operates at admirable speeds; it even operates in the background with or without MultiFinder. GOfer is implemented as a desk accessory and is available within any application. Support for various file types can be customized by the user, including the ability to specify either the resource or data fork for searching. This is very useful when working with unknown file types; sometimes it can be used to search through the data fork of a file that is unsupported by the product. GOfer also offers a rich assortment of ''standard'' file types that it knows how to deal with. These include all of the word processors, all of the page-layout programs, Microsoft Excel, HyperCard, MORE, and ThinkTank.

GOfer offers a breakthrough in working with the multitude of files available in the Macintosh cornucopia. As shown in *Figure 2.17,* the user can specify the type and creator of an unknown file type and GOfer will try its best to search the file for the requested text.

The most significant breakthrough (yes, there is another one) offered by GOfer, however, is its significant additions to the Boolean search routines. Traditionally, Boolean search mechanisms available in most software are limited to the AND, OR, and NOT logical connectives. GOfer, as illustrated in *Figure 2.18,* provides the additional connective NEARBY.

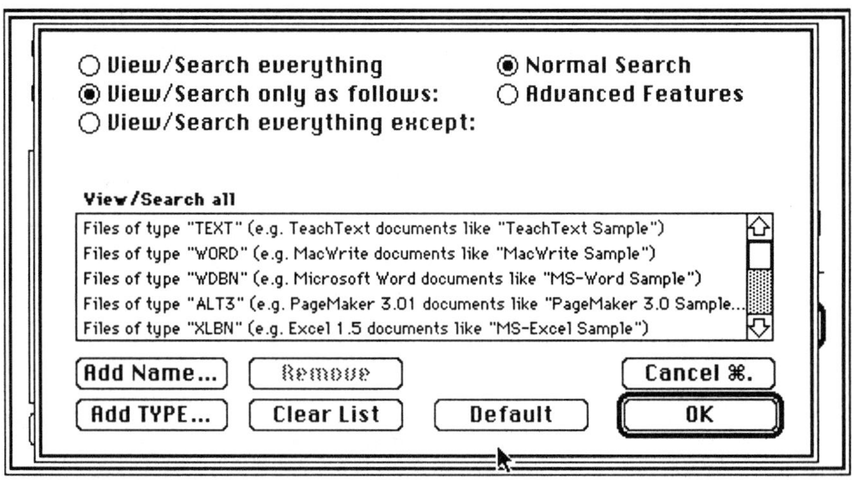

• ***Figure 2.17*** *GOfer's supported file-type customizer.*

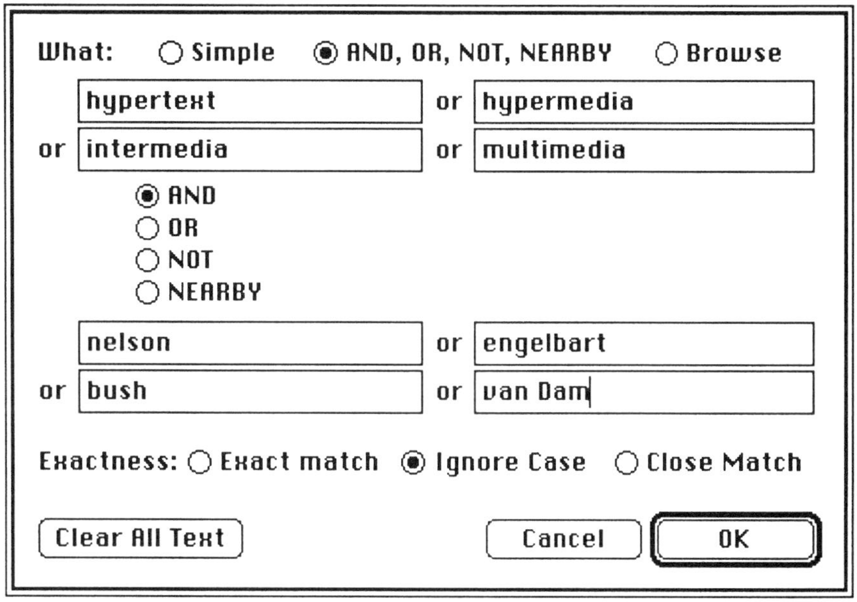

● *Figure 2.18 GOfer's relational Text-retrieval Setup Dialog.*

The NEARBY logical connective, which is very powerful, allows the user to specify the number of lines to limit the search between the AND, OR, and NOT connectives. Using the NEARBY connective, a user could extend his or her search to a much greater number of apparently unrelated documents and raise the level of the search's effectiveness. For example, a relational search within this document for "Nelson" OR "Engelbart" NEARBY "hypertext" OR "hypermedia" OR "interactive multimedia" would yield a much more useful search result than the search for "Nelson" OR "Engelbart" AND "hypertext" OR "hypermedia." The results of the latter search limited to only the first two chapters and front matter of this text are shown in *Figure 2.19* and the more refined former search results over the same information territory are shown in *Figure 2.20.*

GOfer is, without question, the most useful text-retrieval utility currently available for the Macintosh. The fact that it requires no preprocessing of files is enough to warrant the price of admission, and that, combined with its speed and user-customizability, place it head and shoulders above its closest competition. At a price less than half of its nearest competitor, GOfer is also one of the better software bargains available. Frankly, the only way GOfer could be improved would be with an option allowing the maintenance of a virtual index of every file on a given volume. This would be done automatically, in the background, and while the Macintosh was on but not in use.

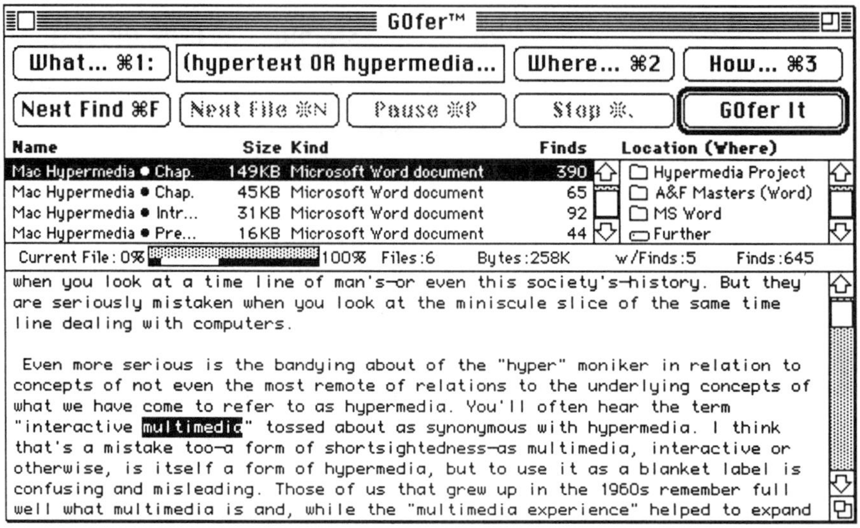

• *Figure 2.19 Results of a standard relational text retrieval using GOfer.*

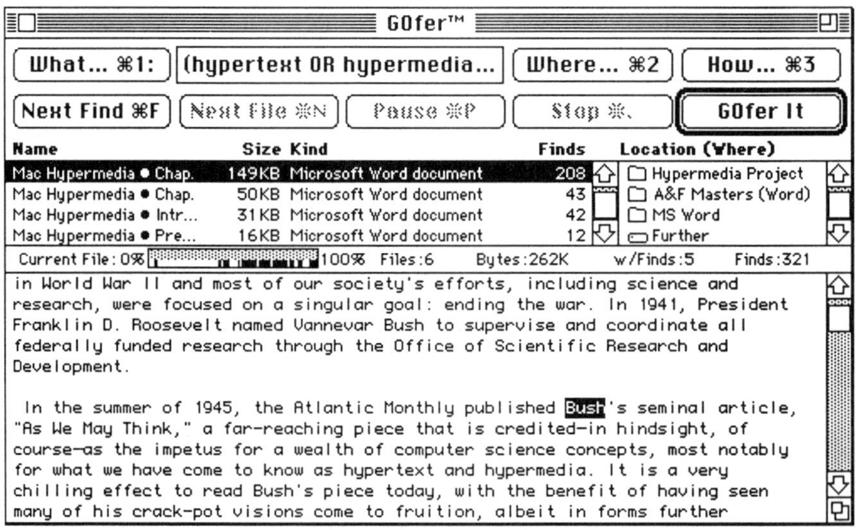

• *Figure 2.20 Results of the search shown in Figure 2.19 using GOfer's "NEARBY" connective.*

GOfer V1.0

Requires: Macintosh 512 or greater.
Retail price: $79.95
Street price: $64.00
Contact: Microlytics, Inc.
300 Main Street
Suite 137
East Rochester, NY 14445
(716) 377-0130

Noncommercial Hypermedia Applications

Several noncommercial hypermedia applications presently are available or under the final stages of development, mostly in the higher education arena. While several of the systems can support the Macintosh as a front-end device, few are written specifically for the Macintosh. This section will focus on a single noncommercial hypermedia system, one that does not run on the Macintosh. This is covered here because its interface is among the most promising and was taken directly from the Macintosh.

Brown University's Intermedia Project

Brown University has been involved in the development of a hypertext system, under the direction of Andries van Dam, since 1968. The Intermedia Project is now continued under the guidance of Norm Meyrowitz and a Macintosh interface recently was designed by Nancy Yaneklovich.

Andries van Dam, together with Ted Nelson and a team of Brown University undergraduates, in 1967 codesigned the world's first hypertext editing system. Several years later, van Dam and his students built another hypertext editing system called FRESS (File Retrieval Editing SyStem). FRESS was implemented as a commercial product in Holland called Philtext.

Ted Nelson recalls Andries van Dam and the rest of the Hypertext Editing System project—as well as the project's initial financial supporters—as infatuated with paper emulation and saw their actions as "pandering to the familiar, this emphasis on paper output, may have set progress back considerably."[78] Nelson saw the reliance on paper as playing to the lowest common denominator and sees the practice as persisting today with what he refers to as an "inane preoccupation with paper: the current stampede for 'desktop publishing,' and the paper orientation of the Macintosh computer, where everything has a 'normal size'—the size of printout."[79]

The Institute for Research in Information and Scholarship (IRIS) was formed in 1983 and some of the people involved in the FRESS project were absorbed into the newly formed project. Van Dam coined the term Scholar's Workstation (subsequently borrowed by Steve Jobs) to describe the educational-use hypermedia system IRIS was working on. What made the Scholar's Workstation different from the hypermedia systems that preceded it was the hardware platform. Suddenly the educators had access to bit-mapped graphic workstations with vastly improved interfaces and levels of power. The main focus of IRIS was, since its inception, the Scholar's Workshop Project and its embodiment in the Intermedia system.

Intermedia is described by its creators as an object-oriented implementation of a multimedia hypertext system built around a Macintosh-based user interface. Norm Meyrowitz, leader of the Intermedia project, put together the Macintosh Toolkit, QuickDraw, and the Macintosh interface (in the form of CadMac from Cadmus Corp.) with a ported version of MacApp (Apple's object-oriented programming shell). The Meyrowitz team subsequently ported Intermedia to the Sun workstation and IBM PC/RTs and is currently converting the system to run on Macintosh IIs under A/UX, Apple's UNIX operating system. At the 1988 Microsoft CD-ROM Conference, Meyrowitz demonstrated a prototype of Intermedia running on a Macintosh II. While the project was originally funded by IBM and the Annenberg Foundation, Apple recently has provided sponsorship for Intermedia.

Intermedia shares a common heritage with Apple's initial hypermedia product, HyperCard. While Intermedia has no programming language (everything not provided must be programmed in C), it is a multiuser system built around a distributed data base that allows for automatic bidirectional links between and within documents, not just cards and stacks.

The dividing point between the van Dam/Meyrowitz/Yaneklovich et al. vision of hypermedia and the other currently available hypermedia platforms is that the Intermedia visionaries stress that hypermedia by nature is not limited to a single user, but by definition is a multiuser tool. Both van Dam and Meyrowitz stressed at the most recent CD-ROM Conference that in order to take hypermedia out of the virtual paper model, three elements must be added: color, motion, and three-dimensional capability. They add that while the cut, copy, and paste mechanisms of the desktop metaphor are powerful, in that they allow for the creation of temporary links between information, what is needed are persistent links that are a basic part of the operating system. These persistent links would be stored separately from the information nodes and would be read at the time of access.

Meyrowitz refers to Intermedia as "a collection of tools that allow authors to set up links between documents created with different applications."[80] The system allows for direct control of videodisc players and appears to the user as a variant of the familiar Macintosh interface. Icons link directly to comments and annotations, as well as initiating full-motion video from a videodisc.

A central concept of the Intermedia project, then, is a campuswide hypermedia network that links vast stores of text and graphics. In mid-1985 the Intermedia development team stated three broad-based goals:

- Provide professors with appropriate tools to create "information webs" for their students;
- Provide an environment to enhance students' ability to visualize and perceive complex, dynamic phenomena, such as music theory and notation and mathematical surfaces;
- Encourage all users to make their own discoveries through exploration of a rich environment.

As graphically oriented as Intermedia is, key words still play a central role in the system, and the key words are what allow links to be created among the various data components available. "Webs" of interlinked information can be created and, more importantly, displayed and navigated graphically on the screen. As an example of such a web, Brown's English department has an information web consisting of Shakespearean tragedies linked to the Religious Studies department's religious symbolism. Other departments, such as Philosophy and Psychology, benefit from the cross-references and also may add their own links to the web. Such an environment places the kernels of information in a variety of rich contexts that were heretofore impossible to maintain. In addition to the faculty-created webs, other university members—students and nonrelated professors, alike—also can create their own pathways through the information structure and also can create their own webs.

The current implementation of Intermedia consists of five applications: the InterText text editor, the InterDraw graphics editor, the InterPix image viewer, the InterSpect three-dimensional object viewer, and InterVal, a timeline editor.

The InterText text editor is almost a direct clone of MacWrite with the exception of built-in style sheets used for quickly formatting text documents. The InterText style sheets allow for fairly complicated document formatting with relatively little effort on the part of the user.

InterDraw is a two-dimensional, object-oriented graphics program, similar in scope and design to MacDraw. A tool palette that is attached to each window in the Intermedia system is the only noticeable difference.

InterPix is used to display bit-mapped images that are brought into the Intermedia system through the use of an optical scanner. The InterPix application is presently undergoing revision to include editing capabilities.

InterSpect is a utility designed to convert three-dimensional data points into three-dimensional graphic representations of that data, which then may be manipulated in virtually any manner by the user.

InterVal is used to create chronological timelines featuring automatic timeline plotting based on the input of the user. The final method of display is fully customizable by the user.

Links in the Intermedia system are constructed through the familiar copy-and-paste mechanism inherent in the Macintosh. In addition to links between complete documents, Intermedia provides specific locations in various documents to be linked through the use of an "anchor point." Anything that can be selected in the document—ranging from an insertion point to an entire document—can be made into an anchor for a link.

The material contained between two anchor points is referred to as a "block" in the Intermedia system. The size of an Intermedia block, therefore, may consist of as little as an insertion point or as much as an entire document. The links may be edited by the user through "property sheet dialogs" that are somewhat similar in function to the style sheets available in some Macintosh word-processing programs. The property sheet dialog contains an "explainer" field that is used to describe the link. These explainer fields are very useful for each link radiating from a block has its own explainer field and the user can select which path to follow from the list of link explainers presented in the dialog box. A simulated Intermedia property sheet dialog is shown in *Figure 2.21*.

User preferences also are configurable to the tastes of individual users through the "viewing specifications dialog" in the Intermedia system. If the user enables the verbose setting of the property sheet dialog in the viewing specifications, the property dialogs are displayed automatically upon block or link creation.

A link is created in any Intermedia application by specifying a region in a document and selecting the Start Link command from the Intermedia menu, as shown in simulated form in *Figure 2.22*. The ending link region is then selected, in any type of Intermedia document, and the link is completed by

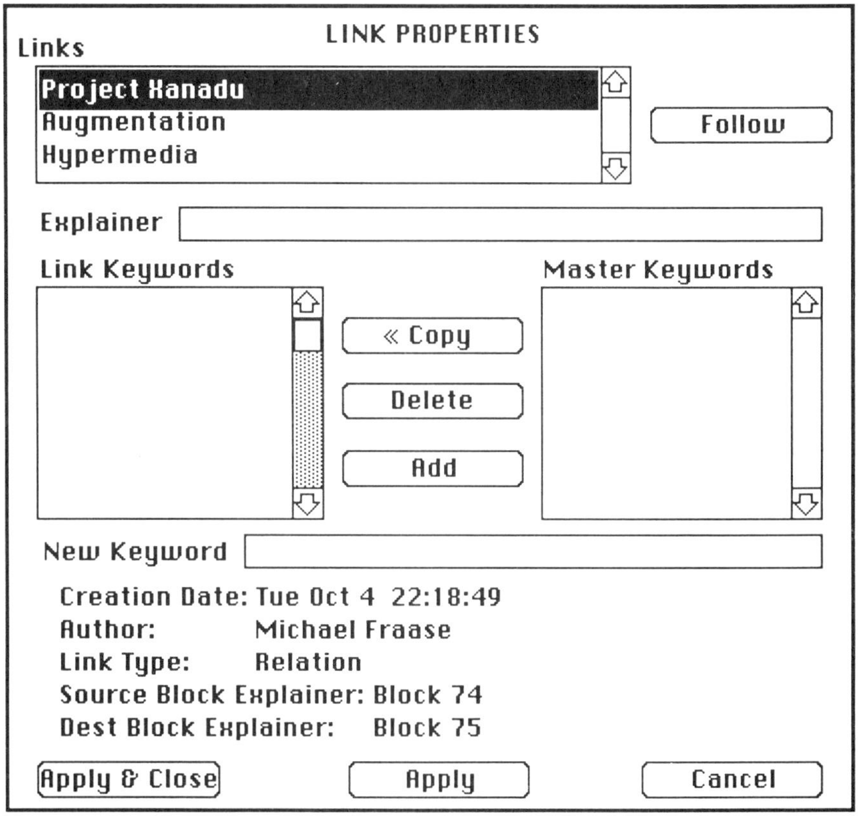

● *Figure 2.21* *A simulated Intermedia Property Sheet Dialog.*

choosing the appropriate Complete Link command (either Complete Reference or Complete Relation) from the Intermedia menu.

To follow a defined link, the user selects a marker icon in any document and selects the Follow command from the Intermedia menu. Alternatively, the marker icon can be double-clicked to automatically initiate the Follow command.

Intermedia varies from other hypermedia systems covered in this book in that its link information is not stored within individual documents, but rather is stored as separate files and superimposed on top of the appropriate documents when they are opened. These separate documents, called ''webs'' in the Intermedia parlance, allow users the option of working within an environment consisting of only their own links and interconnections, insulated from the documents and links of others using the same resources. Opening a web in the Intermedia system automatically opens the appropriate links and blocks within the system and maintains them the entire time the web is open. The advantage to this variance is that any number of people can maintain their own links within a group of documents that are shared with others. Although only one web may be open at a time, any user may access any unprotected web on the system, thus a variety of contexts is available to the individual at any given time.

Intermedia also grants the user a system of access rights that may be assigned to owned documents to help utilize large bodies of material referenced by a variety of users. Standard "read permission" and "write permission" features of UNIX are implemented, as well as a unique "annotation permission." The annotation permission is used to allow others who have read permission to an owned document to add links to a document they are restricted from editing.

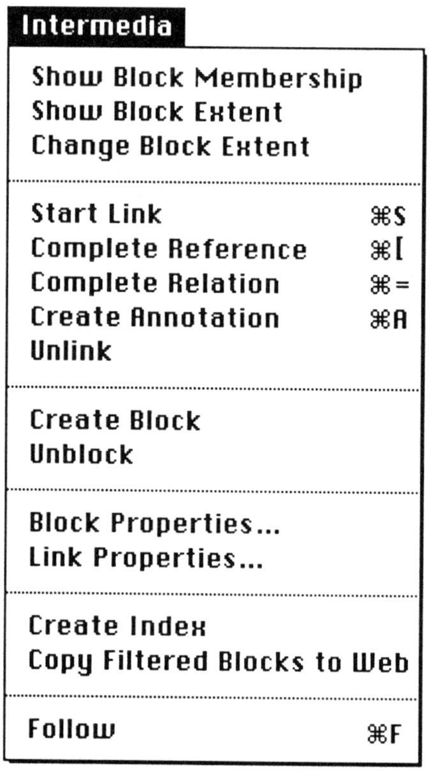

• *Figure 2.22 Simulated Intermedia Menu.*

Another unique interface feature of the Intermedia system (and one that would be a most welcomed addition to the standard Macintosh user interface) is the infinite level of ''undo'' and ''redo'' available to the user. Any number of actions, initiated since the last time the document was saved, may be recalled (in reverse order) through the Undo command. Similarly, any number of undone actions may be recalled (again, in reverse order) through the Redo command. This enables the user to be more comfortable when using the system and allows for free exploration within documents.

Intermedia also departs from the familiar Macintosh interface by not storing applications in the same folders as documents. In Intermedia, applications are stored with related tools in an application window called ''New.'' This relieves the user of having to search through multiple folders to find applications and at the same time aids navigation by allowing the New command on the File menu to display the application window at any time, regardless of other overlapping windows. The application window also enhances ease of use in a networked environment for all applications can be stored in a commonly agreed-on location.

When the user opens a web, a ''local map'' is displayed on the screen. The local map looks like a typical Macintosh opened folder with connection lines drawn between linked documents, as simulated in *Figure 2.23*. The user employs the local map to find his or her way through the connected documents that make up the information web. When the user activates a different document, the local map is updated to reflect the connected links to the new document.

Intermedia utilizes a series of ''marker icons'' to indicate to the user that links exist for the selected document. The linked documents may be alternatively navigated by single-clicking on the marker icon and selecting Follow from the Intermedia menu, which displays a dialog of links attached to the document. The user may click on the link of his or her choice in the dialog and be transported to the appropriate section of the linked document.

The Intermedia development team at Brown University continues to enhance and explore the possibilities of the Intermedia system, particularly in relation to multiuser environments in the realm of higher education. Such explorations involve the development of more sophisticated navigational tools that would allow a user to display the links followed to get to his or her current place in the corpus as well as to implement bookmarks in the form of place holders and that would allow authors to define a reading path for users.

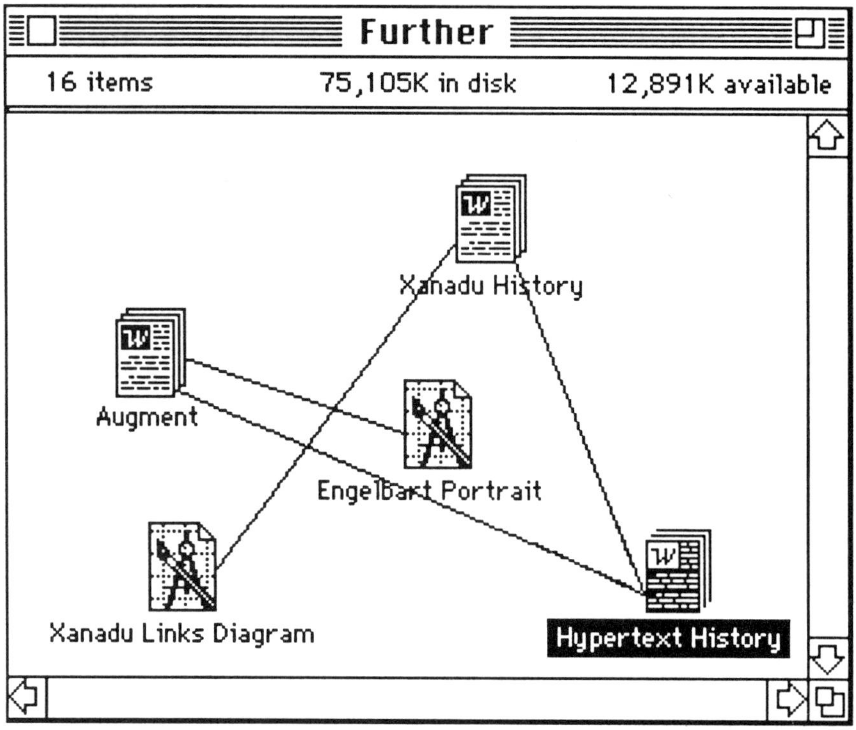

● *Figure 2.23 Simulated Intermedia Local Map with Active Web.*

Commercial Macintosh Hypermedia Products

The first generation of commercial hypertext and hypermedia applications have been available since 1986. The subsequent generations of hypermedia are already undergoing conceptual construction and will begin to be marketed in the 1990s.

Guide, the first commercial hypertext application, was released in 1986 by OWL International, Inc., of Bellevue, Washington. The product initially could run only on the Macintosh, but now has been released in IBM PC format.

The underlying ideas for Guide were developed by Peter Brown, a professor at the University of Kent in Edinburgh, Scotland, who surmised that people would rather read information from paper than from computer screens only because no one had yet presented screen-based documents in an appropriate manner. Brown felt that the key to getting the notion of screen-based documents accepted by the masses lie in the inherent ability of the screen-presentation system to allow the user to customize documents to their individual needs.

OWL International, Inc., was formed in 1985 as the marketing arm of Office Workstations Limited, whom Peter Brown had teamed up with for the actual development effort of his envisioned hypertext system. Office Workstations Limited, which has existed for more than 15 years, specializes in the development areas of hypertext, human/computer interaction, and expert-systems technology. Many of the individuals involved have an extensive background in artificial intelligence as a result of a close association with the University of Edinburgh's Artificial Intelligence Unit.

In addition to the Macintosh and IBM versions of the Guide hypertext system, OWL has released the Guidance toolkit for the development of context-sensitive, on-line help systems for software products and the Guide Library System, hypertext routines for use with CD-ROM. In early 1988, OWL released the Idex system for the IBM, which is an advanced set of networking, file-conversion, security, and desktop-publishing utilities built around an advanced hypertext engine.

OWL International's Guide

Perhaps Guide can be best thought of as a three-dimensional word processor—with a few limitations. You enter information into the Guide document (called a Guideline) as you would with a word processor. But then the fun begins. Say you decide to elaborate on the "few limitations" and this were a Guideline. You would simply highlight the words "few limitations" and pull down a menu to define the selected text as a "button." Immediately, the display would change with the word "replacement" in boldface type. You would then simply type in the text of your "few limitations" ideas. This sequence is illustrated in *Figure 2.24* and *Figure 2.25*.

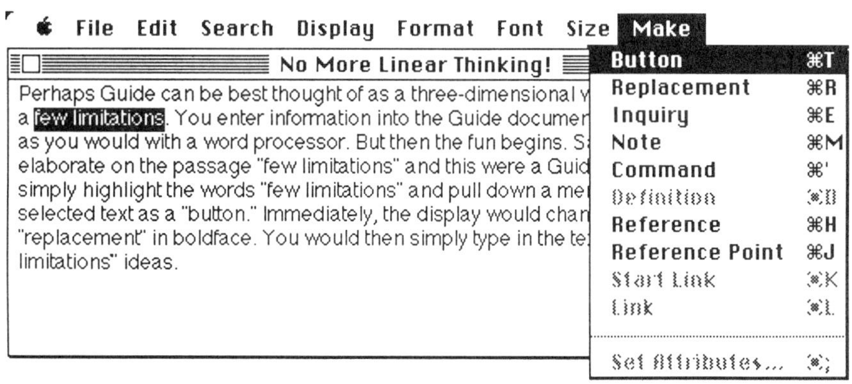

● *Figure 2.24 Unexpanded Replacement Button in Guide.*

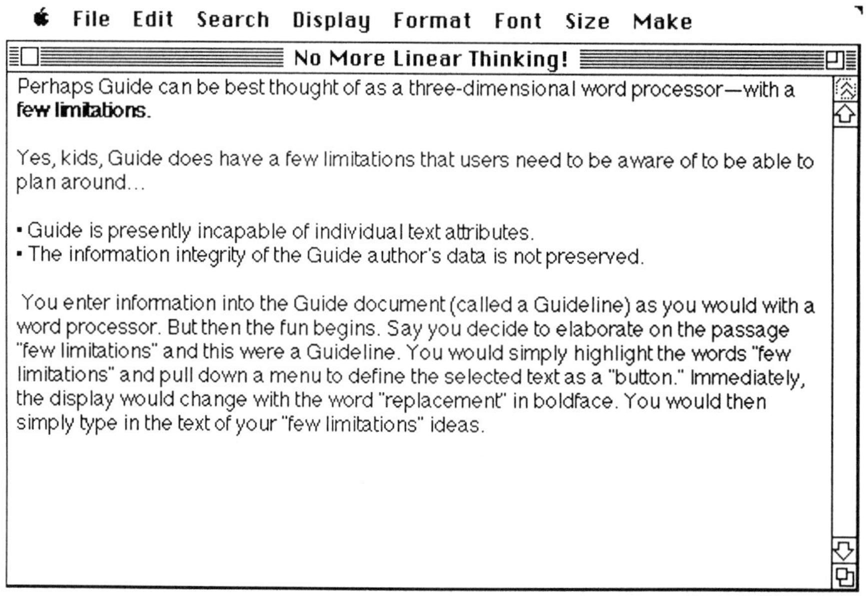

● *Figure 2.25 Expanded Guide Replacement Button.*

Additionally, you could define terms for your readers by using the definition/note button combination as shown in *Figure 2.26.* The definition is expanded by clicking on the underlined term as illustrated in *Figure 2.27.*

You can create that simply a variety of buttons, each button with different qualities.

Rather than attaching an endnote with a graphic of your work group's budget for the next quarter in a report, for example, you can create a ''note button'' in the Guideline. This note button, when clicked, displays the group's budget as a pie chart that you imported via the Clipboard from Excel.

With the Reference and Inquiry buttons, the two remaining button types, 16 other Guidelines can be linked to each other in a virtually unlimited number of reference points. The task of defining a reference button is shown in *Figure 2.28* and the linked reference, opened by clicking on the italicized reference anchor, is shown in *Figure 2.29.*

The Guide hypertext system is incredibly easy to learn to use for only six commands and four cursor shapes must be learned.

Guide, as powerful and as easy as it is to use, is not without problems and faults. Because each text elements style attribute **(boldface,** *italics,* and so on) is used to differentiate buttons from surrounding text, the user cannot

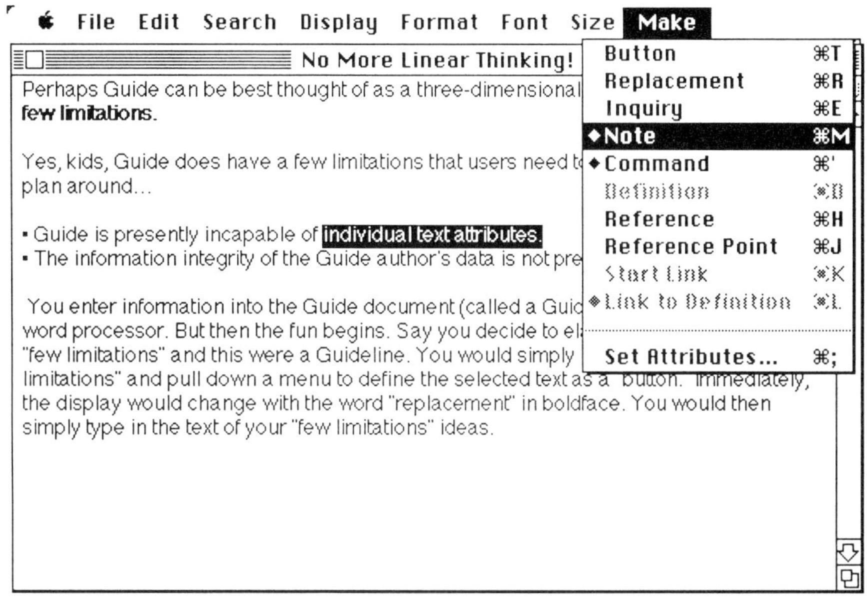

● *Figure 2.26 Defining a Guide Note Button.*

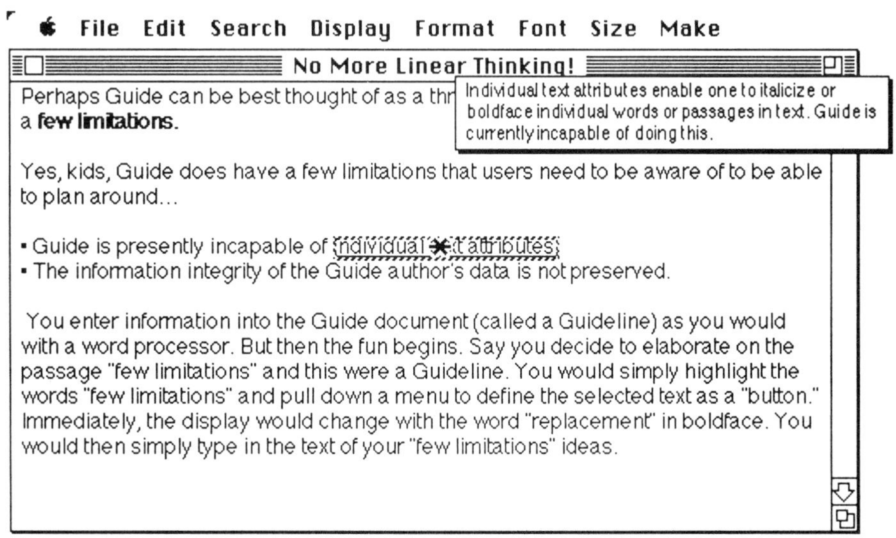

● *Figure 2.27 An Expanded Note Definition in Guide.*

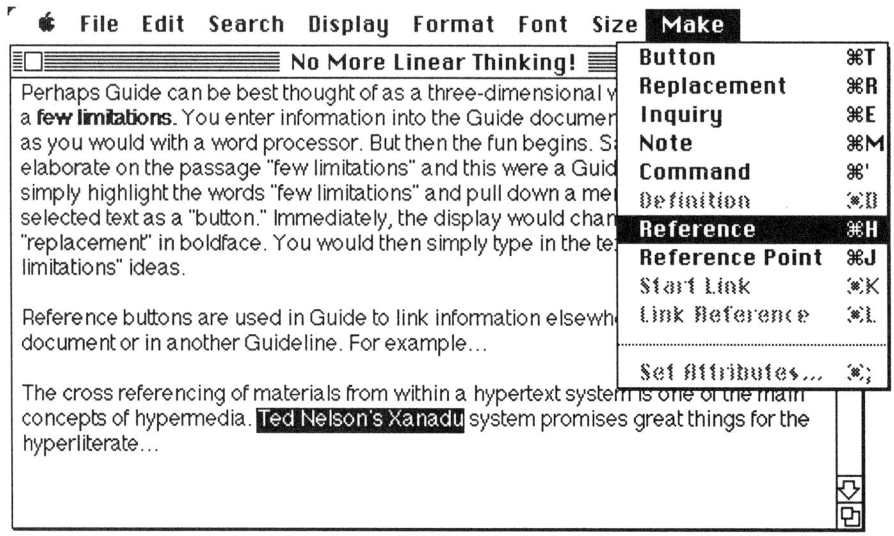

● *Figure 2.28 Defining a Reference in Guide.*

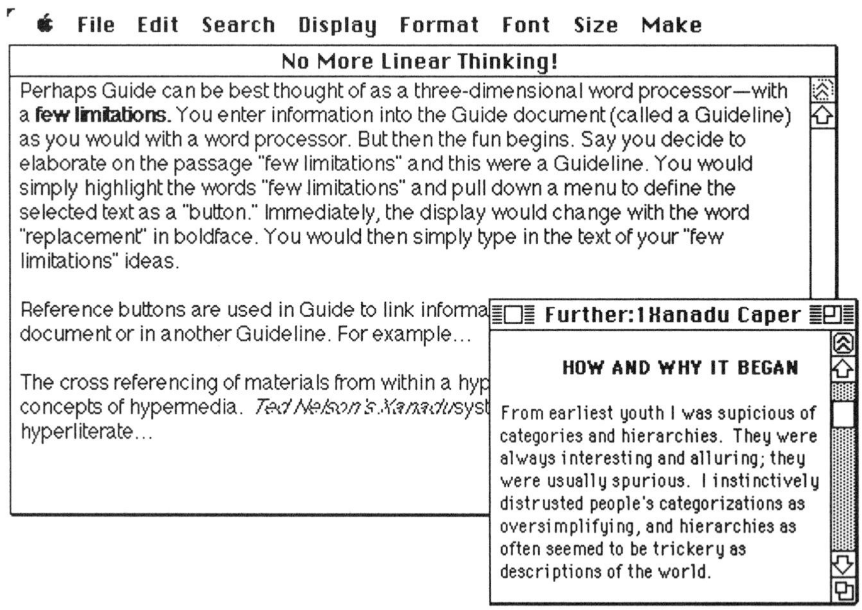

● *Figure 2.29 An opened Reference in Guide.*

set individual text style attributes within the body of the document. This means that the user cannot boldface a word for emphasis, italicize titles, and so on.

According to OWL representatives, this is, in fact, possible, but was left out in the release versions of Guide to date so the product could run faster. OWL International's founder, Alan Boyd, said that allowing the user to set style attributes would make the product run as slow as MacWrite. As faster Macintoshes become available, this feature will hopefully be included in future releases of the product.

Because the level of interest around Apple's HyperCard shows no sign of waning any time in the foreseeable future, OWL released a major update to Guide within a few months of HyperCard's initial debut.

Guide V2.0, which was made available at a reasonable fee to all registered owners of the initial version, is a mostly well-implemented extension to the product's initial release—"mostly" in the sense that individual text attributes still are not available and the Macintosh hardware platform certainly has reached a level to support such an implementation. Other than this shortcoming, however, the product promises to give HyperCard serious competition, especially in text-intensive applications. Larger font sizes and the ability to assign text attributes to entire structures are implemented in the update.

One of the most interesting feature additions for Guide V2.0, and potentially the most useful, is the glossary feature. The glossary allows the user to store a hypertext structure and later recall the structure for placement within any Guide document. This is the first attempt at style sheets for hypertext and is a welcome addition.

OWL's context-sensitive help system, Guidance, now is also included with the product. Aldus's PageMaker V2.0, and the subsequent V3.0 release, is the first commercial application to take advantage of the Guidance help system.

One of the primary limitations of the initial release of Guide was the inability to create buttons on existing graphics. If the Guide author wanted to make a graphical button, it had to be a separate element from those which surrounded it. A new menu item in Guide V2.0, "Insert Invisible," addresses this limitation by allowing the user to insert an invisible graphics box into any element on the screen. This invisible area then may be defined as a button. A companion item also has been included, "Show Invisibles," which makes all invisible graphic elements visible on the screen. The Insert Invisibles convention used to create a graphical button is illustrated in *Figure 2.30*.

Several minor graphics enhancements also have been implemented. Graphic elements now paste to the front of the frame rather than to the back; graphic

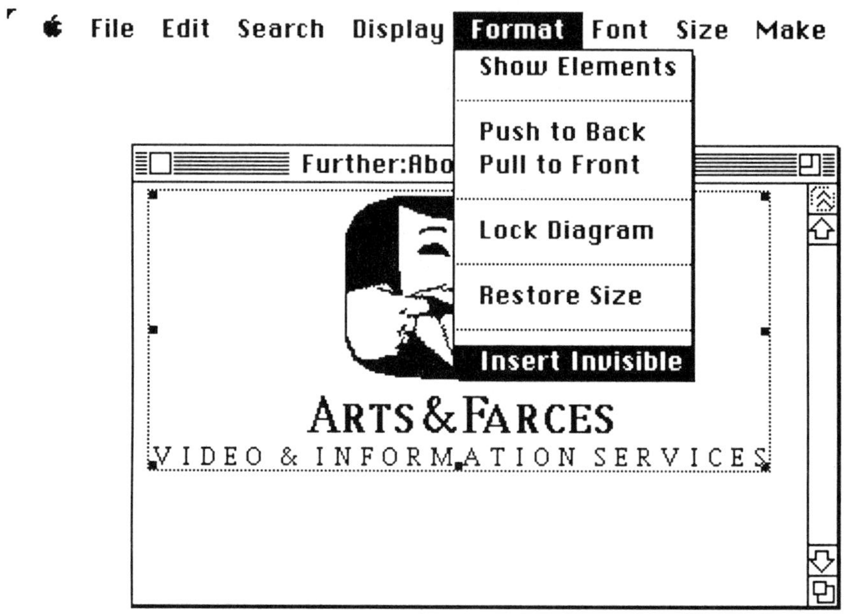

● *Figure 2.30 Guide's Insert Invisible Function.*

frames are aligned to the baseline of text; screen refresh is improved; and the minimum graphic element size is now smaller, allowing for very thin lines and smaller graphic elements. Additionally, a grid has been added that enables the Guideline author to easily align multiple graphic elements.

Another fairly severe limitation in the initial release of Guide, which was subsequently addressed in the product's second release, was the inability to freeze window sizes. The initial version suffered from the anomaly of opening windows that were "never the same size twice," which caused the hypertext hair-ripping syndrome: Hypermedia authors using the Guide system ripped their hair out at regular intervals because they were unable to control where and to what size windows would open after a painstaking and time-consuming screen layout and design process. A "Save Window" check box has been added to the "Set Options. . ." dialog in Guide V2.0 that allows the author to lock the window position and size for his or her documents. Additionally, a "Lock Diagram" function has been added that prevents graphic elements in the selected screen from being repositioned.

One of the more frustrating aspects of working with Guide in the past was that when defining Note buttons *(Figure 2.27)*, which fill approximately a third of the screen when activated, the definition window came up in the full width of the screen. This is modified in Guide V2.0, where the definitions window now appears in the same width as the Note window itself. This allows for accurate Note formatting and saves a fair amount of time in the layout process. Notes now can be formatted "on the fly" rather than by "hit or miss." Similarly, the indent feature was modified to allow the user to set the indents as a number of tabs, although material pasted in from the Clipboard retains its original indentation set.

The second release of Guide introduced a new button type in the form of a Command button. A command button is linked to a script written in Guide's Genesis language and when activated, the definition is scanned for interpreters. If an interpreter (or interpreters; Guide V2.0 can support up to 32 of them at one time) is found, the command is passed to it. Each interpreter can have its own windows, dialogs, and menu. The launch interpreter, for example, allows a launch of an external application from within Guide and then returns control to Guide on exit.

Consider this scenario: You are working on next year's budget for your small business or corporate department and you have an enlightened banker or department head that uses a Macintosh. You want to present your business plan in Guide format, and you need the budget spreadsheet (which is in Excel) accessible from within the complete business plan.

Guide's launch interpreter will enable you to do this. You can define a button that halts execution of your business plan Guideline, opens your budget document in Excel, displays it to the screen where you can make some (hopefully) minor adjustments, and then returns to the exact point in Guide that you launched from.

The provided serial interpreter eventually will enable Guide to communicate with videodiscs, CD-ROMs, and other mass-storage mediums, as well as provide a rudimentary foundation for a front end for Ted Nelson's Project Xanadu.

Both of these features are readily available in HyperCard—either built in (the Launch command) or in the form of external commands (serial port drivers)—Guide's principle competition in the current Macintosh hypermedia field. What will mark the next breakthrough in the Hyper Wars, however, will be the ability to pass messages to and from external applications. Such a development would allow a "message" such as "increase the yearly income figure in next year's budget by ten percent" to an "object" (in this case, Excel) from within either Guide or HyperCard, and then return the resultant figure to your hypertext document (as well as the word-processing document that contains your report and your appropriate data-base file, and related spreadsheets, and so on).

Along with the major enhancements mentioned previously, Guide V2.0 also brings a wealth of small refinements, which is the sign of a maturing product.

Two desk accessories are packaged with Guide V2.0, the previously mentioned Guidance that is a read-only version of the Guide application and a drawing tool entitled Scribbler. Scribbler is an object-oriented graphics editing tool that is useful for creating graphics to use within a Guideline.

Other minor cosmetic improvements also are evident. The Note window now appears to the right of the current window's title bar, and if there isn't room, it will cover part of the window. The Scroll Bar no longer is displayed if all of the active window's information can be displayed, and the end of a file will not scroll past the middle of the window as it did in the previous version. Support for the cursor keys is included and the Backtrack icon can be configured independently for Notes or Replacements.

An ''Expand All'' menu command expands all buttons except that now the top level of an inquiry and all inquiries are folded to show the top levels of the inquiry sections. In a similar vein, the ''Button Remains'' attribute has been modified to allow the reader to click on the same expansion button to collapse the replacement.

As with most things, all that glitters is not gold. Guide V2.0 documents are paged in memory, which allows for faster opening and does not limit file size (other than media space available), but it also considerably slows down screen updating and general performance with large documents.

Another limitation is the compatibility issue. While Guide V2.0 is fully capable of reading documents created with the earlier version, the new documents are incompatible with the older version of Guide. This, in itself, is not serious and probably is even to be expected.

The most serious remaining limitation of the Guide hypertext system is the lack of data integrity. Anyone who has Guide may alter any available Guideline. On the surface, this appears to be a feature, enabling members of a small work group to cooperatively add to and edit a common document. No provision, however, is provided to ''lock'' or protect a document from being altered by anyone other than the most rudimentary Macintosh operating system devices. This is a serious limitation for those considering electronic publishing, although a pseudosolution is provided in the form of the Envelope companion product.

The Envelope product is an adjunct to Guide that acts as a compiler, taking several Guidelines and compiling them into a standard, double-clickable Macintosh application. The resulting Envelope document can be distributed and the intended audience need not own Guide to view the document. Information still can be copied out of the Envelope document via the Clipboard, but the recipient is prevented from altering the original material.

Many reviewers of Guide and other hypertext systems in general complain that the product does not lend itself very well to printing. Because Guide was designed to create documents that are meant to be viewed on the Macintosh screen, I do not consider this a limitation. Any Guideline may be saved, in expanded form, as a MacWrite document, as well as printed to the ImageWriter or LaserWriter.

A radio button has been added to the "Save As . . ." dialog that allows the Guideline to be saved in ASCII text-only format. A new dialog also appears during both MacWrite and ASCII text saves that allows the user to specify tabs, line length, and carriage-return insertion. A check box also appears during ASCII text and MacWrite saves, allowing the entire file to be saved. Checking this box causes all buttons to expand as necessary in order to save the entire file. Along this line, a "Print All" check box has been added to the Page Setup dialog that prints the entire document, again, expanding all buttons as necessary.

It's nearly impossible to compete with a free product, and that's essentially what OWL has to do in order for Guide to be wildly successful. If you work predominantly with text, you owe it to yourself to explore the possibilities of Guide. Its text-handling characteristics are, at this point in time, dramatically better than HyperCard's. If you own a Macintosh with less than one megabyte of memory and you do not intend to upgrade, or use multiple applications under MultiFinder, you also should take a long look at Guide. Its minor shortcomings are far outweighed by the positive aspects of the product, and its publisher has demonstrated a sincere commitment to providing solutions to the existing flaws.

Guide V2.0
Requires: Macintosh 512 or greater; one 800K or two 400K floppies.
Retail price: $199.95
Street price: $160.00
Contact: OWL International, Inc.
14218 NE 21st Street
Bellevue, WA 98007
(206) 747-3203

Apple's HyperCard

On August 11, 1987, Apple Computer, Inc., laid the groundwork for the third paradigm shift in the field of personal computers (the introduction of the original Apple II and the original 128K Macintosh, respectively, being the first two) with the introduction of HyperCard. For the first several months after Apple announced HyperCard, it very carefully referred to the application as "a personal toolkit" and "a software construction kit." The "H" word seemingly was avoided at all costs in the early stages of the product's marketing.

HyperCard changed, by an order of magnitude, the way information is organized, displayed, and navigated and at the same time provided non-programmers with tools to customize their own data spaces and applications. Additionally, HyperCard was the first Macintosh application to implement Ted Nelson's concept of fantics—vaudevillian showmanship combined with a viable information-transfer engine. HyperCard enables the user to present information in a multisensorially pleasing manner, complete with associative links to other bodies of information.

HyperCard was not Bill Atkinson's first software project for Apple. His previous credits included the QuickDraw primitives that allow information to be displayed on the Macintosh screen and MacPaint, the first graphics application for the Macintosh. Atkinson refers to HyperCard, his latest project—almost three years in the making—simply as "an authoring tool and an information organizer,"[81] although he goes on to say that the things created by HyperCard are applications in and of themselves.

Although HyperCard is clearly Bill Atkinson's progeny, it was not a single-handed project. Approximately 20 people were, on a long-term basis, on the HyperCard development team, although Atkinson is responsible for about 70 percent of the actual code. Dan Winkler was the primary author—working from an outline created by Atkinson—of the HyperTalk scripting language that gives HyperCard its programmability, which will be covered in depth in a companion work to this volume.

At HyperCard's initial announcement, Apple president and chief executive officer, John Sculley, referred to the hypermedia system as "arriving just when technology has put more information on a desktop computer than the largest mainframe computer managed only a decade ago. We believe that users need a way to find valuable information quickly as well as customize it in a way that makes sense to them. HyperCard is intended to do just that."[82] Predictably, Apple's press release for the product went on to say, "HyperCard lets users organize and use information the way they think—by association and context as well as hierarchy. Its unique navigational method lets users browse and search quickly through large bodies of information, making it a vital tool with the advent of mass storage optical media technologies."[83]

''Just as Apple opened up the hardware of the Macintosh personal computer to allow new uses and customization, HyperCard opens up the Macintosh software architecture so that users can write programs, organize, and use information in their own way,'' Sculley said. ''It is a continuation of the driving philosophy behind the Macintosh—that powerful technology should be made accessible to people. And that includes developing applications. Our goal is to make creating applications as easy as using the Macintosh. HyperCard is the first step toward that goal. With HyperCard, virtually anyone can become an information provider.''[84] This underlying concept of HyperCard freeing the flow of information is also a strong current through Bill Atkinson's original design, as exemplified in a conversation between Atkinson and Danny Goodman: ''. . . I think what HyperCard is all about is sharing information. A program's soul has a lot to do with the people who are making it and what they're thinking about as they're making it. We're not making this to make money. We're not making this to make Apple happy. We're making this because we want to share something.''[85]

With that sentiment, Bill Atkinson insisted that Apple package HyperCard, free of charge, with every Macintosh sold from that point on. Atkinson, after having control of his initial application, MacPaint, wrested from him and after watching fellow Apple employee Donn Denman spend three years creating a version of the BASIC programming language for the Macintosh that was not published, decided not to let HyperCard suffer a similar fate. ''I went to John Sculley and said, 'I'm leaving. I have to leave Apple at this point because I want to write a really great program for Macintosh,' '' Atkinson told Goodman. ''What I want is to bundle it. . . . I'm going to get this out to people whether I give it away or whether I get Apple to give it away,'' he concluded.[86] Apple agreed, defining HyperCard as Macintosh System Software—bundling the four-disk product with every Macintosh sold and making it available to the installed base of Macintosh owners for the absurdly low price of $49—and the rest, as they say, is history.

In addition to the openness inherent in HyperCard, Bill Atkinson strove for two initial goals for the product. The first was to raise the level of information art ''to where people expect information to be interactive.''[87] The entire HyperCard development team was well aware of the changing nature of information relative to individuals and personal computers and felt strongly that the key to making information more accessible was to build around the expectation of interaction. The form the information fit in was, in many ways, as important as the information itself.

The second aim of HyperCard was to ''raise the level of expectation about customizability.''[88] As we'll see in a later chapter, the notion of

● *Figure 2.31 Welcome to HyperCard.*

mass-customization weighs heavily in this matter. Atkinson goes so far as to call much of the current state of software development "fascist" because a program must be written in such a way as to meet the mainstream needs of 100,000 people, aiming for the lowest common denominator, as it were. A more appropriate solution, according to Atkinson, is to provide "one program that would be useful to 100,000 people, but is customizable so that each of these people with their slightly different needs can tweak it and bend it to be their own."[89]

Atkinson foresaw the potential that a vast market would spring up around HyperCard, based largely on the fact that the product is given away and that the initial gesture of sharing would be returned in vast proportions. Apple coined the term *stackware* to describe the resulting documents created within HyperCard and the volume of resulting stackware to Atkinson's initial gesture has been truly astounding. During the first 90 days of HyperCard's availability, more than a quarter of a million copies of the product were distributed to users, and more than 30 MBytes of stackware appeared on the national telecommunications services. The CompuServe network was so overwhelmed it had to scramble to create a separate forum just for HyperCard.

HyperCard's openness, while an unquestionable boon and blessing for the Macintosh community, does have a major drawback in the eyes of some people. Because HyperCard was designed as a sharing medium, it and the resulting stackware created with it are wide open. Wide open in the realm of information integrity is not a good thing for many information providers, especially those working predominantly with text. There is no easy way to protect the integrity of a stack or a deeply interrelated hypermedia system using the HyperCard platform. Because HyperTalk is an interpreted rather than compiled programming language, the developer also can do little to protect his or her source code. If these concerns cause you to lose sleep at night, you would be well advised to seek out another development and distribution system.[90,91]

Perhaps because of HyperCard's level of openness, accessibility, and free (or very inexpensive) distribution, the product and its associated stackware initially suffered something of an identity crisis. Borrowing from the Rodney Dangerfield school of product marketing, stackware—both commercial products and alternatively distributed shareware, freeware, and public domain stacks—suffered a serious lack of respect. HyperCard itself was almost unanimously praised as being as important to the Macintosh as Applesoft BASIC was to the Apple II line, but it took the stackware market more than a year to shake off the cloak of amateurism.

There were, of course, exceptions. Danny Goodman's Focal Point, for example, quickly replaced Sidekick and most of the FileMaker Plus files on my hard disk. After using the product for an extended period of time during the course of reviewing the product, I gradually became aware that it was, in fact, capable of doing more than my Sidekick/FileMaker Plus combination largely because it was more integrated. Everything worked from a central hub, and everything talked to everything else—with little or no intervention, pleading, or coaxing on my part. It was slow, and it was not putting HyperCard to its best use, but it worked. More importantly, I was able to remold Focal Point to look like and do *exactly* what I wanted.

This was largely a problem of perceived value, a problem that remains to be fully remedied as I write this. The central factor is how does one market stackware that is based on a product that is given away free of charge and touted as being incredibly easy to use. The answer lies in the area of added value, and the simple fact is that it took more than a year for the stackware developers to get their "hyperlegs" and tutor themselves in the finer points of both stackware and software design. That's right, quality stackware design is no different than designing quality software with a more traditional programming language.

Small stackware publishing companies sprang up like mushrooms after the HyperCard rainstorm announcement, but the big-time software publishers still are reluctant to market HyperCard-based applications for mass consumption. Slowly, however, the tide is turning, mostly at the hand of mid-level publishers who are beginning to market applications with a broad base of appeal in the $200 to $250 price range. More importantly, the computer industry itself is beginning to respect the commercial potential of HyperCard stackware. In the spring of 1988, the Software Publishers Association awarded three awards to two of Danny Goodman's commercial stackware products. Focal Point won two awards and Business Class won for the best software user interface.

HyperCard maintains a basic display and underlying structure metaphor of a stack of screen-sized cards, resulting in a semistructured hypermedia environment rather than the unstructured, free-form milieu offered by Guide, Intermedia, and the more traditional hypermedia environments. Stacks of cards are a suitable metaphor for many applications, but may prove too constraining for others.

In the initial stages of HyperCard's development, Bill Atkinson and the rest of the development team were toying with the idea of switching from the underlying structural metaphor of the card to a book metaphor. The book metaphor under consideration would have been much more specific, containing such elements as library card catalogs, bookshelves, and chapters. In the end, the idea was abandoned because, "At a certain point, however, we just realized that, really, a stack of cards was a much better metaphor. People just don't feel good tearing out pages of books and sorting the pages of a book. The stack of things was a much more general metaphor."[92]

The underlying principle of why the card metaphor is inherently better than the book metaphor is because of the greater level of generalness of the card metaphor. Perhaps it is for this reason that HyperCard has been widely misunderstood and criticized as being too broad an approach rather than offering a specific solution. HyperCard is the first wildly successful general hypermedia development platform as opposed to being a solution to a specific set of problems, and that as a generalist it, by definition, is not so adept at solving specific problems. Appropriately one of the guiding principles behind the development of HyperCard was to keep the system simple and therefore accessible. "Keeping it simple, allowing learning by exploration, and presenting a highly graphic interface are the Bill Atkinson traditions that are self-evident in HyperCard. . . . Bill's trademarks are a balance of complexity and simplicity . . ."[93]

HyperCard is best described to hypermedia novices as a graphic, text, and audio information organizer built around the underlying metaphor of a stack of cards. This is most likely where the misperception of HyperCard as a data base arises. The novice is stymied by the fact that HyperCard provides a very gentle, very loosely unified structure to this information repository. The HyperCard development team did not just present us with a toolkit with which to create stacks of cards, but rather with a meta-tool with which we are offered the opportunity to explore our own creative nether regions as well as manage such mundane things as telephone lists and appointment schedules.

All information management systems—hypermedia notwithstanding—require navigational aids with which we can explore the data spaces we and others create. HyperCard provides a means of creating hypermedia links and cross-references as well as a series of mostly linear navigation tools. The mostly linear navigational tools are accessed via HyperCard's Go menu, which is shown in *Figure 2.32*.

The Home, Help, First, Next, Previous, and Last commands in HyperCard's Go menu provide a series of constant anchor points that provide the user with a sense of stability as well as a series of emergency exits. How each command behaves, however, depends on how the hypermedia data space's structure is designed and implemented. If these commands can be seen as moving the user through the space of the structure, the two remaining commands—Back and Recent—can be thought of as moving the user through time, transporting the user to different cards (or even different stacks) depending on where he or she has been.

Of these, the Recent command is the most interesting and in some cases the most useful. As shown in *Figure 2.33,* selecting Recent from the Go menu displays a series of the 42 most recent cards that have been traversed. Any of the displayed cards can be automatically navigated to simply by clicking on the miniature representation of the desired destination.

The Home command is the last-ditch emergency exit as well as the express route to the familiar territory of HyperCard's Home Card, which is the starting point of most excursions. It is shown in *Figure 2.34.* Like all homes should be, HyperCard's Home is a safe haven from which we can venture out, always assured that it will be the same when we get back. Sooner or later you will find yourself so hopelessly lost in someone's (hopefully not one of your own) hypermedia data spaces that the only thing you can do is click your mouse on the Home button or select the Home command from the Go menu.

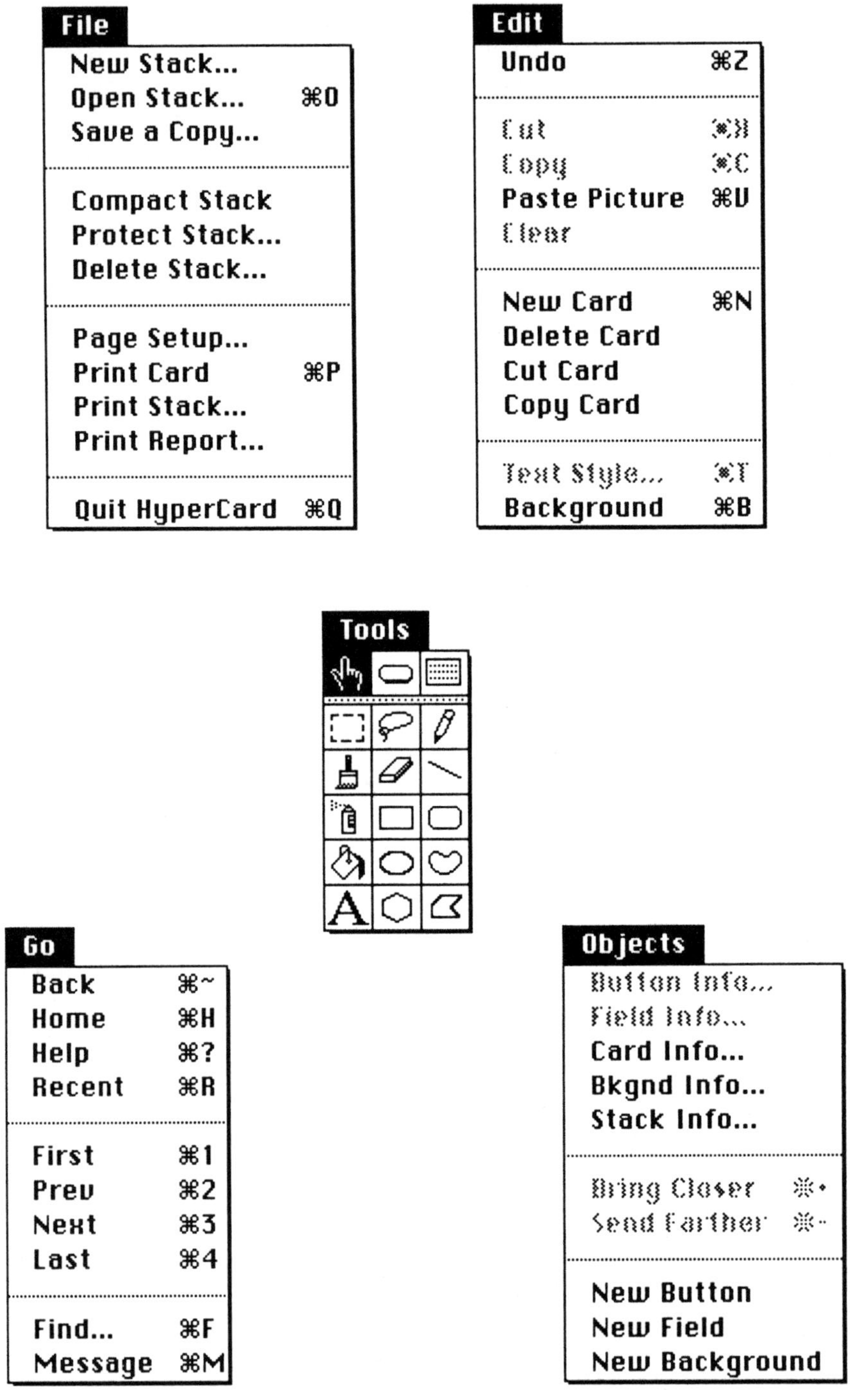

• *Figure 2.32 HyperCard's Menus.*

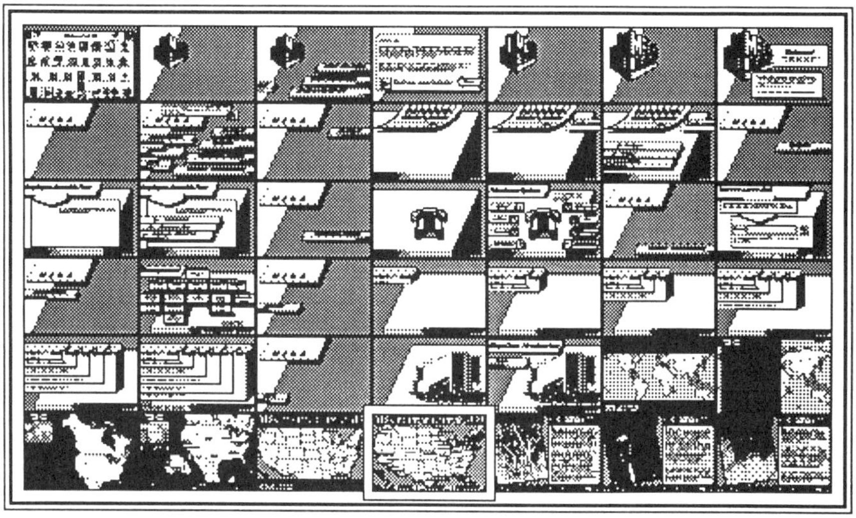

• *Figure 2.33 HyperCard's "Go Recent" Dialog.*

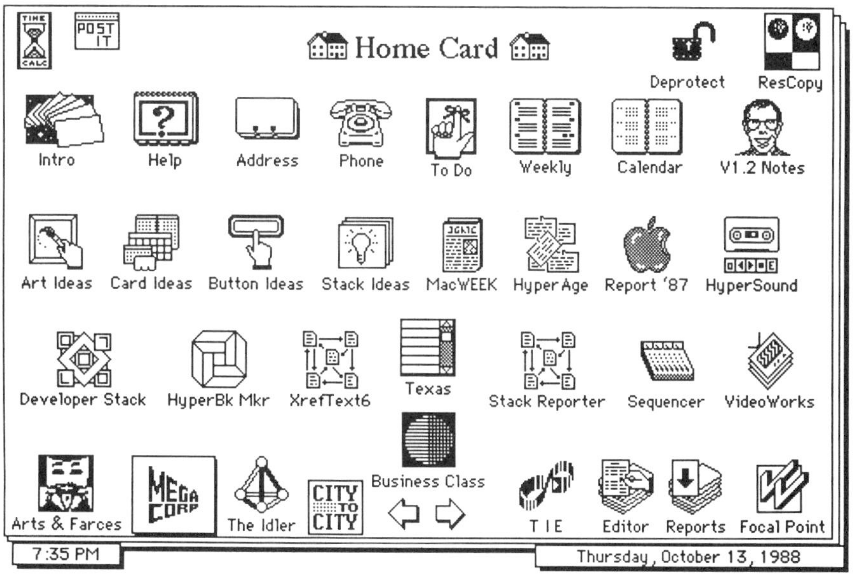

• *Figure 2.34 HyperCard's Home Card.*

Macintosh users are very familiar with buttons on their screens that initiate some sort of action or are used to respond to a query from the application. HyperCard buttons are used for the same things, but they are radically different in some ways, mostly in the ways many of them look. *Figure 2.35* shows a variety of buttons available to the HyperCard user to initiate various actions and *Figure 2.36* illustrates the various button attributes available to the HyperCard author. HyperCard buttons can perform operations ranging from navigating the hypermedia data space to performing mathematical calculations to launching documents in other applications.

Where most hypermedia systems provide a variety of linking structures, HyperCard offers a single type of link, the ''Go To'' command in the HyperTalk scripting language. HyperCard's Go To command is directly comparable to Guide's Reference command. Other types of links may be established within the HyperCard system, but they must be programmed using the resident scripting language, HyperTalk, or implemented as external commands (XCMDs) imported as resources from more traditional programming languages such as Pascal or C.

Herein lies one of HyperCard's shining advantages over other currently available hypermedia systems. If the hypermedia designer needs a command or function that is not available from HyperTalk, he or she may simply write the needed facility themselves using any of the popular programming environments.[94] These commands are compiled in the native language and then added to the HyperCard environment as resources in the form of external

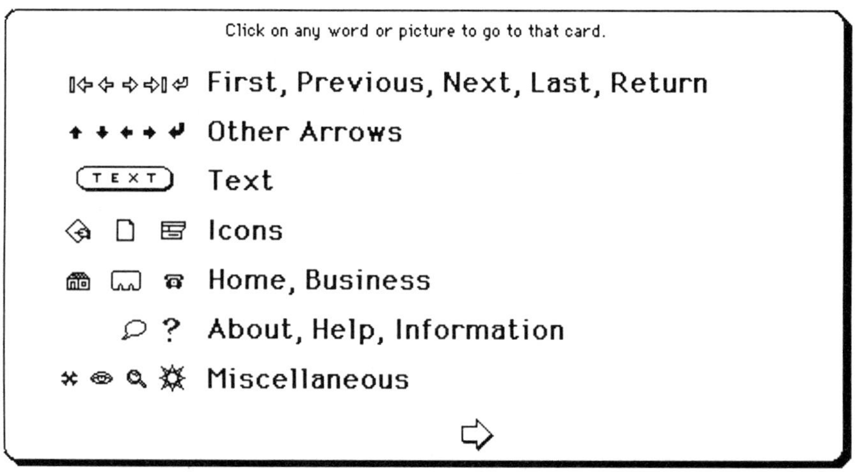

• *Figure 2.35 HyperCard Button examples.*

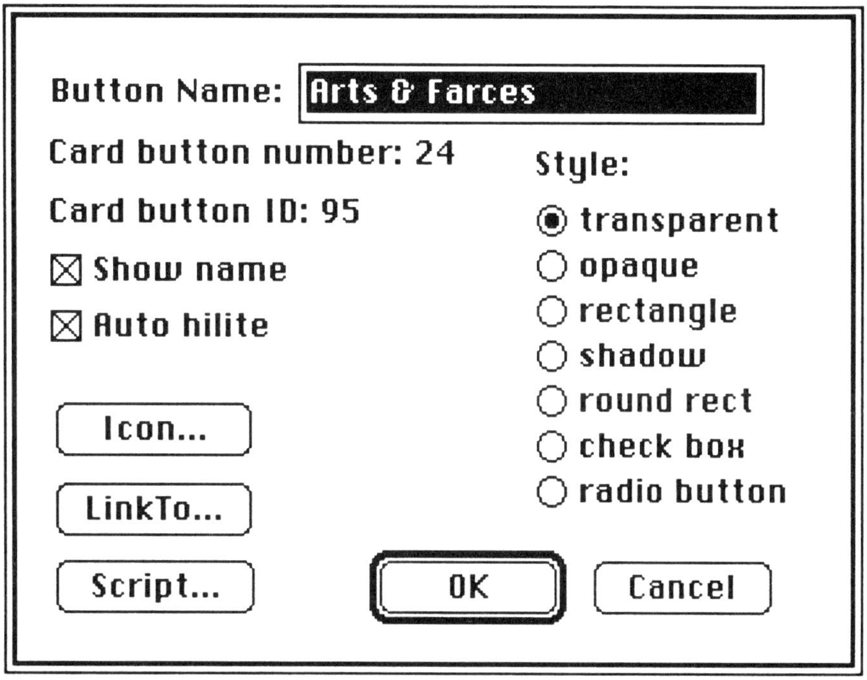

● *Figure 2.36 HyperCard's Button Attributes Dialog.*

commands (XCMDs) and external functions (XFCNs). For the purposes of this discussion, we will refer to external commands and functions in the HyperCard milieu collectively as XCMDs.

An XCMD is a detour taken by the HyperTalk script to perform an action that is not directly available within the HyperCard environment. Because they are compiled into machine language by the programming environment they were created in, XCMDs tend to run much faster than they would if they were possible in HyperTalk. XCMDs also are able to communicate fluently with HyperCard. They can be used to send messages to various cards, retrieve the properties of different objects, and the like.

The singular elegance of HyperCard's support for XCMDs is that the hypermedia author who is not accomplished in one of the traditional programming languages can use readily available public domain and freeware XCMDs without knowing one whit about how they were programmed.

XCMDs also promise to alter the performance of many non-HyperCard applications. Many software publishers are beginning to explore directly supporting HyperCard XCMDs within their traditional applications. The user is the beneficiary in such an arrangement as he or she will be given more and more control over his or her personal computing environment.

HyperTalk usually is referred to as a scripting language rather than a programming language. Although it is both, the scripting nomenclature is more appropriate because all instructions (commands within the script or program) refer to objects and are, themselves, placed inside objects. This is known as an object-oriented approach to programming, which has its origins in Alan Kay's Smalltalk language developed in the early 1970s at Xerox Corp.'s Palo Alto Research Center (PARC). Many professional programmers would argue that HyperTalk is not a programming language because of its simplicity and inability to produce stand-alone applications.

HyperCard consists of seven classes of objects, organized in a rising hierarchy: fields, buttons, cards, backgrounds, stacks, the Home Stack, and HyperCard itself. The HyperTalk programmer can manipulate the objects by sending messages to them through the use of commands, functions, message handlers, and properties from within the HyperTalk language. The hierarchy of the objects comes into play when a message is passed to an object that does not understand it. When this happens the object simply passes the message along to the next higher class of object in the hierarchy.

The HyperCard object hierarchy is best illustrated with an analogy. Consider, for a moment, HyperCard as a ball-bearing factory. Your job is to sort the ball bearings, one at a time, into seven classes. You devise a conveyor mechanism that consists of a track with seven holes of ever-increasing diameter. Each ball bearing is routed through the conveyor until it comes to rest in the hole it is "targeted" for. Your ball-bearing conveyor device is illustrated in *Figure 2.37.*

As each ball bearing travels through the conveyor, it is passed on to the next higher slot until it reaches the slot it fits. If the ball bearing does not fit a slot by the time it reaches the end of the hierarchy conveyor, it falls off into the reject bin and is disposed of. In this analogy, the ball bearing is a message passed along HyperCard's object hierarchy until the message's target (the appropriate slot) is reached. In HyperCard, the user performs an action (such as clicking the mouse on a field), and this event is recorded and sent out as a message to the objects affected by the event. In the case in point, if the user clicks on a field, that field receives that message. If the field does not have a "mouseWithin," "mouseDown," or "mouseUp" Message Handler (the three actions inherent in the click of the mouse), the three messages are passed up the object hierarchy in the order shown in *Figure 2.37.* If the message is passed all the way up the hierarchy without being acted on, it is simply ignored.

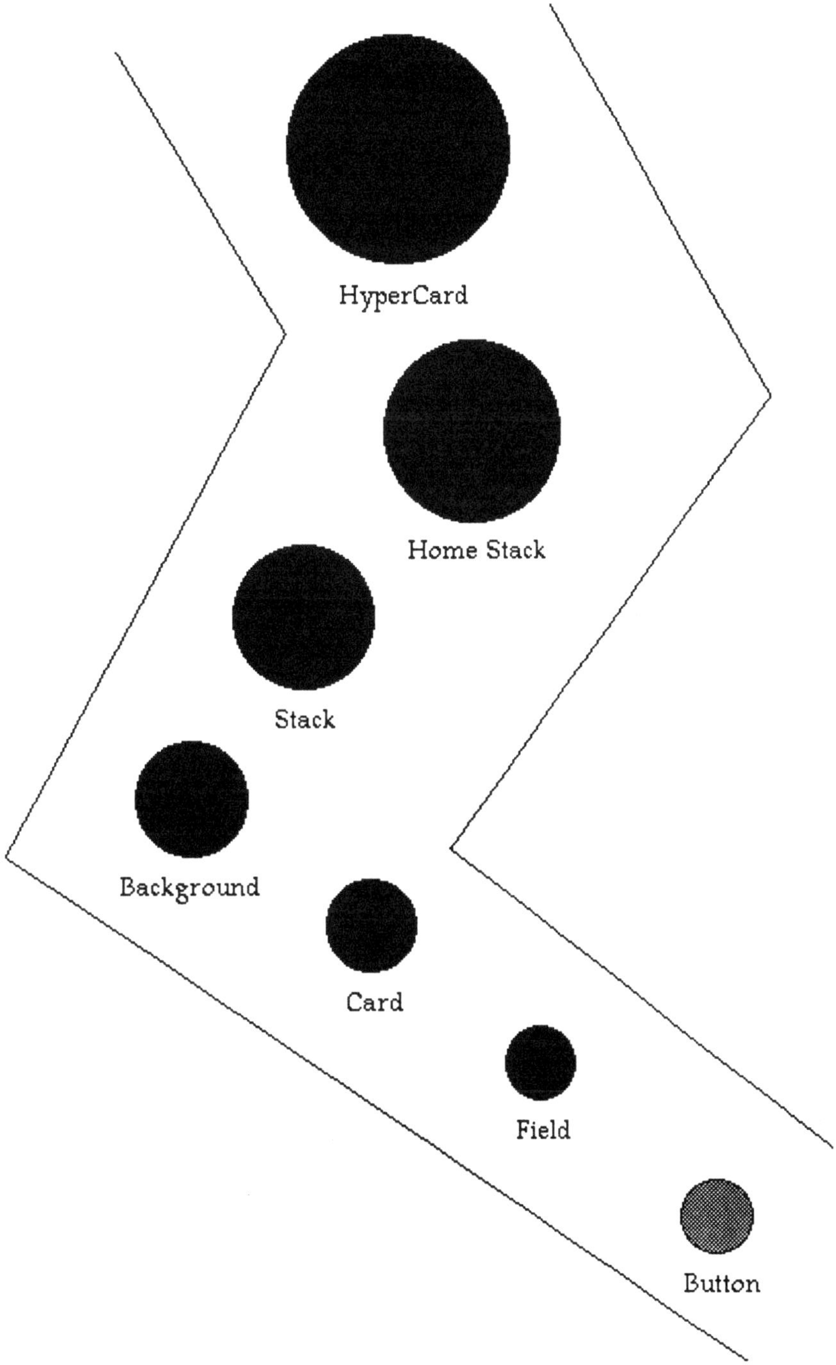

● ***Figure 2.37*** *HyperCard's Object Hierarchy.*

Most hypermedia implementations allow for a body of text to be expanded—in the sense of parenthetical statements or related materials—on command by clicking a region of the screen. HyperCard lacks any sort of text button that could be used for this convention, although given the richness of HyperTalk and the extensibility of the environment through external commands and functions, this can be worked around. As a brief example, consider the use of hidden text fields called up when a specially modified field is clicked on. This technique is illustrated in *Figures 2.38* and *2.39.*

The HyperTalk implementation for this would be quite simply accomplished by entering the desired annotation text in the field shown in *Figure 2.39,* setting the field's lock text property to true and typing "Hide field "PopText" " into the Message Box. Next, the field's lock text property in *Figure 2.38* would be set to true and the script of the field would be edited to the following:

```
on mouseUp
    show field "PopText"
end mouseUp
```

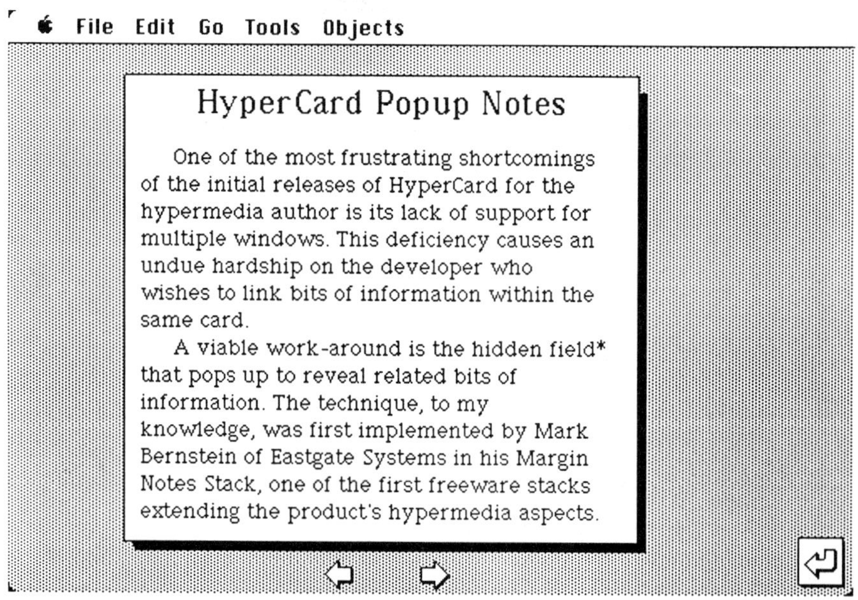

● *Figure 2.38 HyperCard field with locked text and hidden button (covering asterisk).*

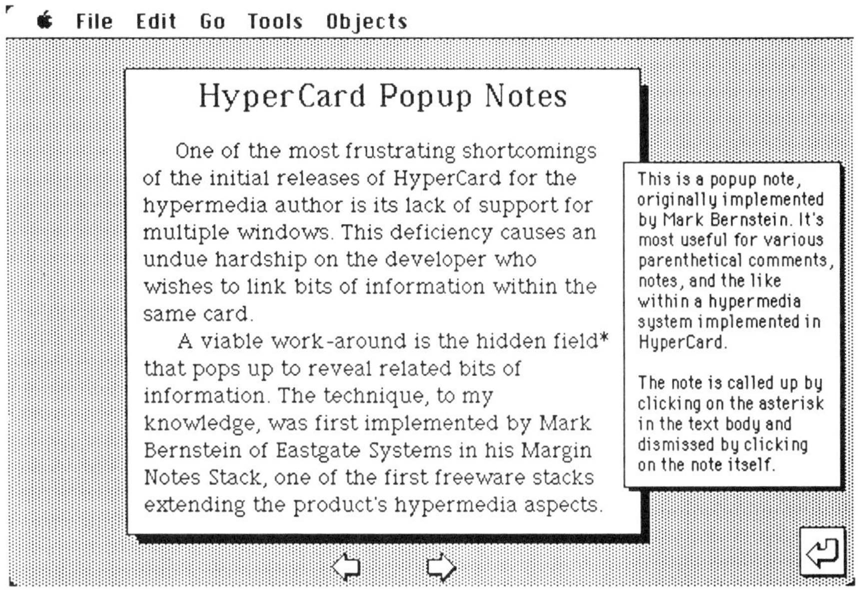

● ***Figure 2.39*** *Expanded popup note in HyperCard.*

Finally, a script for the PopText field also would be created as follows:

```
on mouseUp
   hide field ''PopText''
end mouseUp
```

All advantage inherent in the HyperCard Go To information link, not existing in other hypermedia systems, is that variables can be used within the Go To command statements to allow the use of intelligent reference buttons as location and navigational aids. Such an implementation enables the author to construct a navigational map that appears throughout the information body; a ''crumb trail'' also can be constructed easily through the document, which serves to inform the user of his or her position relative to other parts of the work.

HyperCard is limited because it lacks multiple windows. Bearing the birthmark of its creator, Bill Atkinson, the HyperCard environment presently consists of a single, fixed-size window. This is a major limitation for only a single card of a single stack can be displayed on the screen at a given time. Again, this limitation can be painstakingly worked around by using the Lock Screen command to collect information from a series of cards, copying the required data to the Clipboard, returning to the display card, and pasting the information to a field on the screen. Hopefully, this limitation will be addressed in a future version of HyperCard.

If HyperCard lacks some of the more refined niceties of a variety of information-linking devices offered by some of the other hypermedia development systems, it partially makes up for this by its incredible ease of use. In addition, the HyperCard development team obviously was listening with both ears when Ted Nelson talked about the benefits of fantics in the design of hypermedia systems. HyperCard offers the most advanced support for integrating sound and simple visual effects of any currently available hypermedia development system.

HyperCard provides the user with a wealth of simple but utterly dramatic visual effects that are useful in making a transitional information link from one card to another. Where other hypermedia tools simply open new windows, HyperCard is capable of using common visual effects such as barn doors, scrolling, iris opens and closes, and dissolves. The desired visual effect is as simple to implement as adding a single HyperTalk command to the desired object's script, such as:

```
on mouseUp
    visual dissolve
    go to next card
end mouseUp
```

HyperCard's visual effects are very useful as navigational cues and aids. Using an iris-open visual effect, for instance, implies an expansion of the matter at hand, while an iris close signifies the closing of the opened expansion.

HyperCard includes an integrated paint system that, while limited to the creation and editing of bit-mapped graphics, offers the author the unique opportunity of controlling all of the painting tools via HyperTalk script commands. This environment allows pseudoanimation and other fantic operations, such as automatically generated graphics. Many hypermedia producers consider HyperCard's graphic support lacking because color is not supported and resolution is limited to 72 dots per inch. This has been addressed by the third-party developer community with HyperCard extensions that allow, among other things, animation (MacroMind's VideoWorks Driver for HyperCard) and support for color graphics (various public domain XCMDs).

HyperCard also has been faulted for its drastic memory requirements and the size of its resulting stackware files. HyperCard requires a minimum of 1MByte of RAM and will not run on Macintoshes produced earlier than the

Macintosh Plus. A hard drive also should be considered a necessity, although Apple claims HyperCard is usable with two 800K drives.

With the advent of version 1.2 of HyperCard, the product enters the realm of multiuser hypermedia by allowing multiple users to concurrently access a locked stack on a file server. While multiple users can access the same stack at the same time, no one can alter it. As the Macintosh itself continues to mature relative to multiuser software, this will surely be addressed in future versions of HyperCard.

The single most significant design flaw of HyperCard is its lack of Boolean search, sort, and retrieval mechanisms. HyperCard's native Find command operates admirably well on stacks of moderate size. As the stacks begin to grow to true hypermedia proportions, however, the search times begin to slow dramatically. As with most things HyperCard, If you wait long enough, a solution will be provided by someone, most often a third-party developer. Currently several commercial HyperCard add-ons address this limitation, although they are quite expensive.[95] Hopefully, this issue will continue to be addressed by the developer community as adequate Boolean search and retrieval tools speed the hypermedia development process considerably.

A lesser concern, only because it can be addressed with relatively simple XCMDs, is the lack of a browsing map facility in HyperCard. As we will see in Chapter 3, one of the biggest problems with hypermedia is the ''getting lost'' factor. When a hypermedia document set is browsed, the reader tends to get lost or lose his or her bearings in the information structure. Both the ArchiText and Intermedia systems provide a structural overview of the document set in the form of a browser map or network view. While the HyperCard developer can create such a browser aid after the hypermedia document set has been created, this does not help during the actual development process.

HyperCard, as Apple's initial entry into the hypermedia arena, is an admirable first step. If I seem overly critical, it is because HyperCard is my hypermedia development system of choice and offers incredible potential and opportunities to real people in the real world with valuable bodies of information to distribute.

Bearing that firmly in mind, here is a wish list for the next major revision of HyperCard (in no certain order of preference): multiple windows (smaller ones, at least, or preferably resizable ones that do not detract from the original underlying card metaphor); color support; text buttons; an integrated script editor; external resources that do not have to be installed in a stack or in HyperCard itself; access to the toolbox (menu editor, dialog box editor, etc.); stereo sound; increased speed; and a HyperTalk compiler.

Alan Kay once referred to the Macintosh as the first computer worthy of criticism. HyperCard is the first widely available and used hypermedia development system worthy of the same. It continues to evolve and is better thought of as a work in process rather than as a product.

HyperCard V1.2.1
Requires: Macintosh Plus or greater; two 800K floppies (hard disk strongly recommended).

Retail price: $49.00 or free with the purchase of a Macintosh computer
Street price: $39.00
Contact: Apple Computer, Inc.
20525 Mariani Avenue
Cupertino, CA 95014
(408) 973-1010

Eastgate Systems' HyperGate

HyperGate is a hypertext system developed primarily by Mark Bernstein who admits to first learning about hypertext when he spilled coffee on Ted Nelson in 1977 while they both were at Swarthmore College. In 1982 Bernstein helped form Eastgate Systems, a Boston-based consulting firm that specializes in hypertext software and hypermedia production.

According to a 1987 position paper, Bernstein describes the HyperGate system as an example of what he refers to as pervasive nonlinearity. "Many early hypertext designs evaded the perils of the navigation problem by imposing a dominant linearity upon hypertext documents," he wrote. "Documents created with these tools are often perceived as linear texts augmented by annotations or links."[96]

Indeed, one of the strongest points in HyperGate's favor as a hypertext system is its inherent nonlinearity. There are no such things as scrolling documents or even scrolling pages. There are no indicators of such linear functions as next card or up and down. Yet the system offers an internally standardized form of navigational aids and a welcomed "crumb trail" that informs readers of where they have been and where they are yet to visit. "We created HyperGate to explore the craft of hypertext without the impediment (or aid) of a pervasive underlying linearity,"[97] Bernstein said in his introduction to the *HyperText '87 Digest.*

Navigational aids inherent in the HyperGate system include Bookmarks, which are easily implemented, disposable place markers made available to the user; Thumb Tabs, which are major landmarks within the document that reassure readers of their relative location; Bread crumbs, which show the readers which specific links lead back to recently viewed material; and Maps, which provide a geographical overview of the document.

The sequence employed by the user to create a Bookmark in the HyperGate system is shown in *Figures 2.40* to *2.42*. The user selects the Mark This Page command from the Bookmark menu *(Figure 2.40)*, which calls up the Bookmark Definition Dialog *(Figure 2.41)*. The user enters the appropriate text to be displayed in the Bookmark, and it is then added to the revised Bookmark menu *(Figure 2.42)*. From that point on until the Bookmark is unmarked, using the Unmark This Page command, selecting the newly added command from that menu will return the user to the marked page.

HyperGate also provides the hypertext author and the user with a structured method of annotating hypertext documents that is illustrated in *Figures 2.43* to *2.45*. The user (or author if he or she is annotating his or her own work) selects the Edit Margin Note command from the Notes menu *(Figure 2.43)*, which pops up the Margin Note itself *(Figure 2.44)*. The desired text of the Margin Note is entered, and when closed, by clicking the OK button, a

● ***Figure 2.40*** *HyperGate's Bookmark Menu.*

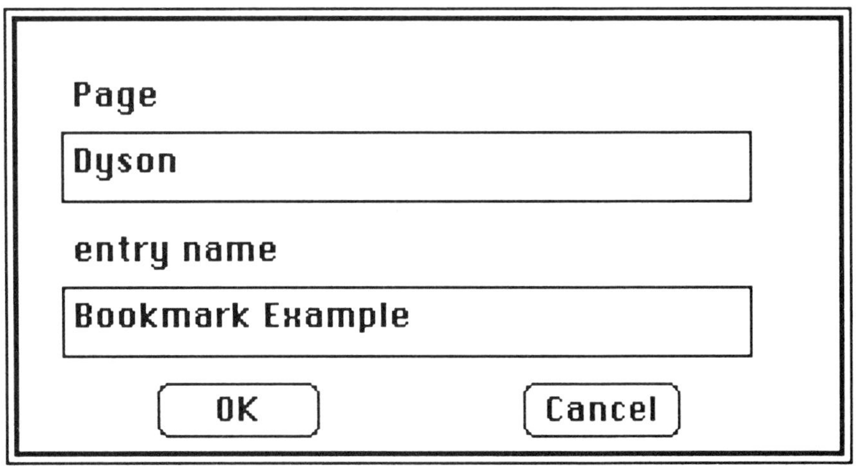

● ***Figure 2.41*** *HyperGate's Bookmark Dialog.*

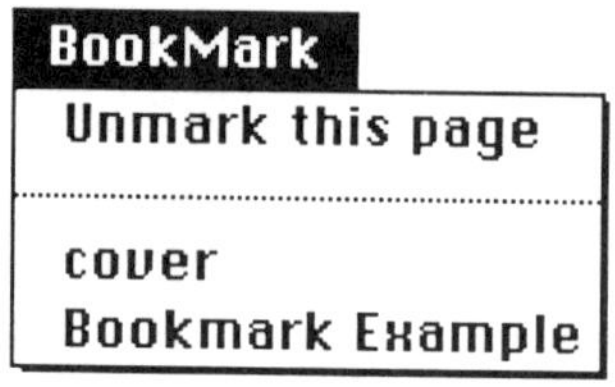

● *Figure 2.42 HyperGate's Revised Bookmark Menu.*

Margin Note dog-ear button is added to the hypertext document *(Figure 2.45)*, indicating that the displayed text is annotated in the form of a Margin Note.

The most extensive indexing and cross-referencing system currently available inherent in a hypermedia system also is provided in the HyperGate system, and this is shown in *Figure 2.46.* The index provides a way for the author to provide data paths through the hypertext and also provides the user with a faculty for creating his or her own paths through the document. The process, which is very intuitive, is a well-done implementation that other hypertext and hypermedia systems could benefit from.

Eastgate Systems' HyperGate is a useful hypertext environment that offers the hypertext author several distinct advantages. The author may create specific data trails through the hypertext that are easily followed by the novice. Data integrity is ensured by disabling any sort of text selection commands or actions, and a facility is provided to print out "pages" of the hypertext. There is also a read-only version of the system, HyperGate Reader, that is available with several very reasonably priced and interesting hypertext documents created by the Eastgate Systems development team.

HyperGate
Requires: Macintosh Plus or greater; one 800K floppy drive.
Retail price: Write for details.
Street price: Not currently available.
Contact: Eastgate Systems
134 Main Street
Watertown, MA 02172
(617) 782-9004

Autodesk's Xanadu

[Note: Although the Xanadu System remains to arise from the vapor during my writing cycle on this project, Xanadu is nearing completion and should be available for public consumption shortly after the initial publication of this book. For that reason, it is being covered here as well as in the Future Hypermedia section.]

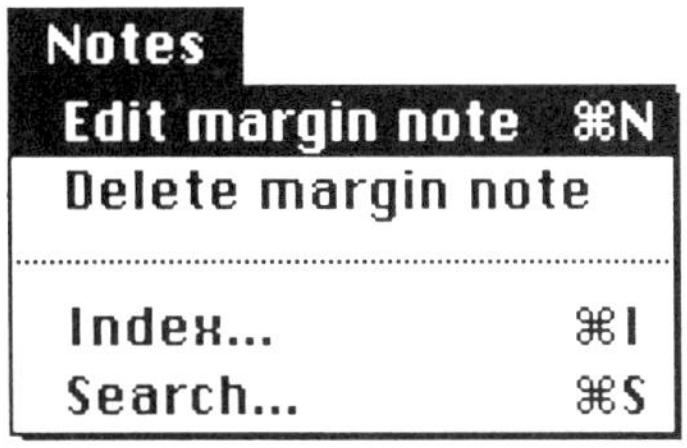

● *Figure 2.43 HyperGate's Notes Menu.*

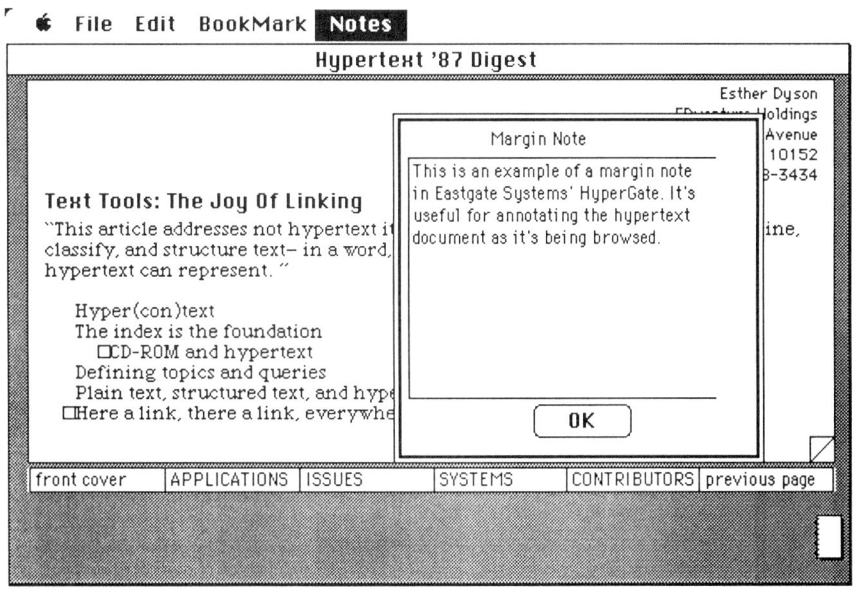

● *Figure 2.44 HyperGate's Margin Note.*

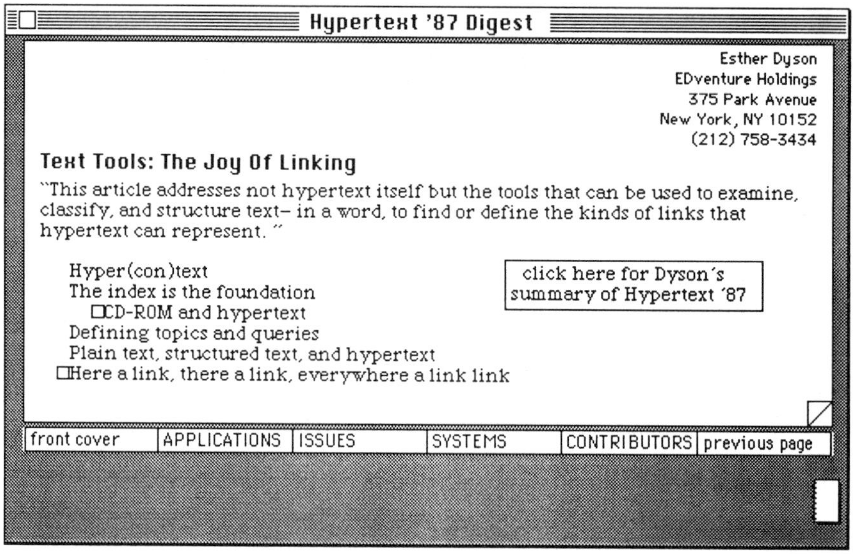

• *Figure 2.45* *HyperGate's Margin Note Button (Dog-Ear Page).*

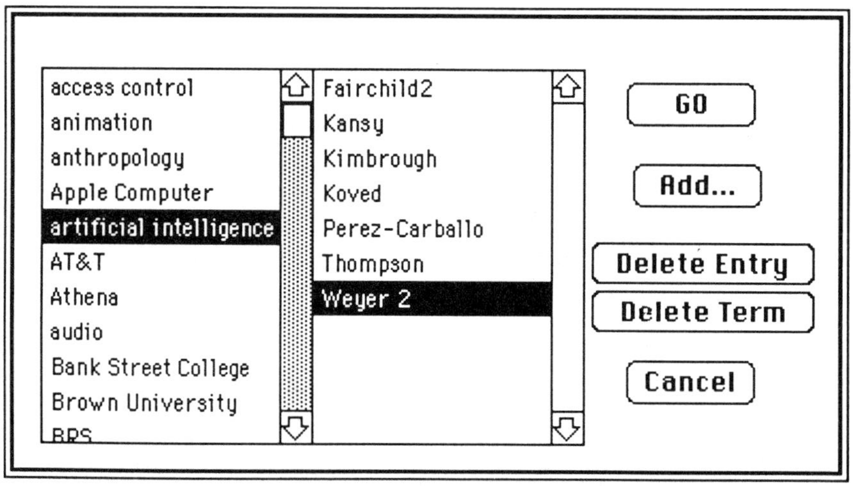

• *Figure 2.46* *HyperGate's Index Dialog.*

Xanadu is the dream of Ted Nelson that appears to be the closet of his many visions that is coming true, which portends great things for the rest of us. According to the updated version of his seminal *Dream Machines,* Nelson alternately refers to Xanadu as a ''Literary System, Storage Engine, Hypertext and Hypermedia Server, Virtual Document Coordinator, Write-Once Network Storage Manager, Electronic Publishing Method, Open Hypermedium, Non-Hierarchical Filing System, Linked All-Media Repository Archive, Paperless Publishing Medium, and Readdressing Software. The Magic Place of Literary Memory.''[98] The name, Xanadu, comes from Coleridge's poem, ''Kubla Khan,'' which Nelson referred to as a ''little story of the artistic trance,''[99] which would offer the electronic author a pleasure dome.

Begun as a Harvard term project on computers in the social sciences in the fall of 1960, Xanadu evolved first into a new set of data structures, proceeded into a single-user workstation implementation, and eventually blossomed into what it is today—a universal data space for everything, everywhere, all at once. The underlying principle of Xanadu is that it allows a user to see, follow, and create a multitude of arbitrary links between nonsequential material. Nelson credits Xanadu's publicity as one of its greatest blessings and simultaneously one of its greatest curses, because it is responsible for the widespread misunderstanding of the project. ''The Xanadu Project is very well known,'' says Nelson, ''many have worked on it over the years. This visibility is both an advantage and a hindrance. Many people know our goals and ideals, but only a few understand our real technical direction.''[100]

Ted Nelson and his cohorts have been hard at work on Xanadu for 29 years, and now it looks as though the dream may be realized as a commercially viable—or at least commercially available—''product'' by the end of 1989. Computer-aided design software publisher Autodesk acquired an 80-percent equity interest in the Xanadu Operating Company in April of 1988 and retained Nelson and his development team to bring the project to fruition. Although Autodesk paid less than $1 million for its stake in Xanadu, the company paid a larger sum for a development with Nelson, Roger Gregory (Xanadu Operating Company's chairman), and the rest of the Xanadu design team. Xanadu initially will be developed for the Sun workstation and the Macintosh II running under A/UX, Apple's version of the UNIX operating system.

Xanadu, in its simplest incarnation, consists of a worldwide network of geographically dispersed, interconnected nodes that collectively provide a hypermedia publishing system. The system will provide users with the ability to publish virtually any kind of document that can be annotated and linked to any other document on the system. All users will have access to the entire body of documents, which Nelson refers to as a "docuverse." In addition, publishers will earn royalties every time someone accesses or links one of their documents.

The Xanadu idea, according to Ted Nelson, is "To give you a screen in your home from which you can see into the world's hypertext libraries.... To make you a part of a new electronic literature and art, where you can get all your questions answered and nobody will put you down."[101]

The system itself consists of software that is capable of running on any computer or workstation running UNIX with a minimum of 2 MBytes of memory (ideally 10 MBytes of RAM) and a minimum of 200 MBytes of hard-disk storage. Versions also are planned for the Macintosh's native operating system, as well as for IBM's OS/2. Front ends to the UNIX back end can be created on any computer system.

Xanadu also promises to address the issue of access to information and what Nelson refers to as the Information Lords. Ted Nelson and his Xanadu design team specifically designed the system to be used by a series of "normal" users, thereby eliminating the need for system administrators and operators as they have come to be called. The design group stipulated the system on the basis of true equality; the design team itself desires nothing more than to be normal users as opposed to gatekeepers. "It is not that our wants are modest, but rather that we want to put an emperor's resources at the fingertips of all users, especially children and scientists and poets."[102]

The Xanadu system is a hypermedia repository for almost any form of material, ranging from ordinary text and pictures to musical notation and recordings to photographs and video material. Furthermore, the system is designed for fast retrieval and delivery of linked documents. According to Nelson, this will provide all of us with the assimilation tools for alternative versions, historical backtracks, and "arbitrary collaging."

Best of all, the Xanadu storage and retrieval system will be completely transparent to the user.

"Bit-map graphics will be stored... to allow panning (graphical scrolling) and zoom (continuously increasing or decreasing magnification) as incremental data deliveries. (How your screen machine will show them is another matter.) Three dimensional objects... may be collaged by users into compound objects, scenes from history, enactments, and artwork."[103]

Obviously, Macintosh will offer a distinct advantage for use as what Nelson refers to as a "screen machine." For the first time a computer will be taken out of the realm of paper emulator on a global scale.

Nelson's concept of a "screen machine" manifests itself as a "front end" to the Xanadu "back end." The Xanadu design team envisions front ends of a variety of flavors, and while any terminal can be connected to the system, the highest potential requires the resources of a relatively powerful personal computer. The Xanadu team refers to a "front-end program" as any application running on the user's local computer, which "delivers to and extracts from the Xanadu storage system."[104]

Publishing on the Xanadu system will revolve around an exquisitely designed (at least in theory) royalty basis. All users will have access to all public hypertext documents. Each time a user accesses a given document, a royalty, albeit a miniscule royalty, will be returned to the originating document. The royalty will be a proportion of what Nelson refers to as the "byte delivery charges," which will amount to between 10 and 20 percent. "If the byte delivery charge for servicing a user is, say $2 per screen-hour, then the royalty will be $0.10 to $0.20 for that hour. This is deducted automatically from the back-end fees."[105]

Material that is published as a "public" document on the Xanadu system may not be removed from the system except by six-month notice or court order. The author or publisher who wants his or her material to be available to everyone but who also wants to reserve the right to withdraw the material at any time can simply publish the material as a private document with unrestricted distribution. Additionally, any user can publish "collaged" or "windowed" documents, with a variety of degrees of "ownership." The origins of these documents are in public documents, which are freely accessible to all. While no user will be restricted from any public document, private documents will contain access restrictions specified by the author(s)/owner(s). Private documents will be accessible only to the owner and to whomever he or she specifies may have access to the material.

A Xanadu publisher will be required to pay a year's space rental in advance, and a publisher who "linked" to the original document will be required to pay only the cost of the pointer storage. On the surface, this appears to give an unfair advantage to the "leech publisher"—one who only extracted pieces of someone else's work. On closer examination, however, we find that this concern is unfounded, for the original publisher receives a royalty each and every time his or her material is accessed.

According to the Xanadu design specification, no limitation or restriction can be placed on the use of materials found on the system, largely because there is no way to implement such a restriction system. For example, if someone wanted to alter one of your documents—completely changing your point through annotation (or worse, drawing a mustache on the Mona Lisa)

—they would be completely free to do so. The beauty of Xanadu, however, is that the unadulterated original always is readily available, just a link away.

Because the user has paid a royalty fee to receive the material, he or she is free to do almost anything with the information within the realm of the existing copyright law. While any published material on the system may be printed out or copied to disk by a user, any link connections are lost and the user is left with what Nelson describes as an "inert, noninteractive copy. . . . Remember the analogy between text and water. Water flows freely, ice does not. The free-flowing, live documents on the network are subject to constant new use and linkage, and those new links continually become interactively available. Any detached copy someone keeps is frozen and dead, lacking access to the new linkage (and, if there were any substantial body of in-links at the time the copy was made, probably most of those as well)."[106]

While inside the Xanadu system, the user has much more freedom with the published material he or she finds. Once the material leaves the system, however, normal copyright law applies. Therefore, any use other than "fair use," for instance, making copies and giving them away or selling them, would be as illegal as would any other form of plagiarism or piracy. Because all material on the system will be time- and date-stamped, a publisher runs little risk by making his or her material public (as opposed to private). Anyone who downloaded material and re-uploaded it under his or her name to obtain royalties would be wide open to an unquestionable copyright violation rap.

The Xanadu development team also designed a system of private sales of materials stored on the system for those not satisfied with the standard royalty structure. In the implementation that Nelson envisions, anyone can store material as private documents that are encoded and may sell access to the material. Because any transaction of this type would be considered private, it is not a concern of the system or its operators.

As complicated as Xanadu sounds (and it gets *much* more complicated, just wait) it is imperative to understand that the system, as it appears to the user, is nothing more than a storage manager—a storage manager that will greatly reduce the amount of time users spend physically managing their data. According to Nelson, "In ordinary computer storage, you have to keep copying files in order to reorganize them—a tedious and dangerous process, which (when done wrong) easily wipes out your work. For every hour spent usefully, perhaps half an hour must be spent copying, rearranging and backing up files."[107]

What Nelson is striving for here, in relation to data management, is release from what he calls the "tyranny of the file." One of the key aspects of the

Xanadu system is what Nelson refers to as ''xanalogical storage.'' The system is built on a single storage container that can not only be shared between virtually any number of users but also simultaneously organized in a virtually unlimited number of ways. The goal is to facilitate the ease with which any user can expand his or her thought process by physically creating new material from bits of preexisting thought-building blocks. Nelson describes the structure of xanalogical storage almost poetically:

> all materials are in a shared
> pool of units, but every
> element has a unit in which it
> originated;
>
> new units can be built from
> material in previous units,
> in addition to new material;
>
> there can be arbitrary links
> between arbitrary sections of
> units.[108]

More than anything else xanalogical storage is defined by three relationships between the units of information contained in the system: origin (the original seed of the various elements); commonality (the process of elemental sharing between the units); and links (the transescalators that add value to the underlying elements of information and synthesize a knowledge base).

In addition to the ''grand idea'' of a universal hypertext, the Xanadu development team has a second, no less grand, vision for the same software and its underlying concepts. All of use are inundated with an ever-increasing amount of information flow. Think of the ''paper blob'' television advertisements for Federal Express translated from a paper mess to an electronic one: electronic junk mail. Everyone who uses a computer amasses large numbers of small files that we cannot even remember what the names mean after a few months, let alone their origins and relationships to other bits of information that clutter our individual and collective data spaces. Xanadu promises to address this issue as well by enabling individuals to create arbitrary links between their own localized documents in their personal data spaces, thereby providing them with the tools to manage their own information more effectively.

To once again quote Nelson: ''We believe we have a unifying technical solution to both problems. . . . We have a model that is rational yet radical: rational because it proposes to keep things orderly to a degree they could never be before; and radical because it requires a fundamental change in the way computers are programmed. Like other new paradigms, this presents an entirely new worldview, and it provokes various forms of confusion and anger.''[109]

Confusion and anger are common responses to things we do not understand that promise, by their very nature, to upset our way of looking at the world. The Xanadu design team is among the most rigorous of boat-rockers I'm aware of, and, if anything, confusion and anger are understatements. And yet, the Xanadu implementation is elegantly simple in its design structure.

If we look at computer storage as we now know it, even on a computer as advanced as the Macintosh, we still are, as users, forced to comply with an external set of stipulations that are mistakenly taken out of our realm of control. Consider Macintosh with its apparently elegant Hierarchical Filing System (HFS): Documents and applications can be placed inside of the electronic equivalent of vast numbers of file folders, as shown in *Figure 2.47.* We can place related documents in a common folder and can add specialized folders ad nauseum inside the more generalized folder as shown in *Figure 2.48.*

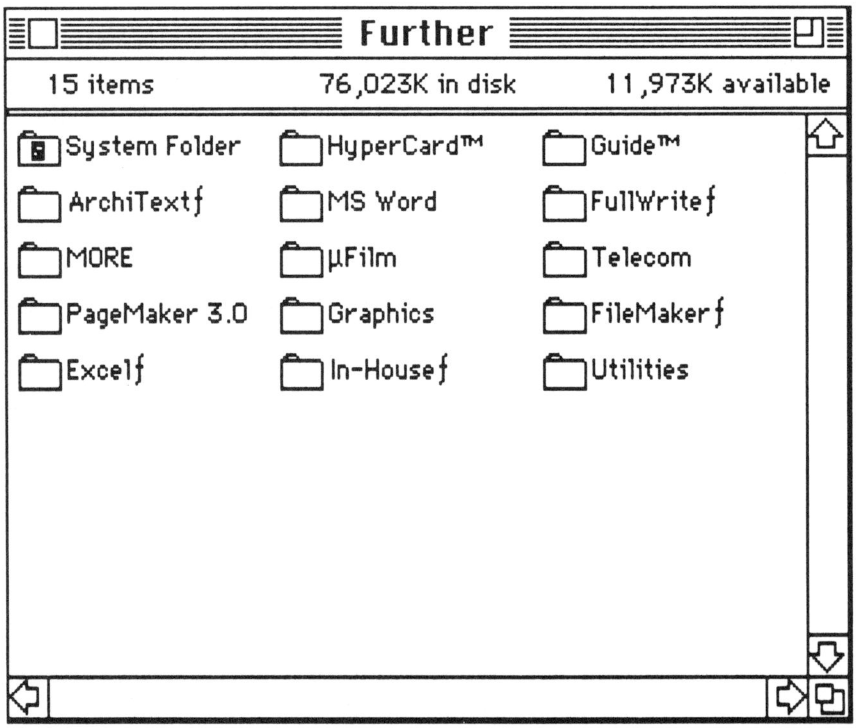

● ***Figure 2-47*** *The Macintosh Hierarchical Filing System (HFS).*

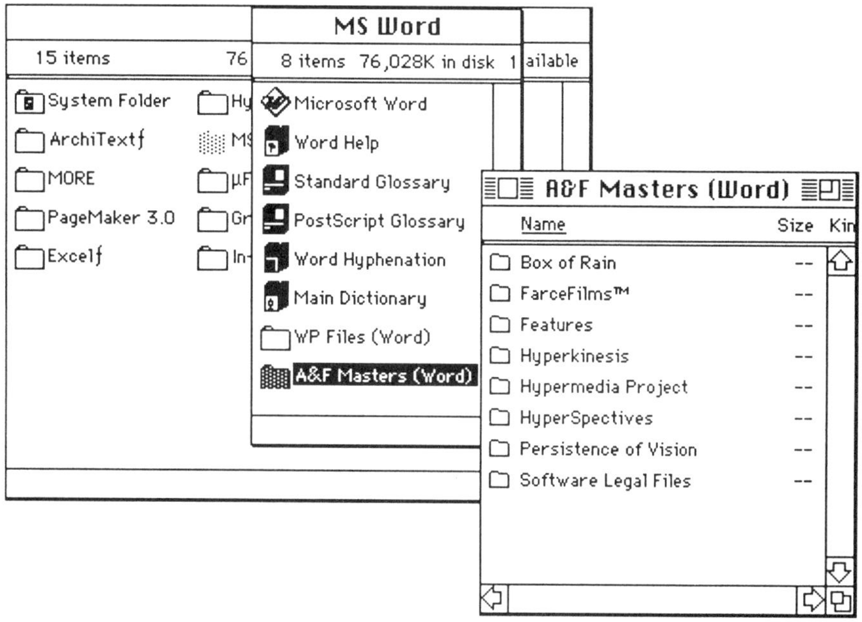

● ***Figure 2.48*** *The Macintosh paradigm of Folders within Folders.*

As I recall the halcyon days of my childhood, I can remember waiting with anticipation for the latest issue of a child's magazine that featured, on the last page, "What's Wrong With This Picture?" This was a line drawing of a scene in which we could discern with just a minimum of effort elements of the drawing that were hilariously quirkish and out of place, things such as a hand iron in a tree, a bird's nest in the bow of a boat, and a man in a suit on a tractor. At first glance, the picture always seemed normal enough, and you only found the outlandish quirks by looking closer.

Consider the Macintosh filing structure as shown in *Figures 2.47* and *2.48* and ask yourself that time-honored question, "What's Wrong With This Picture?" What's wrong is that we still are forced to use naming conventions and manually keep track of all our files. We are forced to manually maintain backup copies of things we do not want to lose, and we are not provided with any way of creating links of relationship between any of our files. Oh, and then there's the niceties of not being able to open a SuperPaint document in MacPaint, even though the reverse is true and the fact is that both are bit-map graphics programs. The Macintosh filing structure is the best that is currently available, at least several orders of magnitude better than "\A\HYPER\MANSCRPT\CHAP1.DOC," but there is plenty of room for improvement.

The point is that "often, apparently simple designs for data storage merely foist complexity on users, requiring many adaptations *outside* the design . . . it pushes onto the user the problem of naming and keeping track of hundreds or thousands of files and their backup copies, and the relations between them. Existing systems encourage clutter; files with unknown contents are saved as a precaution, and the connections between things get lost and deteriorate."[110]

Utilities, such as the previously mentioned GOfer, should not be needed, and if they are needed, they should be built into the computer's operating system.

Nelson goes on to tell us that we do not even know what we need. What we need, according to Nelson, is a "system of storage that keeps track of the origins and variations of everything."[111] As a writer and hypermedia developer, I am in desperate need of just such a device, but the key is that it must be automatic and transparent, or at least painless and transparent. It must provide a way of keeping track of not only origins and revisions, but the underlying relational links between materials that I may want to establish. Of course, it would be nice if it were smart enough to observe my work patterns and the relational connections that I make between materials and would from time to time offer to make for me. The Xanadu development team assures us that their system will provide all but the latter of these in the Xanadu system itself, sooner than many of us think possible. Not soon enough, however, for some of us.

Ted Nelson and the rest of the Xanadu team blame this traditional computer file structure for the tyrannical rule we have all been under these past years. Why can't we just have one big document, with no specialized applications, that contains everything and allows us to create everything rather than having the different specific task-oriented applications we have now. Why can't we process words, graphics, animation, numbers, and everything else in a single corpus with a single tool on the computer? Pie-in-the-sky thinking or at least belonging in the "Future Hypermedia" chapter, right? Not so, according to Nelson: "Conventional files are streams of bits divided into blocks and given a name. Text systems began when someone decided to treat the sequence of bits as text characters, then set up controls for their revision. Data-base programs began when someone decided to treat individual blocks as units and divide them into named and addressable fields."[112]

According to the Xanadu concept, we have been herded, like so many cattle, into believing, as Nelson tells us, "that such programs as 'data base' and 'text' are divinely ordained, and lead us away from designing functions best suited to particular uses."[113]

Of course, not all of us succumb to such constrictions. I regularly receive correspondence from a visual artist who employs MacPaint as her only software tool. My wife, to this day, is convinced that she can convert a Macintosh word-processing file into a folder. She fully understands the underlying and guiding metaphor of the Macintosh desktop; she knows that files go in folders and the folders can go in folders, but for some reason she never managed to grasp what the Finder is for and she's fully convinced that she can perform such transformations simply by deeming it so.

According to the Xanadu method of file structure, an alternative exists. Materials can be stored in their inherent complexity that, by nature, would allow the interrelations between the various components to be understood as part of the system itself. Under the Xanadu storage paradigm, all origins, annotations, and links are maintained automatically as part of the underlying structure of the system. In addition, the Xanadu document saves storage space by not copying all the interrelated data to the various points to which it is cross-referenced, but instead stores only the interconnections and commonalities among all the documents. Because the user is relieved of the mundane burden of maintaining and tidying his or her data space, the Xanadu team fully believes that the system and its filing structure will "lighten office work by as much as 75 percent."[114]

Imagine the benefits of suddenly being able to increase your own productivity by even 25 percent, let alone 75 percent.

This is accomplished in the Xanadu document paradigm by defining a document as consisting only of native bytes (those that originated with the document) and inclusions that are native bytes of other documents that are referenced by the current document. Inclusions are not physically contained in the document(s) they are referenced by, but rather exist only in the document in which they are native bytes. According to Nelson, "Conceptually, there is only one copy of every byte (though for both safety and implementation there are generally other copies). A byte is just as fully a part of a document in which it is included as it is part of the document to which it is native."[115] This allows any particular document to be orders of magnitude smaller than it ordinarily would be, for all references and cross-relationships are stored only as a structure of pointers along with the document's native bytes.

As complicated as this sounds, the Xanadu system is, intentionally, quite simple: basically interconnected computer files that correspond to the interconnection of the ideas behind them, as illustrated in Ted Nelson's original sketch of xanalogical storage (reproduced here as *Figure 2.49).*

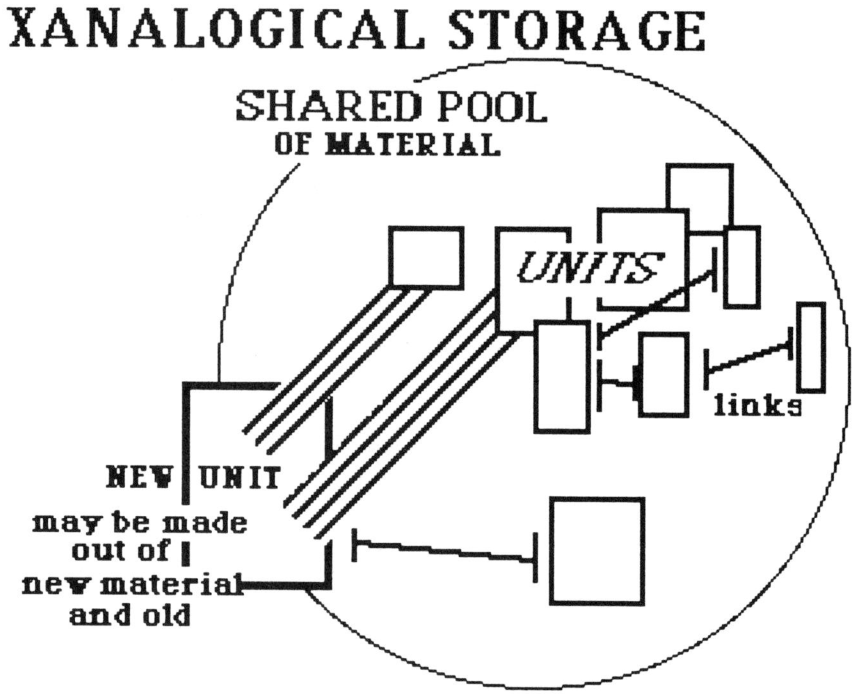

● *Figure 2.49 Ted Nelson's Xanalogical Storage Concept.*

The result is a file structure that, by inherent design, is so extensible that it allows hypermedia links to be of virtually any depth and breadth. Xanadu is simple in underlying concept and incredibly vast in implementation: "In the year 2020, we imagine a network with at least a hundred million simultaneous users, adding a hundred million documents an hour to the system."[116]

Eventually, the Xanadu system, as seen in its final process, will be funded and operated by a series of franchised information stands, called Silverstands in the Nelson parlance. The functional equivalent of the roadside fast-food burger stand, Silverstands will serve as tutorial centers, registration points, and public-relations vehicles for new infonauts and will provide a local access node (via modem connection) for local users. Ted Nelson refers to the Silverstand conceptual scenario as a "marriage of Star Trek and McDonald's hamburger restaurants."[117]

The burger-stand analogy continues on to include the "perky uniforms and accessories" that change on a regular basis and are worn by the attendants who take your order in a reception area and, well, let Ted Nelson explain the scenario: "A cherry young person in futuristic garb will sit you down at a screen, and show you through an area of material of interest to you—text and/or pictures. Then, at the moment of Xanadu Shock, when you get it, when you cry 'Holy ----!'—the kid grasps your forearm and says, 'Mr. Jones, Welcome to Xanadu.' "[118]

Nelson is careful to stipulate that the ambience of the Silverstand is not the sensory overload of the video-game arcade. Business meetings will be held at the Silverstands and people generally will stay for an hour or more. The atmosphere will be one of relaxed concentration. The Silverstand will not be automated. It will be staffed by humans; people will interact face-to-face and no counters will separate the attendants from the patrons.

Ted Nelson designed the Xanadu concept so completely that he even provided design specifications for the actual buildings that house the Silverstands. Designed implicitly for expansion, a Silverstand building is built around a permanent central area that is added to with a "modular hexagonal building-kit system with furniture and monitors built into wall panels."[119] The central hub of each Silverstand, which consists of a central meeting area, cafe, and lounge, is covered with a geodesic dome that is expanded as necessary to fit the configuration.

The computer hardware employed at each Silverstand consists of what Nelson refers to as "main feeder machines," which can be whatever is cost-effective at the time. The computer hardware, except for the storage media and communications equipment, is kept in a central location called the equipment pit, which is a display of sorts and open to viewing through glass windows on all sides. The storage media and communications equipment will likely be stored underground, maximizing each Silverstand's available floor space.

The Xanadu subscriber, whether a patron of a Silverstand or a home or office user, is provided with the material that he or she requests as quickly as possible, although options will be available at extra cost for a higher-priority information delivery. In addition, the subscriber can store his or her own files, linkages to other materials, inclusions, and annotations at the local Silverstand node, for the cost of using something stored on Xanadu is not related to where it is physically stored.

In this capacity, Xanadu is seen basically as an access and storage-management system for a vast array of interconnected networks. This part of Xanadu is the back end and remains standard across all applications and implementations.

The Xanadu front end is described as that group of functions that allow you to do whatever it is that you want to do with the materials stored in Xanadu.

These functions are provided by a front-end application that runs on your local computer. Front-end applications can consist of various types and will likely exist in various forms, ranging from ultrasophisticated, ultraspecialized, and, therefore, ultra-high priced dedicated applications to relatively simple and inexpensive generalized retrieval interfaces. The Xanadu Operating Company continues to actively solicit Xanadu front ends from the development community.

Other Pending Hypermedia Developments

The following hypermedia systems are currently under various stages of development, ranging from pure research to almost-finished products that will be available commercially. Many of these systems were not designed to facilitate the Macintosh, so they are covered, in turn, only briefly. They are discussed here because the issues they address impact all hypermedia developments, present and future.

Electronic Document Distribution System (EDDS)

Electronic Document Distribution System (EDDS) is a UNIX-based system that integrates hypermedia with page composition, computer-aided design (CAD), and mapping technologies across high-speed local area networks using an object-oriented data base. Presently an ongoing research project at AT&T's Network Systems division, the system runs on a network of Sun workstations under the NeWS windowing environment.

EDDS is the only system currently in known use that combines electronic publishing and an electronic distribution system with a full-blown hypermedia system. The system provides users with the ability to create, edit, and eliminate information nodes, links, and the hypermedia documents themselves. Various types of nodes are supported, including text, graphics, video, animation, spreadsheets, and audio. The document is traversed by following reference, annotation, footnote, and other types of explicitly created links. PostScript is used as a display, distribution, and manipulation format as all nodes are stored on optical disk in Encapsulated PostScript Format (EPSF). This allows for an unprecedented level of integration between different hardware and software platforms.

Neptune

Neptune is a hypertext abstract machine (HAM) developed by Mayer Schwartz and Norm Delisle and written in Smalltalk-80. It is unique in its built-in support for a complete revision history of any hypertext object contained in the document, and it also allows the document to be partitioned into different contexts, each of which may have its own version history.

Xerox NoteCards

Originally designed as a single-user hypertext system to support personal data-base applications at the Xerox Palo Alto Research Center (PARC), Xerox's NoteCards system matured into the Distributed NoteCards project that allows multiuser access to a single NoteCards data base. What makes Distributed NoteCards unique is that rather than designing and implementing a central data-base server, the designers chose to focus on a distributed system that allows remote access to any number of data bases.

A significant drawback to the current implementation of NoteCards is the lack of support of an index to allow context searching. Xerox's Content Analysis project is working on this specifically to allow indexing the individual cards on something other than a keyword basis. The project members believe that a semantic profile can be formulated that would allow the construction of relatively small indexes.

The Central Intelligence Agency is currently using NoteCards for "biographical directories, systems for software configuration control and specification management, and displaying and analyzing the interrelationships among events that have been entered in a multiuser data collection environment."[120]

Electronic Information Exchange System (EIES)

The Electronic Information Exchange System (EIES) at the New Jersey Institute of Technology is exploring hypermedia in a variety of ways, most specifically in the area of collaborative hypertext in relation to the EIES Computer Mediated Communications Systems. The EIES system itself always has possessed limited hypertext functions and the research continues under the guidance of Murray Turoff.

This work is presently coming to fruition under the Tailorable Electronic Information Exchange System (TEIES), which is an object-oriented communications data base that incorporates complete two-way links on all text items. TEIES will be readily transportable to other systems through the use of General Markup Language to specify the interrelationships between the text items.

The other major hypermedia project currently under development is the Virtual Classroom, sponsored by the Annenberg/Corporation for Public Broadcasting Project, which will be the first tailoring of the TEIES system and which will allow a group of people to work on the same hypermedia document.

VORTeX (Visual Oriented TeX)

The VORTeX system, currently under development at the University of California, Berkeley, differentiated itself from other hypermedia systems in its capacity to present multiple representations of the same document. Both the source, in TeX format, and the formatted display are available to the user, and both are editable. According to the VORTeX development team's research, some aspects of a given document are easier to deal with at the TeX level, while some are more easily manipulated in their formatted display form.

The current VORTeX implementation is limited to text, graphics, and digitized images; the development team plans to incorporate voice and video in the near future. One of the more powerful aspects of the VORTeX system is its use of PostScript as the underlying image generator, making it possible to present graphics in a dynamic manner by running the PostScript program directly. Also under development is an advanced hypermedia bibliographic system.

CommonTools

Texas Instruments' CommonTools Hypermedia Project is based around the Common Lisp environment and its developers hope it will form the foundation for third-party hypermedia developments using CommonTools as a design and implementation platform. Features of the system, in its current stage of development, include a complete revision management system and an extensible relational data base. An editor that is built around the Explorer text and graphics editors (Zmacs and GED) were combined to support the editing of hypermedia documents that include text, graphics, speech, and digitized images.

Conclusion and Recommendations

Macintosh hypermedia has risen in a few years from virtual nonexistence to a medium offering various development systems at prices ranging from free to reasonable. This area of Macintosh software, more than any other, promises to be a hotbed of activity well into the next decade. The beauty of hypermedia is that it gives individuals with something to say—the information providers—a platform on which to deliver their goods without having to commit extensive amounts of time and resources to learning a traditional programming language. Real people can be doing useful things with the tools mentioned here in a very short amount of time.

Beyond all else, hypermedia is a communications medium. Macintosh hypermedia implementations present us with tools that we can use to make ourselves better communicators. This is exciting, and it is happening now. Best of all, there is no "priesthood" of experts. The level of information sharing is unprecedented and shows no sign of abating. We are suddenly, all of us, on the verge of actually being able to link, index, and cross-reference all the information that we need to inform ourselves adequately on virtually any topic that we wish to pursue. The remaining chapters of this book will address the social implications of the availability and use of these tools and the impact that logical extensions to the present tools will have on each one of us in the future. A companion volume will follow shortly that will address the issues of what we can do with the tools now that they are becoming available.

It is difficult for many to navigate the backwaters of the marketing hype surrounding many of these products, and I think that perhaps it is best to take a cue from Mr. Natural: Use the right tool for the job. OWL International's Guide is extremely well-suited for text-intensive hypertext applications of virtually any size. Apple's HyperCard benefits from a built-in market of well into the millions for the hypermedia data spaces you create and from the development prowess and commitment of its development team. Its widespread acceptance also ensures that a plethora of development tools will become available on almost a daily basis. To date, however, its text-handling capabilities are severely limited.

So take your pick of the tools at your disposal and try your hand at what promises to be the most remarkable communications medium since television.

[78] Theodor Nelson, *Literary Machines,* elect. ed. (Bellevue, Washington: OWL International, Inc., 1987).

[79] Ibid.

[80] David R. Coffman, ed., *Guide to Hypertext,* elect. ed. (Bellevue, Washington: OWL International, Inc., 1987).

[81] Danny Goodman, *The Complete HyperCard Handbook* (New York: Bantam Books, 1987).

[82] John Sculley, Address to the MacWorld/Boston Exposition, August 11, 1987.

[83] Apple Computer, Inc., marketing brochure for HyperCard, August, 1987.

[84] Apple Computer, Inc., press release for HyperCard, August 11, 1987.

[85] Danny Goodman, *The Complete HyperCard Handbook* (New York: Bantam Books, 1987).

[86] Ibid.

[87] Carol Kaehler, *HyperCard Power Techniques and Scripts* (Reading, Massachusetts: Addison-Wesley Publishing Company, Inc., 1988).

[88] Ibid.

[89] Ibid.

[90] HyperCard does offer author-definable security levels that are enabled via the Set Password command. This offers rudimentary data integity, but it is easily defeated by using widely distributed public domain utilities such as Deprotect.

[91] Several HyperCard ''clones,'' which have been announced, will be available by the time this reaches print. HyperCard also is certain to have gone through at least its first major upgrade. Specificially, Silicon Beach Software has announced SuperCard, which adds color, windows, and compiled code to the HyperCard equation.

[92] Carol Kaehler, *HyperCard Power Techniques and Scripts* (Reading, Massachusetts: Addison-Wesley Publishing Company, Inc., 1988).

[93] Ibid.

[94] Some of the programming environments with an example code available in the public domain for the creation of HyperCard XCMDs and XFCNs include MPW Pascal and MPW C from Apple, Symantec's Lightspeed C and Lightspeed Pascal, and Borland's Turbo Pascal.

[95] The first of these Boolean search and retrieval engines was Xearch, from Xiphias, in Marina Del Rey, California. With a license fee of $5,000 and an additional $5 per distributed unit, it is clearly designed for large CD-ROM HyperCard projects.

[96] Mark Bernstein, ed., ''HyperGate: A Very Nonlinear Hypermedium,'' *Hypertext '87 Digest,* elect. ed. (Boston: Eastgate Systems, 1987).

[97] Ibid.

[98] Theodor Nelson, *Computer Lib/Dream Machines,* rev. ed. (Redmond, Washington: Tempus Books of Microsoft Press, 1987).

[99] Ibid.

[100] Ibid.

[101] Ibid.

[102]Theodor Nelson, *Literary Machines,* elect. ed. (Bellevue, Washington: OWL International, Inc., 1987).

[103]Ibid.

[104]Ibid.

[105]Ibid.

[106]Ibid.

[107]Theodor Nelson, *Computer Lib/Dream Machines,* rev. ed. (Redmond, Washington: Tempus Books of Microsoft Press, 1987).

[108]Theodor Nelson, *Literary Machines,* elect. ed. (Bellevue, Washington: OWL International, Inc., 1987).

[109]Theodor Nelson, "Managing Immense Storage," *Byte* (January 1988): 225–238.

[110]Ibid.

[111]Ibid.

[112]Ibid.

[113]Ibid.

[114]Theodor Nelson, *Computer Lib/Dream Machines,* rev. ed. (Redmond, Washington: Tempus Books of Microsoft Press, 1987).

[115]Theodor Nelson, "Managing Immense Storage," *Byte* (January 1988): 225–238.

[116]Theodor Nelson, *Computer Lib/Dream Machines,* rev. ed. (Redmond, Washington: Tempus Books of Microsoft Press, 1987).

[117]Theodor Nelson, *Literary Machines,* elect. ed. (Bellevue, Washington: OWL International, Inc., 1987).

[118]Ibid.

[119]Ibid.

[120]Mark Bernstein, ed., *Hypertext '87 Digest,* elect. ed. (Boston: Eastgate Systems, 1987.)

HYPERMEDIA USES AND APPLICATIONS

CHAPTER 3

- *Current Uses for Hypermedia*
- *The CD-ROM Dilemma and Data-base Publishing*
- *Storage Hope on the Horizon*
- *Networking and Hypermedia*
- *General Hypermedia Problems*

''Information, even when it moves at the speed of light, is no more than it has ever been: discrete little bundles of fact, sometimes useful, sometimes trivial, and never the substance of thought,''[121] Theodore Roszak told us a few years ago.

The time has come, both within this work and within the community at large, to draw distinctive lines, in bright (preferably fluorescent) colors, between the concepts of information, ideas, and thought. Because this medium does not support color, we will make do with black, white, and shades of gray. And we will make do quite well, thank you.

First a little personal background. . .

My background is in psychology, but not the kind of psychology most of us are familiar with. I never ran a rat through a maze in my life and the closest I ever got to ''science'' was experiential exercises in a sensory-deprivation tank. We're talking *humanistic* psychology, you know, having a good time under the guise of self-discovery and a quest for enlightenment that sometimes crossed the line of narcissism. The kind of stuff a lot of good, God-fearing rural Georgians and college administrators sometimes had a hard time dealing with.

If I left that experience with anything it was the ability to think.

You see, information has very little to do with thought. I used to think that information was the raw material we used to think with. I was wrong. We use *ideas* to think with, not information.

The Macintosh, and the concept of hypermedia, is much more of an idea—or set of ideas—than a series of products. Remember when Apple was first marketing Macintosh as a ''tool for knowledge workers'' and an ''appliance''? Remember when Steve Jobs was speaking of a shift in our perception of the computer as a servant to the computer as a guide, as an agent? That is idea-based thought, rather than product-based thought.

Since then, Macintosh has grown up. Kind of. Apple has changed its marketing strategy from the top down, so to speak, getting rid of a lot of ''idea'' people and replacing them with ''product'' people.[122] This has manifested itself in events ranging from Steve Jobs' departure to the termination of Chiat/Day as Apple's advertising agency of record.

Idea and thought are process-based. Information is product-based. The products covered in Chapter 2 are process-building, process-enhancing tools. In addition they are information-builders. What we have come to recognize as ''straight'' data-base managers are information-builders that are devoid of any sort of process-building or enhancement attributes.

For example, consider 4th Dimension, the premiere data-base management system for the Macintosh, published in the United States by Guy Kawasaki's ACIUS. The 4th Dimension is a wonderful *product.* It does not appear to be much of an *idea,* however. I would go so far as to call 4th Dimension idea-anemic. It forces us to fit our data—our information—into field-sized chunks that the program can handle.

It's not fair to single out 4th Dimension for criticism on that point, for it's the nature of a data-base management system to be idea-anemic. All data bases know about and all they concern themselves with is the assemblage, organization, reformation, and regurgitation of information; there is no facility for the broad cross-referencing and vast data spaces we have at our disposal in even the most basic hypermedia environment.

While information is necessary, even crucial, we cannot continue to place it in our hierarchy basket above idea and thought. We think, and are subsequently productive, with ideas not information. We have all had "great ideas"—some of us have "insanely great ideas." We *receive* information, sometimes even "great" information, but we do not speak or feel about it in the same terms that we speak or feel about ideas. We speak of being "struck" with ideas, especially great ideas. We speak of "giving birth" to ideas, of "having" an idea. Undesirables "have" information. We speak of information "leaks." We do not speak of "gathering" ideas as we do of gathering information, as if it were a commodity.

Idea and thought imply an active participation in the process. We passively receive information. Passive-active; white-black; up-down; wet-dry; in-out. It takes both parts to make the whole. When that tenuous balance is achieved between the two, we reach a peculiar state—something akin to a synergy—when, quite suddenly, the information is worth more than it would be alone and the ideas come faster and with more fury.

So, assuming that you agree that a synergy is desirable, what we need is an exchange of ideas in addition to an exchange of information. Such an exchange results in all of us acting as catalysts for each other, sparking ideas, priming the pump, juicing the flow.

Stanley Davis, in his ground-breaking 1987 book, *Future Perfect,*[123] spells out the four earmarks of the information economy: any time, any place, no matter, and mass customization. He saw three underlying principles at work in viewing time as a resource in an information-based economy:

- Consumers need products and services *any time* (i.e., in their time frame, not the providers').

- Producers who deliver their products and services in *real-time*, relative to their competitors, will have a decided advantage.
- Operating in real-time means no *lag-time* between identification and fulfillment of the need.[124]

Such a context shift causes us to rethink the old saw, "time is money." In an industrial economy, that statement implied that money is the most important resource not to be wasted and that time was the yardstick used to measure the effective use of the resource. In an economy based on intangibles, the same statement takes on a completely different meaning; time becomes the resource and money becomes the measuring device used to gauge effective use.

Hypermedia allows us to provide each other with access to information at any time. Moreover, the time resource is under the complete auspices of the individual. As videotape recorders first offered individuals the power to control their own "prime time," so hypermedia takes the control aspect one step further by not requiring any premeditation on the part of the user. Where videotape recorders require the user to preprogram the recording event in order to "time-shift" his or her viewing schedule, hypermedia operates free of such constraints. The information and the intelligent links are there all the time, any time.

The second leg of Davis's quadruped view of an information economy—any place—is defined again by a contextual shift: "The technological ability to transform micromatter, by compacting it in space, is very much at the heart of the new economy: transforming time, space, and mass to be more useful to people. The cornerstone of the transformation lies in seeing them as resources rather than roadblocks. Thus, *when a spatial limitation is reached, rather than viewing it as a constraint, space needs to be redefined so that it can accommodate the new need.*"[125]

Traditional media—film, video, print, records, and so on—are all two-dimensional; they occupy flat planes and store and display static information in sequential or hierarchical form. Hypermedia transcends the two-dimensional limitation by adding layers of textures not only by combining the various traditional media but by adding the intelligent links and cross-references. Any time and any place.

Because the hypermedia docuverse inhabits exponentially smaller physical space than the sum of its two dimensional parts, the end product itself is more valuable, apart from the inherent value of its linkages. As Davis tells us, "In physics, density means the ratio of an object's mass to its volume. Applied to products, density should be used to mean the ratio of product size to its value. Shrinking the size of a product without otherwise changing it, in and of itself, creates greater value.''[126] Suddenly, we each can access all the great works—at our fingertips—at any time and any place, and at no time and no place: They exist as ridges and valleys in optical media or as rearranged magnetic particles in more traditional, magnetic media.

As futuristically pie in the sky as this may sound, it is partially available to us now. At least one of the national telecommunications services, CompuServe, offers a nonlinear message base in the form of ''threaded'' message sections in the special interest forums, ranging from computers to investing to gardening. We can customize our own data spaces in real time, bypassing the topics which are of little or no interest to us. As interconnected hypermedia systems, such as Xanadu, begin to come on-line, this will become ever more widespread and prevalent. From a business and marketing standpoint, it is a generally accepted maxim that consumers are much more likely to purchase products that are available to them where they are. According to Davis, ''The ultimate shift occurs when the producing organization moves *into* the physical space of the consuming unit, and the consumers take over the producer's actions in their own space.''[127]

Davis refers to the process of the producer moving closer to the consumer (metaphorically and physically) as *disintermediation.* As hypermediacians we are both producers *and* consumers—disintermediation to the nth degree, as it were. Disintermediation accomplishes two worthy goals concurrently: As the levels of intermediation are reduced, so are the costs, and each level of disintermediation offers increased efficiency in any system. Thhhhheeeeeyyyyy'rrrrreeeee hhhhheeeeerrrrreeeee . . . and they are us. The consumers are *becoming* the producers, which is an even more far-forward level of disintermediation than Davis saw.

The no-matter element of an information-based economy should be self-evident. Davis is clear, ''Matter is not all that matters! In the new economy, the value added will come increasingly from intangibles, 'things,' whose importance does not lie in their material existence.''[128] Consider this book as an example. Until the time I delivered the manuscript to the publisher, it existed only as a series of magnetic fluctuations on my hard disk. You could see the hard disk (actually, you could see only the case), but you couldn't see the information it held. I was amazed, when I first entered the publishing contract for this work, that the publisher could not accept the manuscript on disk. It had to be printed out. Several times.

In the information-based economy we are moving into, tangible products in and of themselves will begin to lose value, or rather, their value will be based on the level of the value added to the product by intangibles. Consider the Macintosh as a prime example. The Macintosh is made mostly of spare parts from a variety of manufacturers that Apple combines with the intangible ROMs that make the Macintosh unique. According to Davis, "The value added is in the intangible software, in the solution, and the service."[129] Interestingly, the service aspect of the equation is Apple's weakest link and may yet prove to be the company's downfall. Ironically, Apple's concept of providing service to the user is very solid. The notion of providing only board-level repairs, rather than performing repairs on the component level, is something of a breakthrough. This allows the repair to be made in the shortest possible turnaround time. Unfortunately, in practice it is seen as on the borderline of gouging, and Apple's lack of attention to customer frustration is wearing quite thin.[130] As computers begin to become more of a commodity, this will become even more of an issue.

Paul Hawken, economist, author, and partner in Smith & Hawken Tool Company, says that the "single most important trend to understand is the changing ratio between mass and information in goods and services."[131] Stanley Davis takes Hawken's point one step further by extrapolating it into an equation:

$$\text{VALUE OF A DELIVERABLE} = \frac{\text{INFORMATION}}{\text{MASS}}$$ [132]

He goes on to provide the apt illustration of steel containing a lot of mass with relatively little information, while a computer chip contains a great deal of information relative to its mass.

Information generally is seen as an intermediary good—except by the information-providers—that is, it is seen as a tool useful in the creation of other goods and services. What differentiates hypermedia from other information tools is the intelligence and immediate accessibility of the links and cross-references established by the information provider as well as the users themselves. The value of information, in and of itself, will grow and the proportion of intangible goods will increase in the society at large. Because intangibles exist only in time, and cannot be inventoried, it may take us a while to catch on to this reality.

As Davis points out: "Since services dominate the new economy, since they are performed, not produced, and since they don't exist until they are performed, everything depends on executing the performance well. This means that, in implementing strategies, delivery systems play a much larger role in the new economy than they did during the industrial period."[133] Like me, you probably laughed initially at Ted Nelson's concept of the Silverstand as a delivery system for Xanadu. I had a hard time understanding the pains he went to in articulately describing the "tangible" delivery system until I reread Davis several times.

Also inherent to the concept of no matter is the question of physical, geographic location of some of the more esoteric hypermedia delivery systems such as Xanadu. The Xanadu system will enjoy a tangible presence in the form of the Silverstands, but the Silverstands themselves will not *be* the Xanadu system. Xanadu and systems like it—even your own globally connected data space—will exist nowhere, all at once, all the time.

The final Davis earmark of the information economy is mass customization: "The world of mass customizing is a world of paradox with very practical implications. Whether we are dealing with a product, a service, a market, or an organization, each is understood to be both part (customized) and whole (mass) simultaneously."[134] Using the hologram as an illustration, Davis points out that "if the image is broken, any part of it will reconstruct the whole."[135] This regenerative nature of the medium is an inherent aspect of hypermedia. The corpus itself is merely generic information (mass) until the intelligent interlinkings are applied (customization). And if one end of a link is broken, the complete link may be reconstructed from the remaining parts. Marilyn Ferguson stresses the importance of this in relation to the mass customization of information when she states, "The whole code exists at every point in the medium."[136]

Davis also uses the analogy of information on a floppy disk to illustrate his point: "The floppy itself is already a mass-produced commodity; the information any one floppy contains is what customizes it. And the customers have performed the final manufacturing and tailoring themselves."[137] So it is with hypermedia and our personal and global data spaces. The information underlying our links is generic and mass-produced. The value we add to the information—by forging our links—is the final stage of the manufacturing process, hence its customization.

Common sense tells us that a customer would much rather have a custom-made product than one that was mass-produced if they were available for roughly the same price. We can assume, therefore, that there will be a broad market potential for the mass customization of information and information by-products.

It is seemingly difficult for us to address the paradox of mass customization because most of us still cling to an industrial-economy paradigm, one based on tangibles and the economies of scale. The economies of scale dictated that a product could be *either* customized *or* mass-produced and that customized products have a higher unit cost. Using the economies of scale paradigm it is impossible to have both mass-produced and customized goods; we must settle for one or the other. Going back to Davis's hologram example, this is easily addressed. "The power of the hologram lies in the fact that, if the image is broken, *any part that remains will reconstruct the whole!* For this to happen, all information about the whole must be present somewhere in each part. This unique property is unlike the mechanical paradigm of the industrial economy, in which the whole is merely the sum of all the parts. Rather, all information about the whole exists in each and every one of its parts.

"If the whole exists in every one of the parts, as well as in the sum of them, then what space does the whole occupy? If the whole is everywhere, it is, equally, nowhere. The whole has no space dimension to it. If this is always so, if it occurs all the time, then the whole has no time dimension, either."[138]

Similarly, in a universal hypermedia environment, everyone has access to the same information. What makes the information specialized—mass-customized—is the intelligent links, webs, and cross-references forged by the users. And the links exist locally, rather than globally. Everywhere and nowhere. All at once.

Current Uses For Hypermedia

Let's begin by taking a look at Apple Computer, Inc.'s internal use of its own hypermedia product, HyperCard.

Common wisdom tells us that the apple never falls far from the tree. I do not know if that is appropriate here, but there is something comforting—or at least reassuring—about Apple's internal use of HyperCard.

Apple's Information Systems and Technology group, the Cupertino equivalent of an MIS department, I guess, has been developing HyperCard stacks since before the product's introduction in August of 1987, and the seed has begun to bear fruit. IS&T's efforts have been largely focused on developing host system front ends and prototyping and training tools for internal use. Some indication has begun to waft from that part of the left coast, however, that the products may be on their way into the real world from under the protection of the multicolored umbrella.

PRISM, an acronym for Planning and Reporting Information for Sales and Marketing Finance, which has been under development for quite some time by the group, is used internally by Apple employees to retrieve sales and other financial information from the company's IBM mainframe via a HyperCard front end. Prior to the availability of PRISM, only the financial analyst wizards who could run the NOMAD2 data-base language had access to the information that is now as easy to acquire as pressing buttons on the HyperCard screen.

SMART is an acronym for Apple's internal Sales and Marketing Account Reporting Tool, which also was developed by the IS&T group. SMART subsequently has replaced quite a few inches of paper material in binders used by more than 2,000 Apple employees with a single HyperCard stack.

Two other HyperCard projects, both with cute acronyms, also have been developed by the Information Systems and Technology group for internal use at Apple. HyperGOLD is similar to PRISM, but deals with the company's personnel records and is being saved for use with CL/1, another data-base language developed by recent Apple acquisition, Network Innovations. O.L., the fourth internal HyperCard project at Apple, is an order-entry system that eventually may see its way to the dealer channel.

So what does all this mean to those of us out here in the real world, those of us not living in the computer-industry equivalent of Toon Town? Quite a lot, actually. First and foremost, it means that a substantial portion of Apple's hyperbole and swagger surrounding HyperCard is beginning to take on something at least shirttail-related to substance. Apple apparently has put forth quite an effort to apply HyperCard for use in its own complex, multivendor network, and all reports are that it is working.

While in themselves, Apple's internal HyperCard developments are nothing less than that which was expected by the true believers in our ranks, the outsiders are beginning to sit up and take notice of these antics. Apple is reported to have cut down training time significantly through the use of HyperCard-based tutorial systems, and at the same time has raised individual productivity within the company by those who are HyperCard-fluent.

Many of the stackware developers are learning the hard way that stackware development is mostly the same as ''real'' software development and that it takes between three to five times as long as you think it should, given a worst-case scenario. I do not know why any of us ever thought it would be different, but some of us did. Some of us still do.

I would not be too surprised if the Apple mother ship spun off one or two satellite subsidiary businesses within the next six or seven months. Apple's internal work on HyperCard has helped dismiss the naysayers and Hyper-Luddites as well as opened the door for more advanced hypermedia products, including advanced versions of HyperCard. Why shouldn't Apple spin off a subsidiary to publish stackware? This one would be so unsurprising it would almost be a certainty—chartered with the task of acquiring or developing and publishing quality stackware products as well as other hypermedia vehicles.

And what about the chicken-and-egg harbinger of optical media. Who better than Apple to crack the egg and incubate the chick? Apple took a major step when it introduced its CD-ROM drive, but there still is precious little software available for it; and most that is available treats the medium as nothing more than a large, slow, floppy disk drive.

On-Line Help Systems

Aldus Corporation's PageMaker 2.0 page layout and desktop publishing software was the first widely distributed Macintosh application to include an integrated hypertext on-line help system. Aldus continues to distribute the on-line help system in hypertext format in the current version of PageMaker. Implemented using OWL International's Guide and Guidance system, the PageMaker help file tipped the scales at more than 250 KBytes and is quite useful.

A representative help sequence is shown in *Figure 3.1* through *Figure 3.3*. *Figure 3.1* shows the PageMaker Help splash screen that is displayed when

- *Figure 3.1 Aldus PageMaker hypertext help system implemented using Guidance.*

Guidance is selected from the desk accessory menu from within the PageMaker application. The Guidancc system automatically opens an assigned help file if it is found within the same folder level as the application itself.

Figure 3.2 shows the first level of the PageMaker hypertext help system, ''Help with Tasks.''

Figure 3.3 illustrates the specific help topic available for wrapping text around a graphic.

It's interesting to note that the help system within the Guide hypertext system is itself implemented using Guidance. Help systems designed within Guidance may be opened in one of two ways. The Guidance desk accessory may be selected from the desk accessory menu, as in the case illustrated previously with Aldus's PageMaker, or the designer may implement a ''Help'' button within the ''About. . .'' box for the specific application. The latter is illustrated in *Figure 3.4.*

Although OWL's Guidance was the first hypertext system to be adapted for use in on-line help applications, it is by no means the last. HyperCard, for example, comes with an extensive help system—that, quite frankly, is better than the product's accompanying documentation—developed as an

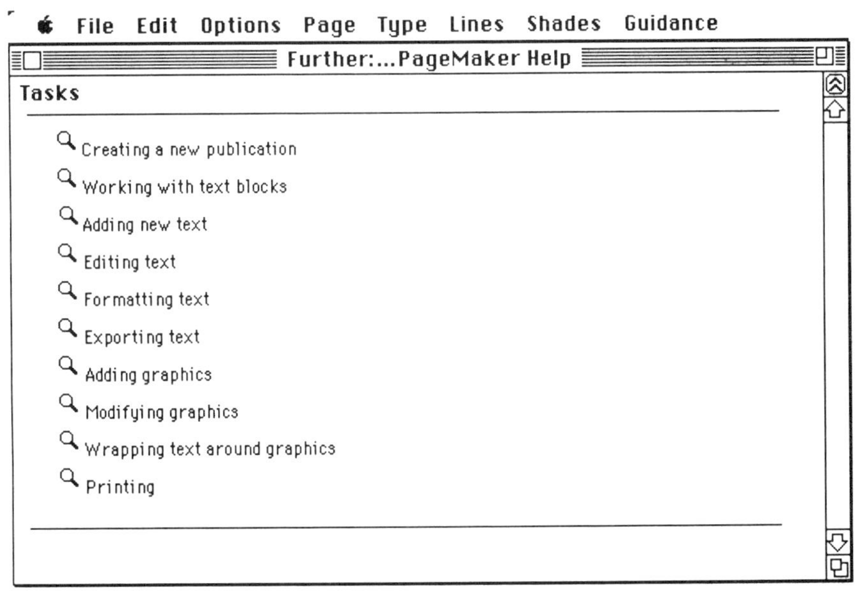

● ***Figure 3.2*** *PageMaker's help system linked to ''Help with Tasks.''*

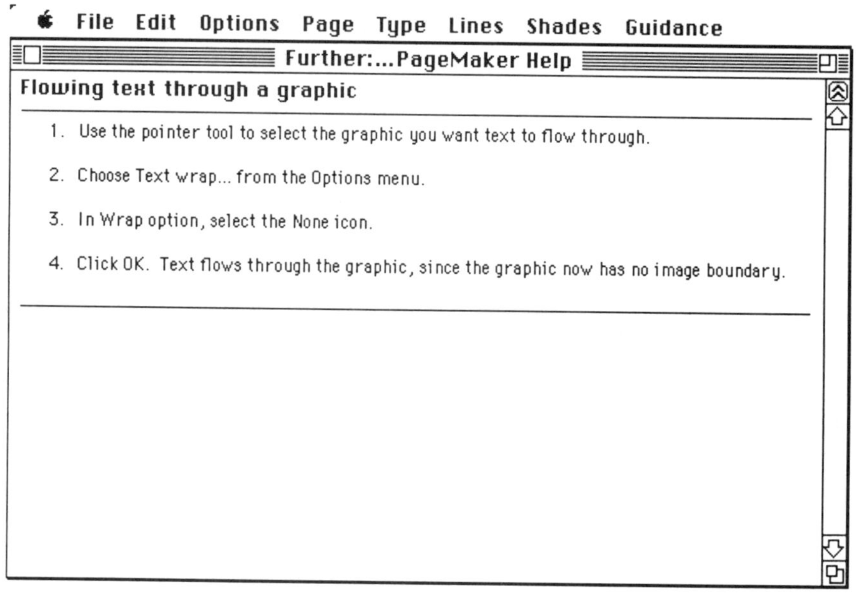

• *Figure 3.3* *PageMaker's Help with wrapping text around graphics.*

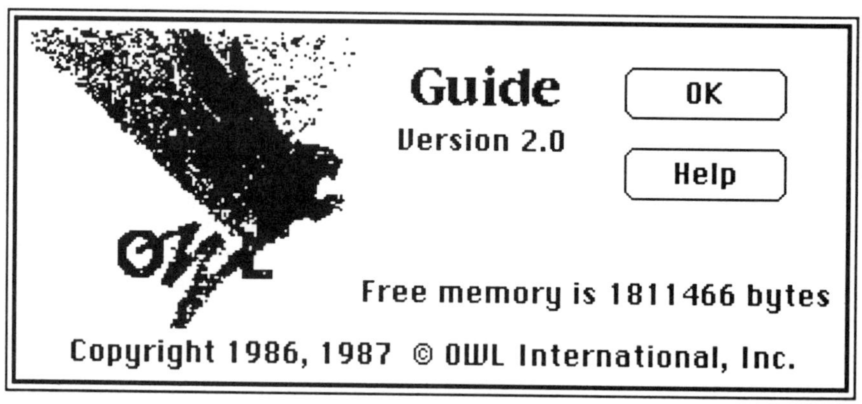

• *Figure 3.4* *The Guidance Help button within an application.*

integrated 579 KByte HyperCard stack with companion index and samples. Examples of the HyperCard help system and its menu command are illustrated in *Figures 3.5* and *3.6.*

The HyperCard help system is accessible via the Help command on the Go menu (shown in *Figure 3.5*) and may be intercepted by the HyperTalk programmer to redirect the help command to a more context-sensitive system or one that is completely unique to the application at hand.

Such a context-sensitive help system was integrated by Danny Goodman into his Focal Point product, one of the first commercially available HyperCard stackware products. The Focal Point daily calendar is shown in *Figure 3.7,* with the resulting context-sensitive help available for that portion of the application illustrated in *Figure 3.8.*

Within a year of HyperCard's introduction, Mesa, Arizona–based Symmetry Corporation had released its HyperDA desk accessory. HyperDA allowed many (but not all) HyperCard stacks to be opened in a read-only manner via a desk accessory. The product also allowed some stacks to be opened on a Macintosh with less than one MByte of RAM, something which HyperCard itself is not capable of doing.

Symmetry hopes to make available HyperEngine, another desk accessory that opens HyperCard stacks in read-only format, which is completely customizable and designed with the intent of enabling developers to create context-sensitive help systems within HyperCard for use in other applications. Symmetry is currently embroiled in a legal scuffle with Apple over who owns what, but if the matter is resolved in a manner that will allow Symmetry to release HyperEngine, an entire mini-industry would spring up around HyperCard with talented individuals and small companies making great strides in the area of on-line, context-sensitive help systems for Macintosh applications.

Electronic Multimedia

Marshall McLuhan remarked on several occasions that "Gutenberg made everybody a reader. Xerox made everybody a publisher." That being the case, hypermedia speeds up the process and enhances the end product by several orders of magnitude. If, as many assert, the only real freedom of the press is to own one, hypermedia addresses that as well, at least for those who have access—a significant problem in its own right that will be addressed shortly.

I have been engaged in the practice of electronic publishing for three years now. My publication, the *Arts & Farces Review,* is a Macintosh-specific

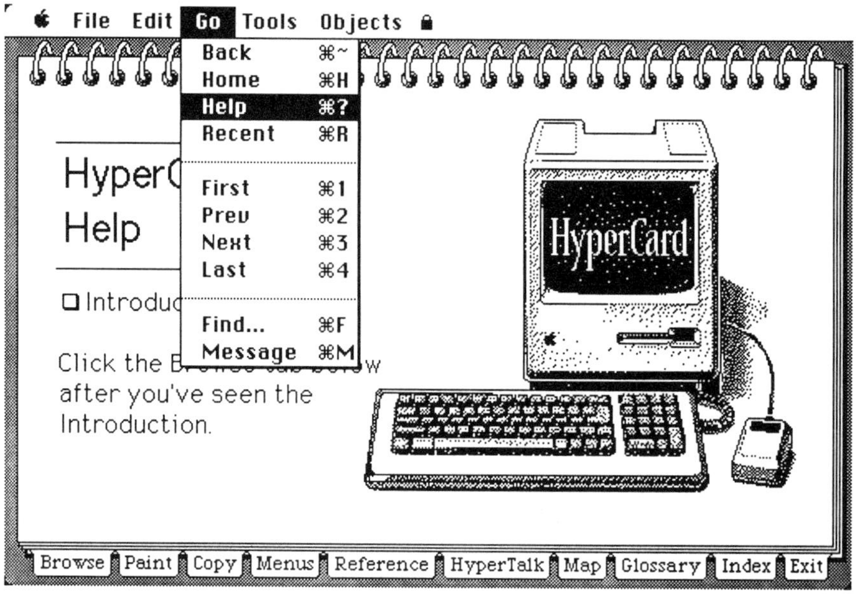

• *Figure 3.5 HyperCard's Help command and associated hypermedia help system.*

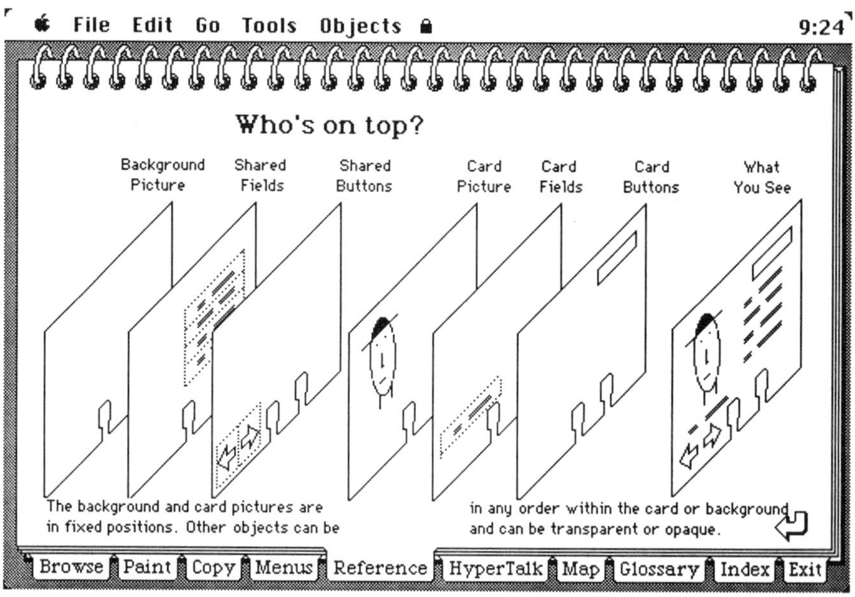

• *Figure 3.6 HyperCard's integrated help system.*

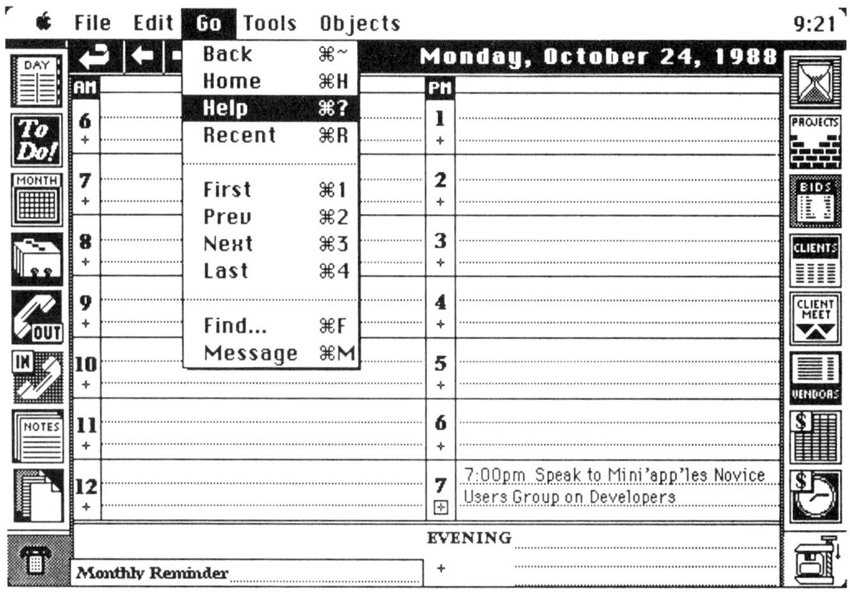

● *Figure 3.7 Intercepting HyperCard's Help command in Focal Point.*

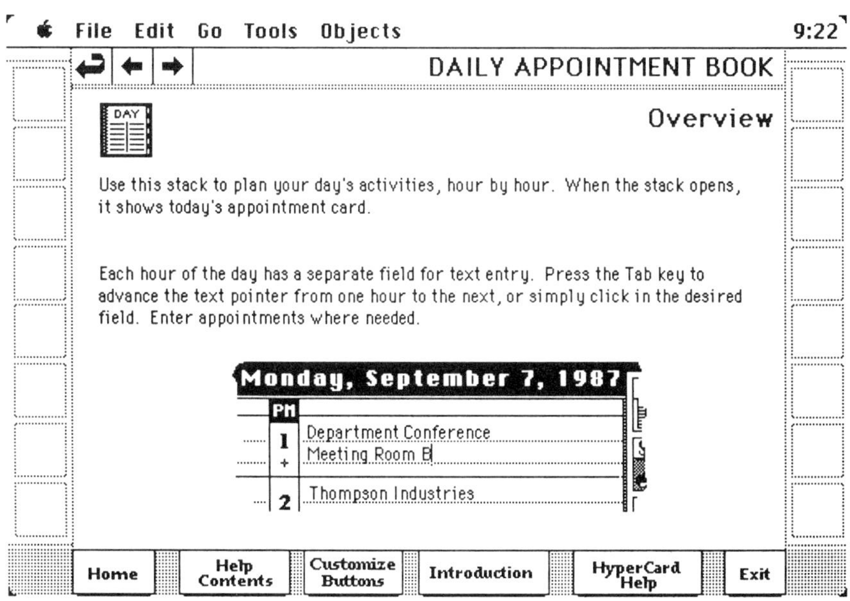

● *Figure 3.8 Focal Point's context-sensitive, integrated help system using HyperCard.*

monthly that is distributed electronically (and on disk to subscribers each month) via shareware.[139] Shareware is an alternative distribution method that relies heavily on the honor of the individuals receiving it to pay for it if they derive value from it. The jury is still out as to whether it "works" or not, although it is by no means a new concept or original to me.

The *Review* was initially published using the Guide/Envelope system from OWL International and subsequently moved to the MicroFilm format using Buck Wheat & Associates' MicroFilm Compiler.[140] The initial Guide/Envelope format is shown in *Figure 3.9* and the currently used MicroFilm format is illustrated in *Figure 3.10.*

The Guide/Envelope format was superb for nonlinear writing, but suffered from several limitations, including the lack of information integrity and support for richly formatted text (italicized and boldfaced passages of text, for example). The limitations will be covered in greater depth later in this chapter.

Shortly after Guide's introduction, its publisher, OWL International, released a "Hypertext Application Construction Kit"—the Envelope companion product—that enabled the hypertext author to turn Guide documents into stand-alone hypertext applications that did not require the reader to own the

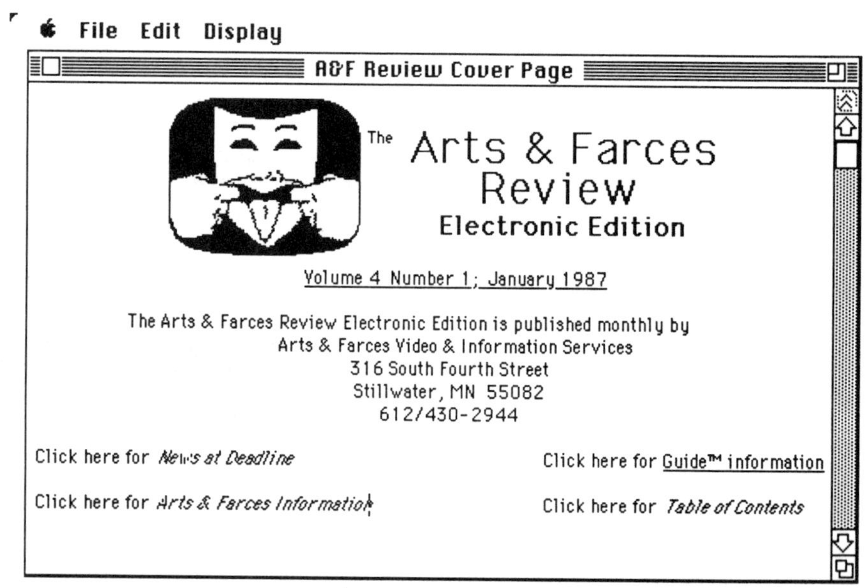

● ***Figure 3.9*** Arts & Farces Review *electronic publication in OWL's Guide/Envelope.*

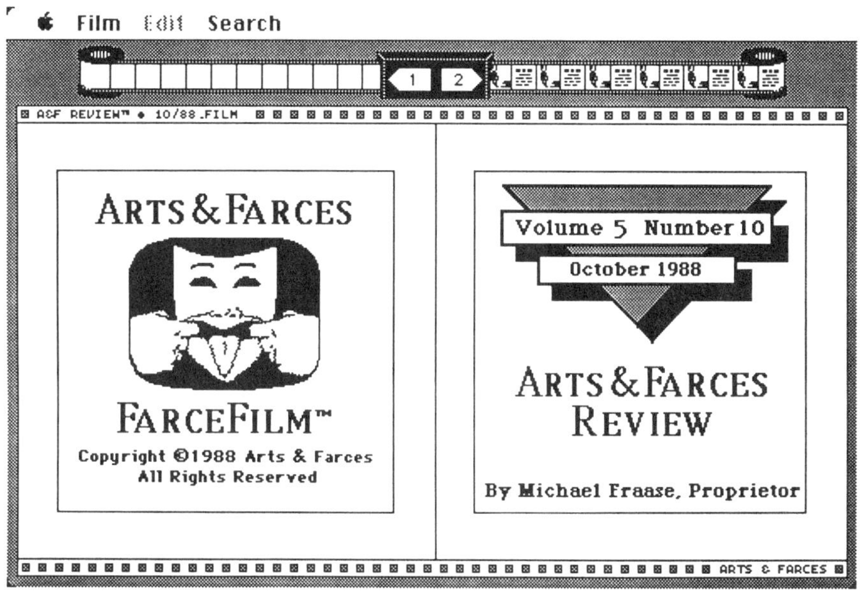

● *Figure 3.10* Arts & Farces Review *electronic publication in MicroFilm format.*

Guide hypertext authoring system. Ted Nelson's *Literary Machines* was published electronically using this system, and is shown in *Figure 3.11.*[141]

An Envelope can contain up to 32 linked Guide documents in a single file, and it adds a minimal overhead (about 60 KBytes) to the resulting file. The Envelope publishing system also enables the Guide user to create and distribute documents called Postcards. Postcards are similar to Envelopes in the sense that up to 32 Guide documents can be contained in a Postcard. The difference is that Postcards do not carry the 60 KByte additional publishing overhead that Envelopes do. The only limitation is that a Postcard must reside on the same disk as an Envelope. The Postcard ''borrows'' the reader portion of an existing Envelope to present the hypertext to the user.

Envelopes and Postcards that are created with the Guide system can be freely distributed with no licensing fee, although the product is limited to producing 1,000 Envelopes at which time the product must be relicensed from OWL International. The Envelope publishing system's method for compiling a group of Guide documents is illustrated in *Figure 3.12.*

MicroFilms, created with Buck Wheat & Associates' MicroFilm Compiler, also can be freely distributed without licensing fee and require the MicroFilm Reader, which is widely available through the on-line services and user

• *Figure 3.11 Ted Nelson's* Literary Machines *electronic edition.*

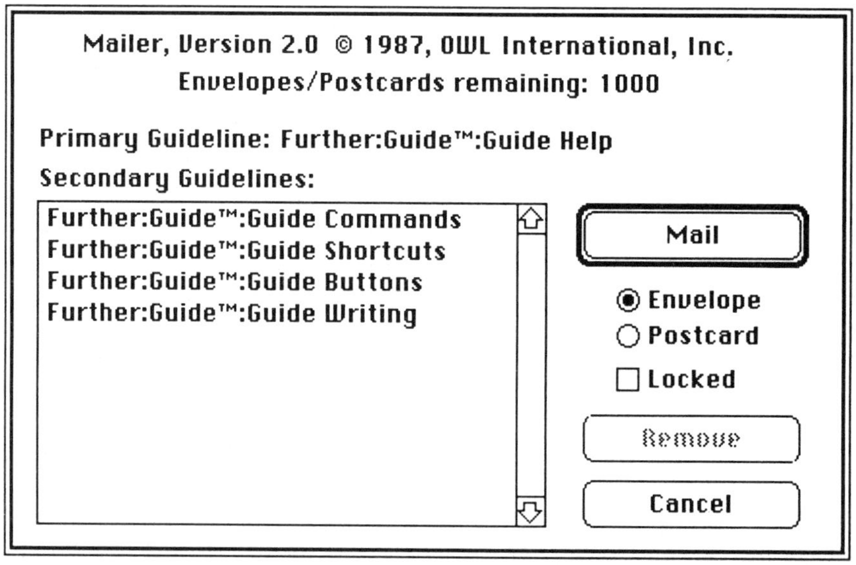

• *Figure 3.12 Document selection dialog from OWL's Envelope.*

groups at no charge. Furthermore, there is no limitation on the number of MicroFilms that can be created before a relicensing situation is triggered. MicroFilms also offers another advantage for those authors who distribute their works electronically—the product does a very good job of compressing the data contained in the MicroFilm.

The MicroFilm Compiler produces a document that is not hypertext in the true sense of the term, although an electronic index can be semiautomatically generated that allows key words to be clicked on and located automatically within the text. It is most useful for the creation of texts that are designed to be read in a sequential manner.

Apple's HyperCard also quickly garnered the attention of electronic publishers shortly after its introduction. Author Danny Goodman has identified four categories of HyperCard stackware products that have emerged since the product's introduction: information publishing, information management, external device control, and utilities.[142] To my mind, electronic publishing—what Goodman refers to as information publishing—is where HyperCard's greatest long-term promise lies. Instructional stackware, technical documentation, general-interest materials, freestanding information kiosks in urban areas, and the like are all examples of electronic publishing well suited to development and delivery in HyperCard. An example of HyperCard as an electronic publishing medium, using hypermedia concepts, is illustrated by a representative issue of *HyperNews* shown in *Figure 3.13.*[143]

Several freestanding HyperCard information kiosks based on Macintosh computers running the "Welcome to MacWorld" stack shown in *Figure 3.14* were available for use by Expo attendees during the MacWorld/Boston Expo at which HyperCard made its debut. Information about the greater Boston area—recommended restaurants, transportation facilities, tourist attractions, and so on—as well as information about the various Expo exhibitors was readily available and easily accessible.

The CD-ROM Dilemma and Data-base Publishing

In April of 1987, Apple became the first major computer manufacturer to endorse CD-ROM (Compact Disc-Read Only Memory) when it released its AppleCD SC, which is compatible with both the Macintosh and the Apple II computer families and also may be used as a shared device over an AppleShare network. Priced at $1,199, the AppleCD SC includes audio circuitry that allows it to play standard audio compact discs.

CD-ROMs are interesting birds to the general computer population and will be even more attractive for Macintosh users because the devices are

● *Figure 3.13 TRU's* HyperNews *electronic publication in HyperCard.*

● *Figure 3.14 MacWorld/Boston Expo information kiosk in HyperCard.*

capable of storing more than 500 MBytes of data. Industry research firm Dataquest estimates that 40,000 CD-ROM units were sold by the middle of 1987 and most analysts agree that the installed base will grow exponentially in the next five years.

Jean-Louis Gassée, president of Apple products, sees Apple's CD-ROM entry as an information enabler that is useful to a wide variety of people. "One by one we have added capabilities that help people deal meaningfully with information: copy-and-paste simplicity, graphics, sound, processing power, systems integration and, finally, in HyperCard, a radically different way of organizing and navigating through information," says Gassée. "CD-ROM complements all of Apple's other strategies by providing a cost-effective and convenient delivery system for vast amounts and varieties of information. It is reasonable to expect that publishers will use the tools we have provided to build a completely new genre of information retrieval products,"[144] he continues.

The AppleCD SC was designed to be compatible with the International Standards Organization's "High Sierra" format although when the initial units were shipped, they were not compatible. The initially shipped units were compatible only with the Macintosh and Apple II file formats and "High Sierra" upgrades, in the form of software drivers, were made available in late summer of 1988.

The Apple product includes a 64 KByte data buffer combined with SCSI interfacing that enables the drive to transfer data relatively quickly. The AppleCD SC also includes an audio chip set (mentioned previously) and a desk accessory that allows the unit to be used to play audio compact discs.

Apple, recognizing the lack of critical mass in the CD-ROM industry, announced a "CD Starter Kit" program for developers and "certified" information providers. This program allowed those with Apple's approval to press a run of 100 CD-ROM disks for about $2,000, which was a step toward hatching the egg.

Two serious problems face Apple's implementation of CD-ROM. The first is its slowness. The premiere authoring and front-end environment (called a search-and-retrieval engine in CD-ROM parlance) for CD-ROM will be HyperCard, Guide, and any forthcoming hypermedia products. HyperCard has a significant problem with its search function on large stacks.

Specifically, Peter Black, author of *The Time Table of Science and Innovation,* one of the first HyperCard/CD-ROM products out of the chute, has found HyperCard's search speed unacceptable—unacceptable to the tune of having to develop a set of external commands for HyperCard to provide

Boolean and range searches.[145] The Xiphias *Time Table of Science and Innovation* CD-ROM stack is shown in *Figure 3.15.*

Black found that HyperCard was capable of finding a word close to the beginning of a stack ("in a second or two," in his words) but took more than 170 seconds to search a four-MByte data base on a standard Macintosh SE. Black's set of external commands, weighing in at under ten KBytes, offers support for full Boolean searching, as well as ranges with wildcards. It uses an inverted index, which means that the material to be searched has to be preprocessed, but once that is done, the search time depends only on the speed of the medium holding the information and the speed of the processor running the search.

The Xearch search yields a hit count and an occurrence list that contains the HyperCard ID numbers of the cards that contain the searched-for material. The HyperCard application can be programmed, through simple HyperTalk, to display either the cards themselves or a variety of information about the results of the search. The Xearch search query dialog is illustrated in *Figure 3.16.*

In addition, more search engines are available from other vendors that adequately address the shortcomings of HyperCard's limited search facility.[146]

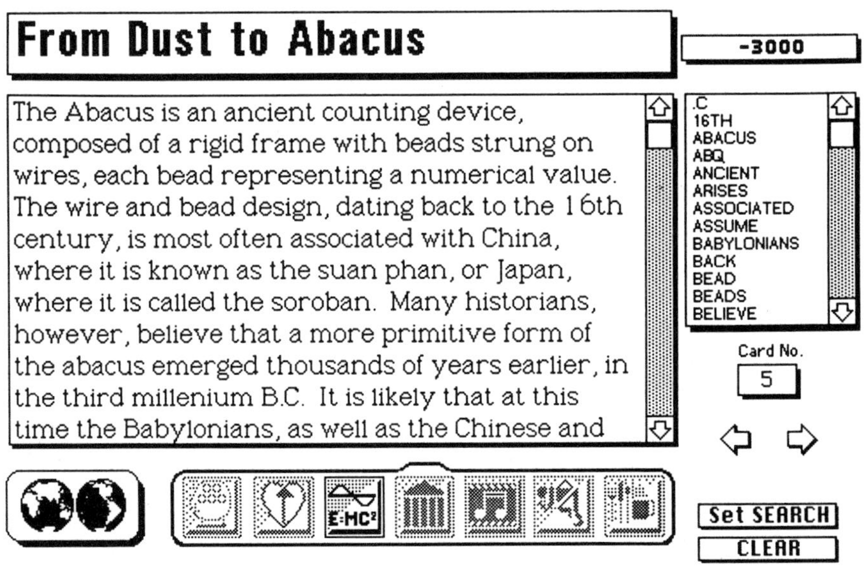

• ***Figure 3.15*** *Xiphias'* Time Table of History *in HyperCard.*

The second problem facing CD-ROM, which is much more serious, lies at the conceptual level. Worst of all, it is not an addressable problem. CD-ROM is only half literate; it cannot write. Think of seven 80-MByte hard drives that you could read from but could not write to. Not a pretty thought, is it? CD-ROM publishers always will be subject to the whims of the pressers. Of course, the major publishers will have their own pressing machines, but what about the rest of us? Are we all condemned to consuming the pap produced to appeal to the lowest common denominator? Ted Nelson said it best: ''. . . a read-only medium in this day and age [is] intrinsically oppressive.''[147]

The read-only nature of CD-ROM only serves to propagate the gatekeeper mentality. Only a select few will have the resources at their disposal to create CD-ROM titles; it costs an absurd amount to master and press a CD-ROM disk. Of course, once the press run is up to what the gatekeepers like to call ''appropriate volume'' so they can take advantage of economies of scale, the cost per unit begins to drop drastically. Oh, my, there's that outmoded concept again.

With the marriage of hypermedia and the now-arriving and forthcoming optical media delivery systems, such as CD-ROM, WORM,[148] and the

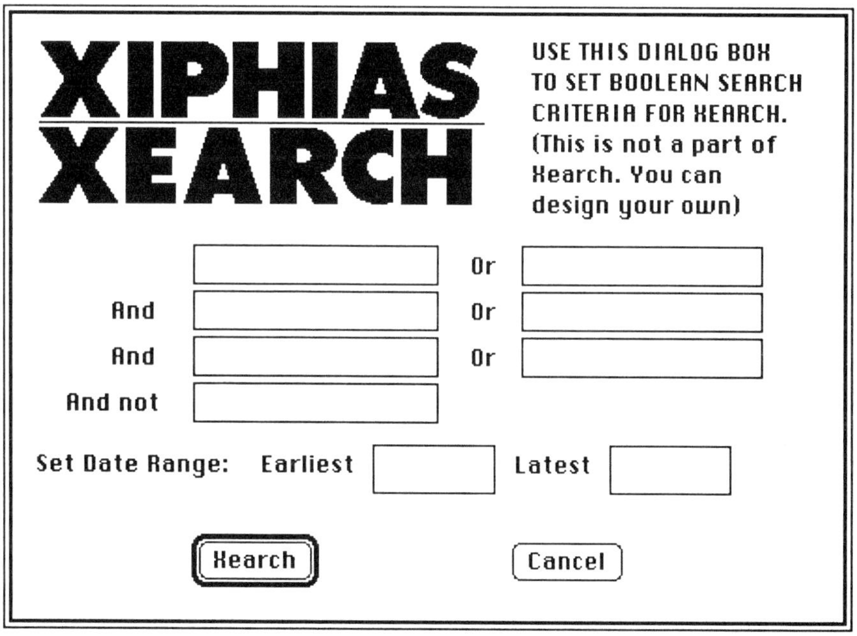

● *Figure 3.16 Xiphias' Xearch Search Dialog for HyperCard.*

erasable magneto-optical systems,[149] various data bases and reference works will be published on optical media combined with hypermedia front ends.

Similar to electronic publishing, data-base publishing generally can be thought of as appealing to a wider audience. The analogy of the difference between broadcast television and some ''narrowcast'' cable television is appropriate as an illustration. Toward this end, several broad-category products already have been announced.

To date, the bulk of the Macintosh CD-ROM titles available tend toward satisfying the lowest common denominator. Representative offerings range from vast stores of public domain, freeware, and shareware software to listings of books in print. Also available are various collections of clip art, maps, and stock photography in digitized image form.

This points to the underlying problem of a read-only medium that is fairly expensive to produce and quite inexpensive to distribute. The bulk of the costs in producing material distributed on CD-ROM are actually in producing the material and in the mastering process. The actual duplication and distribution charges are relatively minor, especially in large quantities. Because CD-ROM is by nature unable to avail itself of the mass-customization qualities mentioned previously, any material published in CD-ROM format must appeal to the greatest number of people in order to be successful.

Of course, in some cases that is not always a negative. For example, consider the Voyager Company's guided tour of the Louvre museum—a beautifully implemented hypermedia environment consisting of a HyperCard stack and a HyperCard-driven videodisc. The company also put together a similar project for the National Gallery of Art. The National Gallery project consists of more than 1,500 images and is driven completely by HyperCard and a series of external commands via an on-screen control panel. By comparison, the Louvre laserstack contains 45,000 images from more than 6,000 works. Tours in either Laserstack may be customized by using an indexing feature and paths are provided for tour by artist, school, date, and nationality. A chronological index enables the user to interactively focus on a specific time period by using an on-screen slide rule time line. Categories are explored and expanded by clicking on the category title that opens to reveal further layers of detail.

Many works in the National Gallery laserstack contain motion sequences that are accessed by clicking on a movie projector button that starts a full motion sequence with sound on the videodisc monitor. Such segments range from a lecture by or on an artist to a tour of an artist's studio. The user is offered complete control over the motion sequences via the on-screen control panel mentioned previously.

On the CD-ROM data-base publishing forefront is the Alexandria Institute, whose charter is to capture all the world's recorded knowledge on CD-ROM and, more importantly, to make it accessible to anyone who wants it. The future, according to the Alexandria Institute, will consist of scholars and researchers with the best libraries in the world at their instant disposal, wherever they are.

This future, of course, is built on a past. In this case, the Alexandrian Library created by Ptolemies in 300 B.C. or so serves as the foundation for the modern-day extension of the idea. Historians estimate the Alexandrian Library contained more than 500,000 papyrus rolls that were constantly revised and edited by the Alexandrian librarians. Scholars traveled from great distances to make copies of the works housed in the Alexandrian Library and, in this manner—copies of copies—the manuscript collections in Europe were established, providing a greater number of people with access to the vast body of information.

In the modern version, Howard Selby, the father of the Alexandria Institute, envisions the capture of recorded knowledge on CD-ROMs with full indexes and cross-references that will be available to all the workstations without anyone having to travel anywhere. Selby, who formed the Alexandria Institute in December of 1984, has been involved in a variety of projects in the past, including computer-controlled water recycling. His vision for the Institute is to center on the process of how we collect, access, and use knowledge.

Robert Kerr is the chief executive of the Institute and oversees the daily operations of the project. He currently is evangelizing the concept of Knowledge Research Centers that are similar in scope, if not implementation, to Ted Nelson's Xanadu Silverstands. Kerr also is designing a copyright system for the Alexandria Institute that is based on a pay-for-use model. Kerr differentiates the Knowledge Research Centers from on-line telecommunications services in that most of the information in a Knowledge Research Center is stored locally rather than centrally at a remote location that the user calls in to.

A typical Knowledge Research Center will contain a KnowledgeBase that consists of electronic versions of traditional books, articles, graphics, motion pictures, sound, and so on, paired with an advanced search-and-retrieval engine. Because the delivery medium is CD-ROM, the material cannot be stolen, lost, not returned, destroyed, or defaced, which are problems more traditional library forms must deal with on a continuing basis. In addition, utilizing CD-ROM as the storage-and-delivery medium bypasses the problem of deterioration.

A consortium of libraries has been formed, called the KRC Project, to implement Knowledge Research Centers at several libraries in small towns, large cities, and universities.

Storage Hope on the Horizon

My first computer was an Apple II. One of the options available was a floppy disk drive with a 143-KByte capacity. When I went to the store to pick up my new computer system I was asked how many floppy disks I would initially need. I responded that I would need, at most, one. Ever. After all, I reasoned, 143,000 characters is a lot of room. My storage need naiveté lasted all of about an hour after I got back to my office.

My first Macintosh was a Mac Plus with internal and external 800K floppies. I figured a total of 1.6 MByte of on-line data storage with a full megabyte of RAM was all anyone would need—at least for a while. (I was no longer naive about storage capacities, remember?) Actually, that storage setup served me almost adequately for about a year and a half, and I never had to fret through a hard-drive crash.

When I was initially seeded with HyperCard, I knew I had to have a hard drive. I supposed I could live, quite comfortably, with a 20-MByte SCSI drive, but by now I was very wizened about these sorts of things and decided what I really needed was a 40-MByte drive. When one of the hard-drive manufacturers needed a manual written for one of their software products, I saw a way, through barter, to get more storage capacity than I conceivably would need—a 40-MByte hard drive with an integrated 40-MByte tape drive. Less than a year later I found myself spending each Sunday evening clearing space on the hard drive for the upcoming week's work. Once upon a time, those in the know would look at you out of the corner of their eye and tell you, "Buy twice the size that you think you need." It was sage advice until the advent of hypermedia. You will never have enough disk space. Trust me.

It was a hard lesson to learn that, no matter what, an individual could never have access to enough local storage space.

Many, including this author, have warned of the threat of the impending information glut. Most of us, again including this author, were wrong about our time frames. The information glut, exemplified by the geometric and exponential growth of available and pertinent data, has arrived and by all indications has been here for quite some time. This makes you wish it would have knocked. And that's not even the bad news—on top of not knocking, it didn't shut the door.

So, serious information workers are confronted with a serious problem: how to store all the information they need within a reasonable reach. Serious information *providers* are confronted with an exasperated version of the same problem: how to master and *distribute* their information products. For most hypermedia producers, the single biggest problem with each project is deciding on an appropriate distribution medium. Large amounts of data require large amounts of storage space, and that is not going to change until systems such as Xanadu are on-line, reliable, and affordable.

One of the problems with the optical media currently available is its size. Ironically, 250 MBytes to 550 MBytes is seen as ''too big'' by many information providers. For example, consider the current raft of ''buddying up'' in the community to fill all that electronic real estate. As the notion of hypermedia begins to mature—especially on the individual level, with many of us maintaining our own data spaces—there certainly will be a need for all that and more. Currently, however, most of the electronic publishers are scrounging fill material from wherever they can, and unfortunately this shows. This will change. Trust me. For the time being, several alternatives to the CD-ROM route currently are available and even one or two are on the near horizon.

Let's take a look at what is available, both for storage and distribution, in the realm of appropriate production media. We will also take a peek at what looms on the near horizon. We will break down each storage/distribution medium into hardware and software costs based on a typical 40-MByte project and 40-MByte backup. We will then factor in a somewhat subjective ''bulk factor'' based on the tedium of working with the medium on a project of this scale as well as physical storage size and the like. This will be based on a scale from one to ten, with one being the most oppressive bulk and lowest level of convenience and ten being the least bulk and most convenient.

Then we will consider a ''usability'' index, based on another scale from one to ten, with one being the least usable and ten being the most usable. This factor will consider such subfactors as speed, amount of storage on-line, and the literacy level of the medium (whether or not it can read *and* write).

Finally, we will consider a ''production'' index, based on standardization, ease of use, accessibility, and cost of production facilities, and the like, which again will be based on a scale of one to ten.

When we add up these subtotals we will arrive at an "appropriateness" total that will give us something of a handle with which to compare the various media. The higher the total, the more appropriate the medium. This is not rocket science, folks, it is just a way for us to get our balance and bearings.

800-KByte Floppy Disks

Hardware cost: $0.00 (included in the cost of the computer)
Media cost: $63.75 (51 disks at 1.25 each)[150]
Total cost: $127.50
Bulk factor: 3
Usability factor: 2
Production factor: 5
Appropriateness total: 10

The only common denominator for Macintosh users, the venerable 3.5-inch 800-KByte floppy has the advantage of good data stability, relatively low cost for small-project distribution, and complete data compatibility. For information-based projects of even medium size, the 800K floppy becomes cumbersome and expensive at best. Consider a project that occupied 40 800-KByte floppies—a moderately large undertaking by today's standards, but small by tomorrow's. Quality control, shipping and media costs, and a system for tracking the hierarchy of the media become substantial problems.

Apple recently began marketing Macintosh computers with a 1.44-MByte 3.5-inch floppy drive. The media costs are likely to eventually fall to just above the current prices for double-sided (800-KByte) disks. The added benefit of the new Apple SuperDrive is the ability to read and write various IBM data formats.

10-MByte and 20-MByte Removable Floppies

Hardware cost: $1,000.00
Media cost: $200.00 (4 disks at $50.00 each)
Total cost: $1,200.00
Bulk factor: 6
Usability factor: 5
Production factor: 7
Appropriateness total: 18

The next step up, in capacity, from the floppy is the 10-MByte and 20-MByte removable floppy drives, such as the Jasmine MegaDrive and the Bering Totem. Standardization is minimal, and data stability and transportability is reportedly quite poor. The bulk factor is acceptable. Take a few points off because they are not any faster than standard floppies.

40-MByte Tape Cartridge (3M DC-2000)

Hardware cost: $1,500.00
Media cost: $60.00 (2 tapes at $30.00 each)
Total cost: $1,560.00
Bulk factor: 8
Usability factor: 2
Production factor: 6
Appropriateness total: 16

The 40-MByte DC-2000 tape cartridge manufactured by 3M has the advantage of a higher capacity and a lower bulk than any of the previously mentioned media. It is slow, unwieldly, and painfully unreliable to work with, however, and is nothing of a standard even though Apple has halfheartedly endorsed it by marketing a unit of its own. Its transportability between hardware environments is only fair, and then only through the use of third-party software.

Several companies, including 3M, recently have announced the availability of storage capacities of up to 80 MBytes on the same DC-2000 tape cartridge. The prices of these units should approach the same level as the existing 40-MByte units by the fall of 1989.

45-MByte Removable-Media Hard Disk (Syquest)

Hardware cost: $1,775.00
Media cost: $250.00 (2 platters at $125.00 each)
Total cost: $2,025.00
Bulk factor: 7
Usability factor: 9
Production factor: 9
Appropriateness total: 25

One of the more popular mediums for small hypermedia projects are the Syquest removable-cartridge 45-MByte hard-disk platters. Marketed by several original equipment manufacturers, all are built around the same hardware and offer similar features. Because the removable-cartridge hard disks use voice-coil technology, they format to a full 45 MBytes and most offer at least an 8-KByte data cache that allows the unit to be formatted to use a 1:1 interleave on all Macintosh models.

Although 45 MBytes will look very constricting in less than three years, right now, it is a workable size. Syquest already has a 100-MByte removable platter, the IQ89, that should be available by the time this is in print. In addition, capacities approaching the 400-MByte mark already are being designed, using the same platter and case size, and many observers see no severe obstacles to reducing the form factor (the physical size) of the units for use with portable computers in the near future.

Because the Syquest removable platters are true hard disks, access times are quite respectable: in the 19 millisecond range, comparing with CD-ROM's 200 millisecond average access times.

Like everything else, however, there are no free lunches; one factor severely impedes the broad acceptance of Syquest's drives: price. The 45-MByte cartridges can be bought on the street for about $125 each, which puts it out of the reach of many. This is at least partially addressed by the fact that the Syquest units can be used as backup devices as well as primary storage media.

250-MByte Magneto-Optical Erasable Media (Canon)

Hardware cost: $2,500.00 (estimated)
Media cost: $50.00 (1 platter)
Total cost: $2,550.00
Bulk factor: 8
Usability factor: 9
Production factor: 9
Appropriateness total: 26

Standard-issue equipment in the NeXT Computer System, the 250-MByte removable media, magneto-optical erasable media developed by Canon promises to advance the state of the art of storage and distribution for hypermedia producers in the near future. Although end-user pricing currently is not available, media costs are expected to be in the range of $50 per 250 MBytes of storage. Canon also announced a 512-MByte version of the subsystem and both units should be available through various original equipment manufacturers by the time you read this. Units of this type will become even more appropriate as data spaces begin to grow exponentially.

Hot on the heals of the NeXT/Canon announcement, Sony announced that its magneto-optical drive now is available to original equipment manufacturers in both internal (SMO-D501) and external (SMO-S501) configurations. Both Sony ''floptical'' drives offer a capacity of 650 MBytes and a 20-millisecond average seek time. The Sony drive conforms to ANSI and ISO standards and both Hewlett-Packard and 3M have announced support for the device. The Canon drive relies on proprietary technology and is compatible only with itself. The Sony drives also are significantly less expensive in OEM quantities than the Canon models: $4,650 for the Sony compared to $6,000 for the Canon.

Where does that leave us?

The synergetics and anticipatory design gurus would tell us that we are currently in a state of phase transition, waiting for an order parameter event and a subsequent state change. Rather than try to explain it myself, we would do a lot better to get some straight answers from experts in the field. As it happens, I happen to know two, and I spoke with them about this issue. Jerry Daniels and Mary Jane Mara are hypermedia producers[151] and the authors of *Applied HyperCard: Developing and Marketing Superior Stackware.*[152] Please refer to that work for an in-depth discussion of synergetics and its attendant phase transition and state change relevant to Macintosh hypermedia.

Daniels was emphatic on the storage and distribution issue: "We can't go back in speed and nobody needs that much storage for the kinds of projects we're seeing now. The average access time is about 25 milliseconds and nobody's willing to put up with the slowness of the CD-ROM. 40 MBytes is enough even though everyone's concentrating on volume but no one has any large properties they're putting together yet anyway. The 45 MByte removable cartridge Syquest drives would be great if they can get the price of the main unit down to under $1,000."[153]

When I asked Daniels if such a price drop would set the order parameter to begin the state change, he replied, "No, we won't get through the phase transition until we get rid of the ugly stacks. It's like an eight-year-old looking at dirty pictures—he can't interface with that product. Thinking in multimegabytes rather than hundreds of kilobytes is completely new and it has a whole learning curve of its own. People are so hungry for quality stacks that they're willing to download 700 KByte material from the national networks. . . . A great stack will cause the order parameter to be set and the distribution media will fall into place. If CD-ROM performs as badly as we expect, I can't see anyone getting worked up. People are still questioning whether they want to look at information on a screen, and artwork is going to make the difference. Unless it makes you hot or wet it won't fly. People still think computers are for looking things up and printing them out. I envision someone doing a really great stack that is really large and distributing it via freeware or shareware on the nets and one of the publishers picking it up. That would cause the distribution media problem to correct itself and set the order parameter."[154]

This assertion seemed to run in direct contradiction with the common wisdom that held that the publishing-distribution dilemma of hypermedia products was a chicken-and-egg situation that wouldn't budge until "something happened." According to Daniels, "The Beatles' *Sgt. Pepper's* album was made on the worst four-track studio that was available at the time. We should be working toward that end. If you have something to say you should be saying it now. It may not make you a millionaire, but you'll make enough to have a fajita dinner with your sweetie."[155]

Networking and Hypermedia

As hypermedia becomes a more and more prevalent mode of communication, networking on all levels will be impacted. Unfortunately, most computer manufacturers (and their satellite peripheral manufacturers) tend to focus on local area networks rather than geographically dispersed work groups that will become more and more prevalent in the near future.

Apple's much-touted "Macintosh Office" was quickly and quietly laid to rest after it was discovered that most AppleTalk networks were initially used as long printer cables. Until very recently, local area networks on the Macintosh were more trouble than they were worth for small work groups. And the geographically dispersed individuals who made up a small work group that did not exist at any given location (anywhere) were virtually ignored until recently.

Thankfully, this has begun to change with innovations such as CE Software's QuickMail[156] electronic mail system and high-speed modems such as the Telebit TrailBlazer Plus.[157]

QuickMail provides remote access to the electronic mail system on a local area network that is a welcome addition for individuals such as myself who work with a variety of far-distant organizations and individuals. In addition, it provides software bridges for remote mail exchange with CompuServe, GEnie, and MCI Mail. Many people have needed a tool that provided geographically dispersed decentralized electronic mail and file transfers for a long time, and QuickMail is the first attempt at addressing that need without relying on external hardware in addition to the software.

For a first attempt, it is a great stride forward, but there still is room for improvement. QuickMail supports baud rates up to 9600 bits per second. With market penetration of the Telebit TrailBlazer Plus, boasting a performance level of 19.2 KBaud, growing on an almost daily basis and even faster baud rates just around the corner, this is a fairly severe oversight.

Referring to the Telebit TrailBlazer Plus as a modem is something of a semantic mistake, along the same lines as calling the LaserWriter II NTX a printer. The LaserWriter II NTX was, until recently, the most intelligent computer Apple manufactured. And the Telebit TrailBlazer Plus is the smartest communications processor on the planet. It is still a modem to you and me, but a blindingly fast modem with the most advanced set of features currently available. It is also probably the most widely misunderstood piece of hardware in existence.

The TrailBlazer Plus is not just an ordinary, everyday, household modem; it is a communications machine built around the Motorola 68000 processor and equipped with a plethora of features that will make your telephone line sizzle. Through the use of what Telebit calls a Packetized Ensemble Protocol (PEP), the TrailBlazer Plus is capable of achieving throughput data speeds of up to 18,000 bits per second over normal telephone lines.

Or, rather, less than normal telephone lines. Let me give you an example. I used to live just far enough outside of the Minneapolis-St. Paul metropolitan area not to be a suburb. This was one of the oldest towns in Minnesota, and one of the annoyances of this community was an antiquated telephone service. My telephone lines were so bad that a normal US Robotics Courier 2400e modem could not even recognize a dial tone, much less connect to anything.

When I heard that the TrailBlazer Plus was capable of up to 18,000 bits-per-second throughput, I was excited but wary. I figured that if a standard 2400-baud modem could not negotiate a connection, fat chance for one boasting 19,200-baud support. You see, the TrailBlazer Plus works by splitting the standard carrier into 512 subcarriers. Imagine my surprise when it managed to consistently attain 18,300 bits-per-second throughput on the Worst Telephone Lines in America.

At speeds above 2400 baud, the TrailBlazer Plus can communicate only with another PEP modem (currently limited to Telebit and Ventel products) and is technically capable of only half-duplex communications. At these higher speeds, however, it uses what the manufacturer calls an adaptive duplex that optimizes overall throughput by automatically varying the transmission of data to match the load between both ends of the connection. At speeds of 2400 baud and less, the modem is fully compatible with the Bell 103 and 212A standards as well as the V.22 standards for both 1200 and 2400 baud.

The modem also features automatic transmission-speed determination, which allows the TrailBlazer Plus to automatically select the correct transmission speed based on the speed of the remote modem—whether it is a PEP modem or not. Also included is real-time line-quality analysis and adaptation that allows commands sent to the modem to report back the relative quality of the telephone line and to renegotiate the connection for optimal throughput if necessary.

The remaining major feature of the modem is its self-testing and diagnostics abilities, which are performed automatically each time the modem is turned on. Additionally, the modem constantly monitors signal-to-noise ratios, frequency offset measurements, data-flow analysis, and error rates, in addition to the line-quality analysis. Finally, the TrailBlazer Plus is capable of remote diagnostics, that is, another user can call in to your modem for troubleshooting purposes.

The Telebit TrailBlazer Plus uses a superset of the Hayes command set, although it would be misleading to call it Hayes-compatible. The modem has no dip-switches; all settings are controlled in writable and erasable memory within the modem through manipulation of various registers. Although not truly Hayes-compatible, I have found ways to manipulate the TrailBlazer's registers to provide compatibility with most software that appears to require Hayes compatiblility.

We have been hearing talk of gateways between the electronic services for years, and we are no closer to such an arrangement now than we were when the discussions and fantasies first began. Although you can, with more pain than necessary, send CompuServe electronic mail via MCI Mail and vice versa, I should not have to remember that I contact Don Brown on CompuServe and the editors of *MacWEEK* on MCI Mail. I should be able to drop a message to Don Brown at CE Software, West Des Moines, Iowa, on a local telecommunications node, and the back end of the telecommunications link should be intelligent enough to figure out that Don Brown can be reached almost anywhere electronically, but the account on service A is more appropriate than the account on service B because he is there more often. Or, alternatively, that service C is more appropriate for nonurgent correspondence because while he is not there as often, the transmittal rate is cheaper.

As geographically dispersed hypermedia systems begin to come on-line, the telecommunications tools such as QuickMail and the Telebit TrailBlazer Plus will grow in penetration rate. The original design specification for Xanadu, for example, calls for the interconnection of individual and collective data spaces as well as for the interconnection of the relationships between various bits of information. As powerful as the individual personal computer is, its power begins to grow exponentially when connected with other computers. Similarly, the cumulative nature of a vast network of interconnected personal data spaces takes on an exponential growth quality as well and develops a data, information, and knowledge synergy that is truly mind-boggling.

General Hypermedia Problems

Two types of problems confront the hypermedia author/producer. The first of the two, mostly of a technical nature, will be covered in the remaining portion of this chapter, while the broader social ramifications of hypermedia will be covered in the next chapter.

Getting Lost

The single biggest complaint most hypermedia users express is concerns of "getting lost" in the system and "missing things." Both of these problems are symptomatic of underlying design deficiencies on the part of the hypermedia author/designer. My own early hypertext efforts are pretty good examples of how not to provide navigational tools for your users. The point is, however, that I learned from my own and others' mistakes.

Several times a year I am asked to address user groups of various levels of expertise. My favorite ones are the novice groups that are made up predominantly of new users and inexperienced beginners. I like these groups the best because the individuals do not already possess a frame of reference about what menus, dialog boxes, buttons, and screen designs are "supposed" to look like or do. They are great for showing new designs to and getting immediate, unbiased reactions. If they cannot figure out how to use the major portions of an application, on their own, in about 15 minutes or so, you know you have a lot of redesign work to do.

Readers get frustrated when they cannot easily and quickly navigate a body of information. One of the biggest problems with most hypermedia authors is that they implement the links in a single direction—usually from the general to the more specific—quite well, and either give minor treatment to the reverse direction links or ignore them completely. This is likely a result of the current state of the art of hypermedia tools being largely paper emulators. Mostly, we sequentially read paper publications, from front to back. Hypermedia, by nature, is not a sequential medium, and the author must provide adequate navigation facilities for the user.

Apple began to address the navigation problem with the initial few releases of HyperCard by providing button ideas that revolve around navigational themes, as shown in *Figure 3.17.* Unfortunately, HyperCard is mostly a paper emulator right down to its most basic underlying metaphor: the stack of cards.

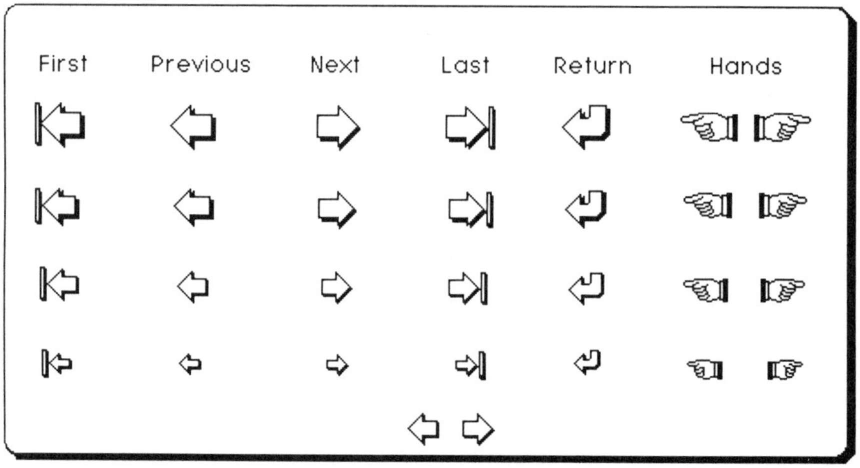

● *Figure 3.17 HyperCard's mostly linear navigation buttons.*

Most of the resident navigation buttons provided by Apple revolve around sequential concepts, such as "next," "previous," "first," and "last." Additionally, few Apple-produced HyperCard stacks have adequate navigational aids.

I ceased producing an electronic publication in hypertext format and moved to a more sequential format specifically because I received letters of frustration from readers. They invariably told me that what I thought were adequate navigation controls and cues were not enough for the average user. Consequently, I spent the next two years exploring various interface issues with hypermedia systems. While my explorations continue, I feel that I have come up with one and possibly two interface methods for the production and subsequent navigation of data spaces of various sizes that are fairly easily implemented in hypermedia systems.

The best current example of a stack designed with appropriate navigational tools is Danny Goodman's Business Class[158], which was one of the first commercially available stacks after HyperCard's release. Business Class is designed as an aid for international travelers and contains information on a variety of countries, such as currency, customs, transportation facilities, lodging, etc.

As you can see from the following Business Class screens, there is no concept of "first" or "next." Navigation is accomplished simply by clicking on the desired area of the world *(Figure 3.18)*, which brings up a more detailed map of the desired area *(Figure 3.19)*. Following the zoom-in map

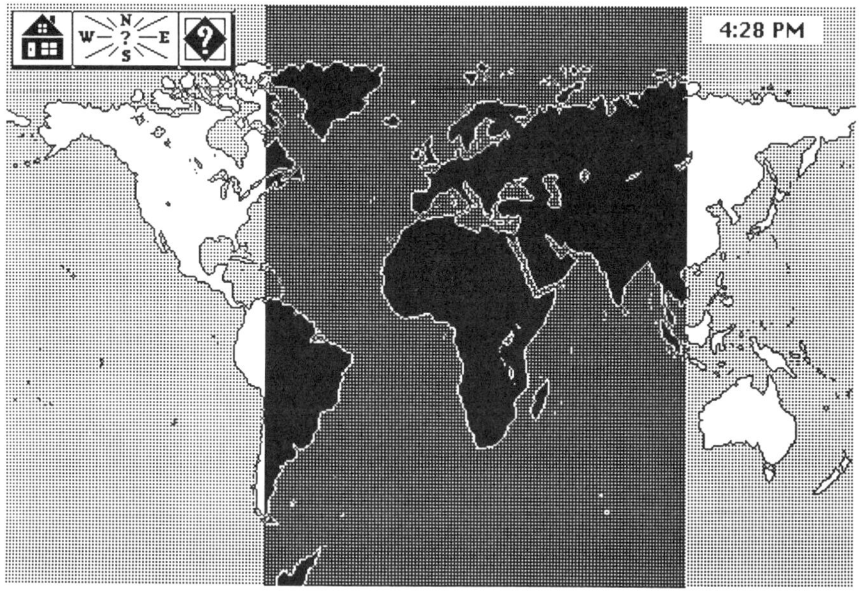

● *Figure 3.18 Business Class's world screen.*

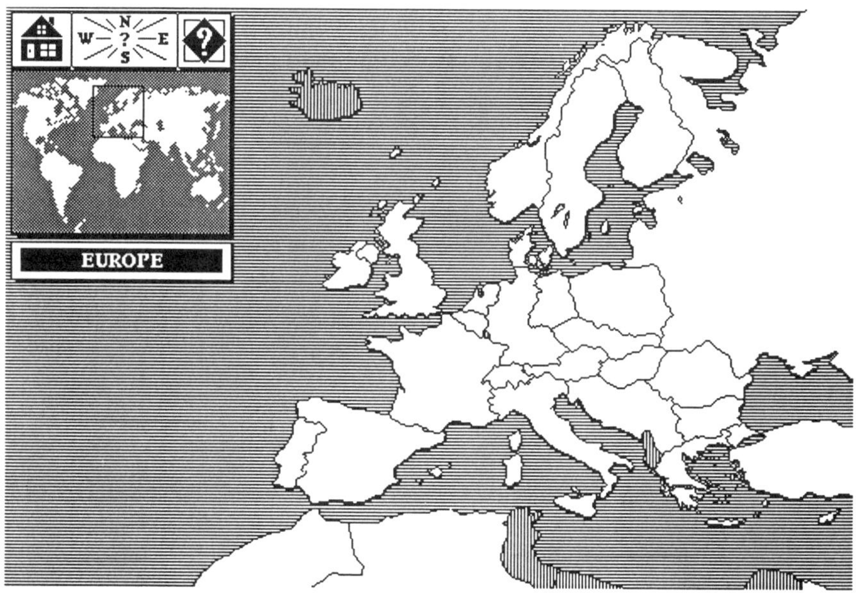

● *Figure 3.19 Business Class's Europe screen.*

metaphor, the user simply clicks on the country of interest, which brings up the final layer of general geographic information *(Figure 3.20)*, which also shows the major cities of the area in question.

To receive specific information about the transportation facilities in France, for example, the user would click on the airplane icon for information on air transportation and the highway/train track icon for ground transportation information. Such a navigation metaphor and implementation allows the user to quickly locate the specific information he or she is interested in with a maximum of three or four mouse clicks.

Frame of Reference Problems

Somewhat related to the getting lost problem, mentioned previously, is the frame of reference problem—how does the user view both the generalized information overview (the forest) and the more specific information (the trees) simultaneously; and, moreover, how are transitions implemented between the two. This, like the getting lost problem, is symptomatic of underlying design flaws and must be appropriately addressed.

Again, referring to *Figure 3.18* through *Figure 3.20,* Danny Goodman's Business Class always keeps the user informed of where he or she is in the data space. The user has constant access to more specific *or* more general

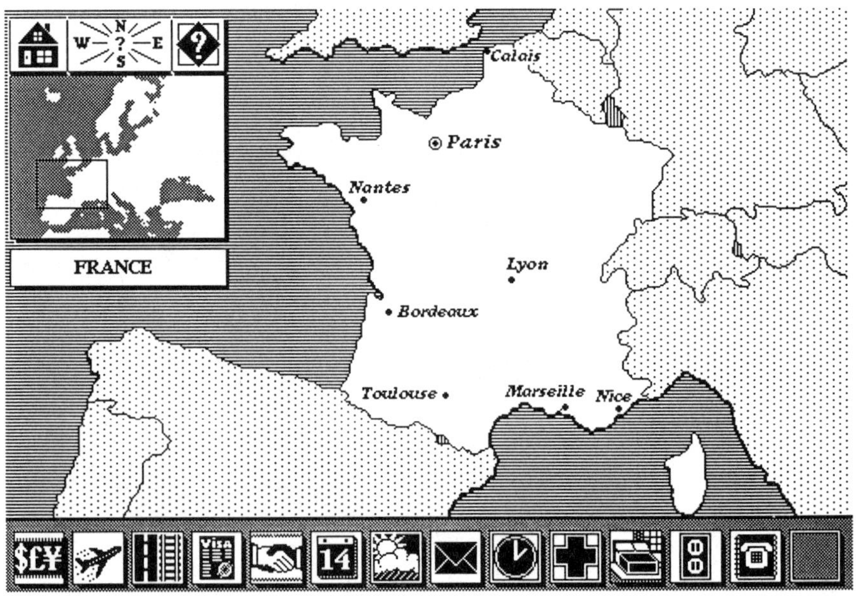

● *Figure 3.20 Business Class's France screen.*

information at all times; more specific information is obtained through clicking on the desired sections of the large map, while more general information is navigated to through the smaller map superimposed in the upper left corner of the screen. If the user clicks outside of any country in the superimposed map, he or she is returned to the most general level of information, the initial world map displaying what parts of the world are experiencing daylight and what parts are in darkness.

Business Class is a good example of a hypermedia that provides adequate bidirectional links from the general to the specific and vice versa. Such implementations significantly enhance the hyperness of a data space as well as making it more accessible and useful. By providing access to context shifting buttons, the user is given complete control over the data space and his or her confidence in navigating the information is bolstered.

Version Control Problems

With multiple versions of electronic publications, data bases, and other data comes version control problems. How are users kept abreast of new version changes that may make their hypermedia links obsolete? This is sure to become a more serious problem as the hypermedia networks begin to come on-line, and is also a significant problem with huge storage media environments that are erasable. Both situations allow a shared data space to be constantly updated. Never the same information twice becomes a serious problem that is best addressed at the most basic design levels.

Apple employee Sioux Lacy has released a version control utility, in the form of an XCMD and an XFCN distributed in the Version Control stack, for HyperCard that allows the HyperCard author to maintain a version history. The Version Control update dialog is shown in *Figure 3.21,* and is displayed each time a stack that contains the utility is updated. This is useful for HyperCard developers but does nothing to address the problem of information updates from the user's perspective.

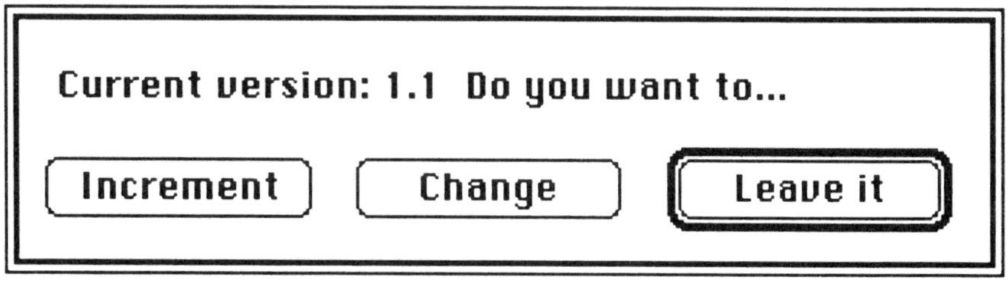

• ***Figure 3.21*** *Update Dialog from Sioux Lacy's Version Control.*

The Interleaf page layout software for UNIX workstations provides a workable solution that hypermedia creators can build on. The Interleaf software supports the concept of linked copies that enables each person on the network to have a copy of a shared document that is automatically updated when any of the other members of the networked work group changes one of the linked copies. In the case of hypermedia this would be an appropriate solution for both stored links and information that would automatically be updated each time the user logged onto the networked hypermedia system or opened a nonupdated hypermedia document on a local node.

Networked publishing systems like Interleaf provide a series of solid clues and starting points for the designers of future and existing hypermedia systems. On a system such as Xanadu, facilities must be provided for the sharing of data while at the same time ensuring the integrity of the information contained on the system. As long as the links are stored separately from the actual document(s), as is the case in the Intermedia project, this is not such a problem for data integrity, although there must be a way of updating the links while maintaining various levels of link histories.

The Aesthetic Problem

Because the vast majority of hypermedia practitioners are rank novices, and all are learning the ropes, we will continue to be plagued with unattractive implementations for quite some time. This is a serious problem in the short term, but is likely to take care of itself in the long term.

Just as we experienced the ''ransom note'' syndrome when the Macintosh first became available—documents printed with virtually every typeface available—and desktop publishing survived and even flourished, so will the hypermedia ugly-duckling stage correct itself in due time.

Exquisitely designed hypermedia documents are already beginning to appear. Clement Mok's MacWorld Expo press kit from 1988 is exceptionally well done, while his design for Apple's 1987 Annual Report Supplement leaves a good bit to be desired. So, we are all learning collectively, although not quickly enough for the likes of some (including myself from time to time).

The potential uses for hypermedia are as varied as the users, and only a few basic existing implementations have been presented here. There are many others, already in existence, which are contained in the broad categories covered here. For example, Guide is used in the automobile and airplane manufacturing and service industries to maintain automated maintenance systems that have replaced many linear feet of manuals.[159]

Hypermedia is also in widespread use in training implementations ranging from the Cornell Medical School[160] and the University of Mississippi's School of Veterinary Medicine[161] to any number of HyperCard training stacks for Macintosh software products.[162] Closely related to the training implementations is something OWL International refers to as "reader-defined information delivery," which many users at a variety of installations are using to replace more traditional media, such as books, manuals, reports, and correspondence. Reader-defined information delivery offers distinct advantages in the communication of information that requires interaction, analysis, or cross-referencing.[163]

As more powerful hypermedia development systems become available and as more users become hypermedia-literate, the usefulness of the systems themselves will begin to mushroom, resulting in usable and accessible applications that are well beyond the scope of what is currently available or even hoped for.

[121] Theodore Roszak, *The Cult of Information* (New York: Pantheon Books, 1986).

[122] To be sure, Apple retained a great many ''thinking'' and creative individuals. It's just that the company has made a transition from an ''idea'' company to a ''product'' company, much for the worse as far as I'm concerned.

[123] Stanley Davis, *Future Perfect* (Reading, Massachusetts: Addison-Wesley Publishing Company, Inc., 1987).

[124] Ibid.

[125] Ibid.

[126] Ibid.

[127] Ibid.

[128] Ibid.

[129] Ibid.

[130] I'm speaking mainly of computers marketed by Apple prior to the Macintosh II and SE. Earlier models were plagued by a woefully inadequate power supply, and the initial Macintosh SEs were hindered by a fan of mediocre quality whose noise drove users to distraction. Apple benevolently offered a $90 replacement. The company continues to deny any problems with the Macintosh Plus and earlier power supplies.

[131] Paul Hawken, *The Next Economy* (New York: Holt, Rinehart & Winston, 1983).

[132] Stanley Davis, *Future Perfect* (Reading, Massachusetts: Addison-Wesley Publishing Company, Inc., 1987).

[133] Ibid.

[134] Ibid.

[135] Ibid.

[136] Marilyn Ferguson, *The Aquarian Conspiracy: Personal and Social Transformation in the 1980s* (Los Angeles: Tarcher, 1980).

[137] Stanley Davis, *Future Perfect* (Reading, Massachusetts: Addison-Wesley Publishing Company, Inc., 1987).

[138] Ibid.

[139] The *Arts & Farces Review* is available from Arts & Farces Video & Information Services, 2285 Stewart Avenue, Suite 1315, St. Paul, MN 55116; (612) 698-0741.

[140] MicroFilm Compiler is available from Buck Wheat & Associates, 332 Sunderland Court, Lee's Summit, MO 64603; (816) 795-0074.

[141] Theodor Nelson, *Literary Machines,* elect. ed. (Bellevue, Washington: OWL International, Inc., 1987).

[142] Danny Goodman, *Danny Goodman's HyperCard Developer's Guide* (New York: Bantam Books, 1988).

[143] *HyperNews* is available from Training Resources Unlimited, 31849 Pacific Highway South, Suite 115L, Federal Way, WA 98003; (206) 874-6760.

[144] Jean-Louis Gassée, address at the announcement of Apple's AppleCD SC CD-ROM drive, Seattle, Washington, March 1, 1988.

[145] The product is entitled Xearch and boosts HyperCard's average search time to 2.0 seconds, using a Macintosh SE and an AppleCD SC. This speed differential

is more than 70 times faster than HyperCard's native search function. Xearch is available, as a licensable product, from Xiphias, 13464 Washington Blvd., Marina Del Rey, CA 90292; (213) 821-0074.

[146] Xearch and the other third-party search engines are listed in the Appendix section of this book.

[147] Theodor Nelson, *Computer Lib/Dream Machines,* rev. ed. (Redmond, Washington: Tempus Books of Microsoft Press, 1987).

[148] WORM is yet another of the acronyms that the computer phrase masters love so dearly. It stands for Write Once Read Many media platforms that now are beginning to become available.

[149] Magneto-optical storage systems are optical media systems capable of reading, writing, erasing, and rewriting, which is a significant breakthrough not expected in the general consumer market for several more years. On October 12, 1988, Canon announced both 256-MByte and 512-MByte versions of a magneto-optical drive that would be available to original equipment manufacturers by the end of 1988. Canon, at the same time, announced that the 256-MByte model would be the standard storage medium for the NeXT Computer System.

[150] These prices are current as I write this. Current maneuvers by the government, however, may result in drastic price increases in floppy-disk media; most analysts predict price increases in the near future of between 40 to 60 percent.

[151] Jerry Daniels and Mary Jane Mara are the designers/developers for Mac TV, Macintosh Bible: STAX! Edition, Sound Effects Studio, and STAX! Helper. All are HyperCard products available from STAX! Inc., 8008 Shoal Creek Blvd., Austin, TX 78758; (512) 467-4550.

[152] Jerry Daniels and Mary Jane Mara, *Applied HyperCard: Developing and Marketing Superior Stackware* (New York: Brady Books, 1988).

[153] Jerry Daniels, telephone conversation with author, August of 1988.

[154] Ibid.

[155] Ibid.

[156] QuickMail is available from CE Software, Inc., 1854 Fuller Road, P.O. Box 65580, West Des Moines, IA 50265; (515) 224-1995.

[157] The Telebit TrailBlazer Plus is available from Telebit Corporation, 1345 Shorebird Way, Mountain View, CA 94043; (415) 969-3800.

[158] Business Class is available from TENpointO, 3885 Bohannon Drive, Menlo Park, CA 94025; (415) 329-0800.

[159] The Hewlett-Packard Service Bay Diagnostic System, which consists of a customized computer system running the PC version of Guide coupled with a CD-ROM, will be used to service Ford vehicles throughout the world beginning in 1989.

[160] The Cornell Medical School has placed its entire second-year curriculum on a hypermedia system using Guide and Macintosh computers linked to a videodisc player.

[161] Students at the University of Mississippi's School of Veterinary Medicine have access to a hypermedia system implemented in Guide that allows them access to various levels of information.

[162] An entire subindustry has sprung up around HyperCard as a training tool for Macintosh software products. Implementations currently include accounting, computer-aided design, desktop publishing, and networking.

[163] For example, a major corporation currently publishes its 100-page sales reports using Guide and Macintoshes. Such a delivery mechanism allows individuals within the company to focus easily and quickly on the areas of expertise. Additionally, the United States Environmental Protection Agency is using Macintosh-based hypermedia to publish its very complex regulations for underground gasoline storage tanks.

SOCIAL IMPLICATIONS OF HYPERMEDIA

C H A P T E R 4

- *Data Navigation and Management*
- *Privacy and Free-Speech Issues and Implications*
- *Copyright and Intellectual Property Issues and Implications*
- *Ted Nelson's Bill of Information Rights*

Hypermedia is indeed an interesting development for computer users and offers a wealth of benefits that appear to be available to all. Hypermedia is not, however, a panacea. There are some inherent problems of a far-reaching nature that we must begin to address now.

It is interesting to note that with the introduction of any new technology—and make no mistake, hypermedia is definitely a new technology—it has taken an overly long time for the legal issues and societal impact to catch up with the actual introduction and subsequent availability of the technology. Hypermedia, to date, is no different, notwithstanding the efforts of many hypermedia pioneers to the contrary. In this chapter we will take a step-by-step look at the underlying issues relevant to potential access to an overwhelming amount of information.

Data Navigation and Management

Within five years, each of us will be inundated with virtual mountains of data. How will we sort through it; how will we navigate to specific information we need; how much will it cost us? Perhaps, more importantly, what new intellectual equipment will we need to possess, and are we properly preparing our children to develop an acuity in dealing with massive amounts of information?

Before we can address those specific concerns, we must address, briefly, the notion of inherent value of access to information via hypermedia running on various computer systems.

Computer experts generally make the argument *for* the computer stating that the computer is a neutral machine that can be used for either good or evil or that people who question the value of computers are nothing but Luddites. Or they find it hard to believe that the machine they are constantly patching and debugging could be perceived as a threat to anyone.

It is time for all electronic publishers, information providers, and hypermedia developers to realize that what we are really doing is selling drugs. Jerry Garcia claimed that computers were the new drugs, and Jerry Daniels points out the good biochemicals we experience when we work with the Macintosh. They are right. We are pushers, not publishers, and we have a responsibility. In fact, we have a series of responsibilities.

Consider the grandly connected, intricately interwoven hypermedia system that is Xanadu—and the electronic community surrounding it and other information utilities—as a nervous system with all the dendrites and synapses that go along with it. Consider the information that travels the electronic byways of the system as chemical agents causing a *reaction.* It is not the hardware that Garcia considers a new drug. It is not the software that Daniels sees as good biochemicals. It is the *information,* the *flow* of that information, and the *interface* in which the information is presented that produces the reaction.

This is at least partially why people play with Macintosh and work with IBM. Our anal-retentive society cannot grasp the notion that something that is as fun as Macintosh can be work. This is where Apple Computer, Inc.'s concern about "personal productivity" comes from. It might even be where Apple's constant attempt to sell computers to big business comes from.

So the providers of these chemical agents have a series of responsibilities, not the least of which is to have fun. Other responsibilities include integrity and impeccability. Impeccability is impossible. Integrity is imperative. One out of two is not bad.

Advertising, for instance, has an adverse effect on integrity, in this case integrity of the information. Advertising is misleading, ineffective, not cost effective, and intrusive. In an electronic medium, such as hypermedia, these negatives are exacerbated.

Advertising industry analysts estimate that each of us is exposed to about 3,000 advertisements each day. They also maintain that the more ads people see, the more ads they tune out. The vast majority of these advertisements are deceptive and misleading.

A recent study conducted by the Ogilvy & Mather advertising agency showed that 72 percent of the United States public feels that advertising insults their intelligence. Another study by the R. H. Brushkin Associates research firm showed that almost half of the United States public feels that advertising produces "very little useful information." But the ads keep coming. In 1986, $94.7 billion was spent on advertising by United States advertisers.

Yet another study, conducted by the Opinion Research Corporation for the Harvard Business School in 1967, found that 53 percent of Americans disagree that most advertisements present a true picture of the product advertised.

Discerning customers have an ingrained bias against claims made in advertisements. They assume claims made in advertisements are false. Regis McKenna, no marketing slouch by anyone's standards, bears this out in *The Regis Touch:* "Increasingly, people are skeptical of what they read or see in advertisements. I often tell clients that advertising has a built-in 'discount factor.' People are deluged with promotional information, and they are beginning to distrust it. People are more likely to make decisions based on what they hear directly from other people—friends, experts, or even salespeople. . . ."[164]

Advertising people maintain that if you can measure the benefits of advertising on your business, advertising works. They further maintain that if you cannot measure the benefits of advertising, it is because your measurements are not good enough and the only sure solution is to continue advertising.

Dr. Julian L. Simon of the University of Illinois conducted in-depth research on the effectiveness of advertising in 1970 and concluded, "There is not one single piece of strong evidence to support the general belief that increasing returns exist in advertising... there are a great many studies that show diminishing marginal returns...."

Advertising carries a highly inflated self-image. Along with that inflated self-image comes a high price tag. The fact is that for a business that thrives on repeat customers—hypermedia, by definition, requires repeat customers—advertising is simply not cost-effective because you generally reach the same audience over and over again.

While bankers expect to see advertising costs as part of a business proposal, this is mostly because of the advertising community's misrepresentation of things such as "your ad didn't work because it wasn't good enough, make a better ad," and "the effects of advertising are cumulative, keep trying."

Aside from simply not being cost-effective, advertising is ineffective mostly because it does not generate customer loyalty. In order to survive, a business requires customers, not consumers. Ads generate consumer interest, but customers—real customers—will not be swayed one way or the other by even the flashiest advertisement. The sales that are generated as a result of advertisements generally pay for the ads themselves, thus creating a vicious cycle: You have to run more ads to generate more sales to pay for the last batch of ads.

Advertising is not the be-all and end-all to making a customer base aware of a product or service. The best vehicle available, and most appropriate in the promotion of public hypermedia systems, is word of mouth. This works quite simply. Provide a quality product or service and your clients will tell folks they know about you and what you do. The key word here, however, is quality. Most of the people who bad-mouth word of mouth offer, at best, mediocre products or services.

Publicly accessible hypermedia systems can be introduced to potential customers via the computer industry infrastructure without advertising. I propose that the publicly accessible hypermedia systems be kept free of advertising. As an alternative ancillary income generator, I have no problem with the services providing listing opportunities in lieu of advertising space. Listings, placed where people are accustomed to finding them, can be very effective. Because people are generally looking for the information contained in a listing, they are not intrusive. Advertising, which has become a mainstay of popular culture, is generally intrusive and unwelcome. Advertising, more than any other single phenomenon, has degenerated television to the state it currently occupies. Hypermedia, like television before it, has incredible potential. It need not be sullied with zero-information content advertisements.

What Good Are Computers and Why Should We Want Them?

Everyone can tell a horror story about the "computer." An electronic funds transfer did not arrive on time because the "computer" went down. An automated teller machine failed to credit an after-hours deposit because the "computer" glitched. A credit-card purchase is denied because the "computer" failed to update the purchaser's payment last month. Everyone has a story; here is mine: Twice during the preparation of this manuscript I had a hard-drive crash, resulting in several weeks' work being lost on both occasions. It seems like this happens to me at least once during every major project. It has occurred so regularly that I have considered factoring it into my scheduling: Let's see, I can complete that piece in three weeks; ordinarily, it would take two, but let's factor in a minor hard-drive crash to be on the safe side.

So what good are these computers, anyway, and why in the world should we want to entrust our most valuable information to them? Moreover, aren't there inherent dangers in an information repository as vast as something like Xanadu—what about all the bad things we hear about Big Brother and his even bigger computer? Why should we choose to create even more connections between information bases? Good questions, so let's start with looking at why, perhaps, we should not use computers.

More than 150 million individual credit records are contained in computers belonging to the five largest credit-reporting companies in this country. In the mid-1970s it was discovered that one of the largest credit-reporting companies had access to the patient personal records of 90 percent of the nation's hospitals. More than 250,000 times each day, business subscribers of these credit-reporting companies make inquiries as to the credit-worthiness of customers and receive responses within three seconds. Every year, more than 350,000 formal complaints are registered with the single-largest credit-reporting company concerning the accuracy of the credit records held in its computer data bases. Each year, more than 100,000 of these complaints result in the information being changed.

David Burnham, in his landmark *The Rise of the Computer State,* quotes Kent Greenwalt, a professor at Columbia University's Law School, about the effect of such vast amounts of information in the hands of a few: "If there is increased surveillance and disclosure and it is not offset by greater tolerance, the casualties of modern society are likely to increase as fewer misfits and past wrongdoers are able to find jobs and fruitful associations. The knowledge that one cannot discard one's past, that advancement in society depends heavily on a good record, will create considerable pressure for conformist actions. Many people will try harder than they do now to keep their records clean, avoid controversial or 'deviant' actions, whatever their private views and inclinations. Diversity and social vitality is almost certain to suffer, and in the long run independent private thoughts will be reduced."[165]

Shuddering reality, that. As we attempt to connect computers to provide very real benefits to the society at large, we also are providing kindling and a strong draft to the already raging wildfire of what has amounted to nothing less than computer surveillance.

The Mass Merchandising of Information

We have been hearing about the "information bomb [that] is exploding in our midst"[166] now for the better part of a decade. Alvin Toffler, John Naisbitt, and others have been warning us of the impending information explosion that we must steel ourselves against. Invariably, the solution lies in the anthropomorphizing of computers and the mass merchandising of information according to those who would point the way.

California State University history professor, Theodore Roszak, minces few words to describe these would-be futurologists and their musings: "an ungainly hybrid of potted social science, Sunday supplement journalism, and soothsaying . . . pitched at about the intellectual level of advertising copy."[167]

The ill-conceived notion of the mass production of information is traced back to one of these soothsayers, John Naisbitt, in his immensely popular *Megatrends.* One of Naisbitt's central megatrend themes, possibly the *only* one if the material is closely examined, is that we have moved from an industrial society to an information society. Naisbitt's view of the information society is very different from Stanley Davis's concept of an information-based economy of intangibles covered previously. Naisbitt holds that "we now mass-produce information the way we used to mass-produce cars. In the information society, we have systematized the production of knowledge and amplified our brain power. To use an industrial metaphor, we now mass-produce knowledge and this knowledge is the driving force of our economy."[168]

Here Naisbitt has clearly jumped from the Sunday supplement into the realm of intentional obfuscation. While we have, without doubt, begun the process of mass merchandising information, in no way can the leap be made from information to knowledge. Again, according to Roszak, "Information, even when it moves at the speed of light, is no more than it has ever been: discrete little bundles of fact, sometimes useful, sometimes trivial, and never the substance of thought."[169]

Clear, clean distinctions are to be made between the notion of information and knowledge, that Naisbitt would apparently deny. According to Roszak, we have always judged the value of knowledge on three factors: depth, originality, and excellence. With the inflated valuation of information comes a blatant, if unconscious, attempt to blur the distinction between what constitutes knowledge and what is merely information. Little, if any, substance lies behind this intellectual equivalent of junk food, although Roszak attentively points out that this has not fallen completely on deaf ears.

Theodore Roszak points out that the pop futurology that is currently so popular is seen as a panacea by the political New Right, citing Georgia Congressman Newt Gingrich's now apparently defunct Conservative Opportunity Society.[170] Insisting that growth is the only way to ensure economic survival in this country, the Conservative Opportunists assure us that huge tax concessions to high-tech industries are sure to help us avoid the pitfall of the "antitechnological bias of the Left [which] overshadowed the possibilities of the computer age."[171] Gingrich's book carries such notary endorsements as Ronald Reagan, Jack Kemp, and Alvin Toffler.

Perhaps even more disturbing than the New Right's infatuation with cancerous economic growth and voodoo bookkeeping is the nature of the base of technological development in this country. Since World War II, and the very seed of hypermedia, technological development in America has been funded and fueled by the defense industry—what Roszak refers to as the "militarization of our economy." Roszak specifies that "the nation's two most important computer development investments are also funded and controlled from military sources. Most importantly these include the Defense Department's Information Processing Techniques Office and the recently formed twelve-company consortium, the Microelectronics and Computer Technology Corporation at Austin, Texas, which was launched under the chairmanship of a member of the National Security Council and CIA."[172]

This shows no sign of abating and is of grave concern to many within the computer industry itself, those in other industries, and within the general population. The numbers of the concerned in this area appear to be growing at a small but steady rate.

The economic impact of high-technology advancements, according to many, also tends to exacerbate the growing chasm in society between the haves and have-nots. As we quickly approach the danger of becoming a two-tiered society, high-technology enterprises in general, and the computer industry specifically, show no overt signs of attempting anything to check the slide. Everett Rogers and Judith Larsen, in *Silicon Valley Fever: Growth of High Technology Culture,* are quite indicting as they point out that "Silicon valley means low-wage, deadend jobs, unskilled, tedious work, and exposure to some of the most dangerous occupational health hazards in all of American industry. It is a dark side to the sparkling laboratories that neither barbecues, balloons, nor paid sabbaticals can hide."[173]

Information depends on knowledge, not vice versa. Many in the computer industry, however, would have us believe that they are on the verge of creating intelligence in their machines. At any given time for the past decade we have been told that artificial intelligence—and, specifically, a thinking machine capable of more and better thought than humans—was five years in coming, and, at most, a decade. This is illustrated by an ongoing process of what Roszak refers to as the "anthropomorphizing of the computer as a surrogate human intelligence."

As a culture we have accepted and even adopted this anthropomorphizing with little tension. Many Macintosh users have named their computers and spend an inordinate amount of time with their electronic friends. We have personalized our electronic workspaces with customized background screens and specialized beeps for various system functions. We speak of interfacing with our associates and we solicit feedback from them. Most likely, this started when we began to refer to the computer as having a memory.

The anthropomorphism of the computer seems to have peaked with Apple chief executive John Sculley's much-publicized notion of the Knowledge Navigator. Sculley's vision focuses on the computer as an electronic buddy with very human traits that carries out our bidding for us. There seems to be a glimmer of hope within the general computer community, however: In the early winter of 1988, the Society of Computer Professionals for Social Responsibility called Sculley to task for his attempts at promoting the anthropomorphism of the computer.

Some computer enthusiasts find it hard to bear in mind that a computer is little more than a series of electronic switches that open and close at lightning-fast speeds. Many begin to speak in terms of computers that are capable of more advanced thinking than humans. Many of the artificial-intelligence researchers posit that computers are potentially more capable of thought than humans are because computer memory is much less fallible than human memory. Indeed, computer memory exists as distinct pieces that, barring system crash or media failure, are subject to total recall. Human memory, on the other hand, is fuzzy, and what Roszak referred to as "the invisible psychic adhesive that holds our identity together from moment to moment . . . it is fluid rather than granular, more like a wave than a particle. Like a wave, it spreads through the mind, puddling up here and there in odd personal associations that may be of the most inexplicable kind."[174]

Stanford University professor Avron Barr, for example, tells us that "the human mind not only is limited in its storage and processing capacity, but it also has known bugs; it is easily misled, stubborn, and even blind to the truth. . . . Intelligent systems, built for computer and communications technology, will someday know more than any individual human being about what is going on in complex enterprises involving millions of people."[175]

Views such as Barr's are based on the notion that humans are obsolete, reducing the idea of thinking to simple information processing. If, indeed, thought and knowledge are nothing more than information processing, then indeed, computers are better suited for the task and we all may just as well go into hibernation. I have yet to see, however, any evidence that any computer is capable of anything more than advanced information processing and inference. Information processing and inference do not knowledge make, so maybe there is hope for us yet. The fact is that we think with ideas, not with information, and ideas are created by other ideas not by facts, data, or other information.

Men are creative beings by virtue of their ideas, and the computer is nothing more than just another one of man's ideas. Roszak addresses this point adroitly by pointing to the human mind's capacity for self-transcendence. "The mind, unlike any computer anyone has even imagined building, is gifted with the power of irrepressible self-transcendence. It is the greatest of all escape artists, constantly eluding its own efforts at self-comprehension. It can form ideas about its own ideas, including its ideas about itself. But having done that, it has already occupied new ground; in its next effort to understand its own nature, it will have to reach out still further. This makes it impossible to invent a machine that will be the mind's equal, let alone its successor. The computer can only be one more idea in the imagination of its creator."[176]

While the computer only can be just another idea of its creator, its meta-tool nature—the quality computers possess of being tools used to create other tools—is what fascinates and absorbs the initiated. This phenomenon especially is apparent in the Macintosh community as the tool itself—as well as the tools it is used to create—become regenerative in nature and build on previous iterations. This, too, should come as no surprise, for this is the "difference that makes a difference" in the realm of hypermedia: that which transforms from simple information to rich knowledge.

The Politics of Information

Information theory, as a science—OK, as a pseudo-science—dates back to the late 1940s, when Claude Shannon founded it while working at Bell Labs. In those days, information was seen as almost physical. According to Shannon, paraphrased in the McGraw-Hill *Encyclopedia of Electronics and Computers,* "The information contained in a message unit was defined in terms of the average number of digits required to encode it."

In other words, information was the signal part of the signal-to-noise ratio. Aren't we glad we know better now. . . .

In 1979, Gregory Bateson finally came up with a more comfortable—and accurate—definition of information: "Any difference which makes a difference." Data, the "news of a difference" according to Bateson, is not information until it means something—"makes a difference."

Subjectivity entered the equation.

At first blush, information seems to be void of political volatility, and most certainly, if we take Claude Shannon's view. Following Bateson's more enlightened approach, however, a preconscious gnawing begins. "Weeeellll, everything's political," we assure ourselves, sidestepping the issue.

In the old days, the days when our society and its economy were product-based, wealth was created by the creation and distribution of tangible products, which was quite simple, actually. If you created a product and sold it to me, I had it and you did not. We are in the midst of a severe paradigm shift that is so far-reaching and is occurring on such a huge scale that most of us do not even experience it; the only apt analogy would be the speed at which the earth itself revolves and circumnavigates the sun. Things are not so clear any more. As we shift from an economy based on tangibles to one based on information, the notion of product distribution becomes murky indeed.

The comfort we place in our notion of the "old days" generally is misplaced, and in the case of information is severely misplaced. Problems of the politics of information were just as rampant then.

In the early 19th century, the English Utilitarians managed to completely reform the Old Poor Law almost solely through the politicization of information. While today we take the gathering of information by governments as a given, in the "old days" things were different. The English Utilitarians were among the first to put to use the notion that the control of facts or, more appropriately, the *perceived* control of facts breeds power, which is a very political notion, indeed.

The English Utilitarians—precursors to the modern political action committee and think tank—headed by Jeremy Bentham, brought about this change by amassing immense amounts of statistical information in the Victorian Blue Books. With the Blue Books as a basis, the Utilitarians claimed that the Poor Law[177] was inefficient in the extreme and that it should be replaced with a more efficient and less-expensive system, the one proposed by the Utilitarians. The Utilitarian solution was the severe workhouse system that was adequately documented by Charles Dickens. The new system was based on the broad-brush assumption that poverty was equated with parasitism and that punishment was the only cure. Interestingly, these same Victorian Blue Books formed the foundation for Karl Marx's indictment of capitalism.

The only thing about the politicization of information that has changed since 19th-century England is that we are now better at producing it. Now we have think tanks and various policy study centers that purport to be pondering reams of information to arrive at appropriate policy decisions. In effect what really is happening is that these groups are arriving at appropriate information to support their concept of appropriate policy.

Ithiel de Sola Pool, in his *Technologies of Freedom: On Free Speech in an Electronic Age,*[178] points out that political forms shape communication forms. He points out the fact that until the mid-1960s, the Soviets received radio transmissions over hard-wired speakers. In 1964, the total number of regular receivers finally outnumbered the wired speakers. The inherent political quality in the nature of information simply cannot be denied.

According to Theodore Roszak, "It is not the facts that determine policy, but more often policy that determines the facts—by selection, adjustment, distortion."[179] In many cultures, censorship is a way of stifling the flow of information to individuals. Most fair-thinking people regard this as inexcusable, yet the censorship issue continues to boil. In our own culture, however, we suffer from the opposite: *too much information.*

On the surface, this phenomenon seems to lack any redeeming merit of mention as a problem. On deeper inspection, however, it is a problem just as real and just as threatening as overt censorship. According to Roszak, ". . . in our society, the strategy of government is not to censor but to counter fact with fact, number with number, research with research. It even becomes advantageous to have lots of contention about facts and figures, a statistical blizzard that numbs the attention."[180]

Even John Naisbitt's Pollyannaesque vision bodes ill: "We have for the first time an economy based on a key resource that is not only renewable but self-generating. Running out of it is not a problem, but drowning in it is. Data is now doubling every twenty months."[181]

One of hypermedia's greatest promises is to bring a sense of supple structure to the information glut. The difference that makes a difference in hypermedia is the addition of intelligence in the interlinking structure and a level of refinement to the raw, unprocessed information. Moreover, networked hypermedia systems foreshadow the likelihood of the individual being able to maintain a footing on the same level as that of our spookish government.

David Burnham appropriately pointed out that personal computers would never be able to match the computing power at the disposal of the United States government, and that we were condemned to being subject to electronic surveillance of the most intrusive kind. Burnham pointed out that our government wields a tremendous amount of power because of the projection powers of its collective computing iron. "With the computer, organizations can analyze information about the activities, opinions, and social characteristics of individuals in ways that allow them to anticipate the future actions, desires, and fears of the groups of people with whom these individuals associate."[182] "The ability [to amass and analyze vast amounts of information] may be used to allow the people in control to say only what they already have determined their listeners want to hear," continues Burnham. "The ability also may be used to develop a series of different, but not necessarily inconsistent, statements about a problem that raise complicated ethical questions about the nature of truth. The ability, in short, can be used for cynically manipulative purposes that tend to undermine the democratic process," he concluded.[183]

Burnham goes on to point out that no matter what level of power personal computers may reach, the government's computers always will be more powerful. "Because this particular application of the computer requires a large amount of sophisticated expertise and equipment, it usually is available only to the richest and most powerful institutions of our society. The isolated citizen sitting in front of his personal computer cannot be a player in this very special league."[184] And he is certainly correct, so far as he goes.

One of the most encouraging breakthroughs of late in the field of computers is that of parallel processing.[185] Briefly, parallel processing involves the coupling of large numbers of processors, each of which are assigned a specific and singular task to perform. The idea is that parallel processing allows several things to happen simultaneously, more closely emulating the way the human brain works, and significantly speeding up the computing process. As networked hypermedia systems come on-line, a sort of parallel-processing environment is set up by default.

For example, consider the impact of an announcement made in late 1988 by Dow Jones Information Services that it had developed a new on-line information search-and-retrieval engine called the Connection Machine that enabled on-line searches to be conducted using Englishlike command queries. Scheduled to be available on-line by the end of 1989, subscribers to the Dow Jones News Retrieval Service will be able to perform text retrieval using English queries to search various publications, including *The Wall Street Journal, Fortune, Forbes,* and *The Washington Post.*

Dow Jones' Connection Machine is a text search-and-retrieval engine designed specifically to allow users to communicate their queries in English rather than the archaic search commands in use on other systems. Combined with the English-language query interface, the Connection Machine relies on the Thinking Machines' parallel-processing computers as the "back end" of the system. The Connection Machine employs a Macintosh II as the front end and allows the user access to the computing power of 32,000 small processors. "The paradigm of the Connection Machine," according to Robert Millstein of Thinking Machines, "is the notion that you have a processor for every data element of a problem you are working on."

Subscribers will be able to query the system with an English question, such as, "What is the extent of the involvement between Steve Jobs' NeXT, Inc. and IBM and what are the implications for Apple Computer, Inc.?" and receive an abstracted and annotated bibliography in a matter of seconds. If a search yields too broad an answer, the scope of the question can be narrowed, interactively, using a "relevance feedback" feature that researches the compiled articles based on a relevance algorithm.

The front end for the Connection Machine consists of a Macintosh II and the query program written in LISP. Analysts and principals both hasten to point out that while the system is a great step forward in easing the use of on-line search-and-retrieval engines, the Connection Machine is not artificially intelligent. The addition of artificial intelligence to the formula will likely be the next breakthrough in the technology although it still is more than a few years in coming.

The importance of the Connection Machine lies in its wresting of the control of access to information from the information brokers and placing it in the hands of individuals. In fact, William Dunn, executive vice president of Dow Jones Information Services, states the control of access as a central impetus for the project. Dunn goes so far as to describe an addition to the Dow Jones News Retrieval Service that will provide an ongoing stream of data to corporations and universities through a permanent 9,600-baud connection to the service.

While the Connection Machine is a far cry from systems such as Ted Nelson's envisioned Xanadu—where a user would have potential access to all the information in existence on a given subject—it is certainly a big step forward from what we have now.

Presently, the state of the art in information retrieval is the black art of complex Boolean logic, which is not very accessible to untrained humans. This places the information lords at a significant advantage in the access to information. This disparity of access to information has been one of the barriers Apple has continually pledged to shatter, and it looks to me like the Connection Machine offers a pretty hefty chunk of hand-sized barrier-shatterer.

Which is why it is hard to understand why Dow Jones has not been able to elicit even a modicum of cooperation, interest, or support from Apple.

Chalk it up to another instance of Apple's inbred good-old-boy network. Like the old-timers in the South used to say, "That boy's got some good ideas, but he ain't from 'round here." Translation for the rest of us: The Connection Machine does not have a multicolored Apple logo on it, and our friends in Cupertino do not pack quite enough wallop to "acquire" Dow Jones.

While nothing can compete on a processor-to-processor basis with the supercomputers available to the United States government, developments such as the Connection Machine provide a glimmer of hope for the individual casting about in the sea of information.

The Economy of Information

Interestingly, or perhaps not, one of the main factors absent from the Dow Jones announcement of the Connection Machine parallel-processing information-retrieval engine was any mention of the price. Naisbitt told us in *Megatrends* that "the new power is not money in the hands of the few, but information in the hands of the many."[186] It would have been more accurate if he had rephrased the last clause to reflect the availability of information in the hands of anyone who can afford it.

Most telecommunications networks levy connect-time charges in single-minute increments. The charges range from a low of about $5 per hour to well over $100 per hour of connect time. This obviously takes the access to information out of the hands of "the many" and places it firmly in the control of "the few." According to Roszak, "There is obviously a significant political public for whom the connect-time charges, let alone the price of the basic equipment, would be prohibitive. Networking may for some time to come remain a strictly middle-class medium."[187]

As an example, consider my own electronic publication, *The Arts & Farces Review.* For two years, the publication was distributed as a shareware product. Subscribers purchased a tangible product from me (a floppy disk containing information) that I delivered to them. In a product-based economy, I would have depleted my inventory by distributing the disks. But the nature of electronic publishing is that I still had the product after it was distributed. In fact, as a collective corpus, it was worth more to me than it was to the subscriber.

Stewart Brand, in *The Media Lab,* addresses this paradox in a unique way. "Information wants to be free because it has become so cheap to distribute, copy, and recombine—too cheap to meter. It wants to be expensive because it can be immeasurably valuable to the recipient. That tension will not go away."[188]

As an example, Brand cites the Lexis search-and-retrieval system for lawyers. The information contained in the Lexis data base—in the form of judicial decisions—are in the public domain. "Multimillion-dollar Lexis succeeds by charging handsomely for them," says Brand, "by owning copyright on the *page breaks.*"[189]

Ithiel de Sola Pool, in his 1983 *Technologies of Freedom: On Free Speech in an Electronic Age,* takes the point of copyright one step further by declaring, "The recognition of copyright and the paying of royalties emerged from the printing press. With the arrival of electronic reproduction, these practices became unworkable. Electronic publishing is analogous not so much to the print shop of the eighteenth century as to word-of-mouth communication, to which copyright was never applied."[190]

Brand states emphatically what I and other electronic publishers have experienced firsthand: People are reluctant to pay for quality information. According to Brand, this is because the "valuing is retroactive." He points out, however, that people will "pay for quality of *source,* because the constancy (reliability) of source makes value somewhat predictable."[191]

My own experience is that people will not necessarily pay for the reliability, either. For two years, The *Arts & Farces Review* maintained a rigid publication cycle, never being so much as a day late with delivery. People were reading the publication on a regular basis, but simply refused to pay for it when it was available as a shareware product, perhaps because they felt they already had paid for it through their connect-time charges on the telecommunications services. Whatever the reasons, I find that Brand is correct as far as the *distribution* end of the information food chain goes, but he's dead wrong about the *production* end.

In the United States, we have an abundance of communications media open to us. We have had our collective bouts with the gatekeepers and the ticket-takers of the information byways, but for the most part, we have had pretty easy sailing.

The government continues, for example, to insist that the radio frequencies be controlled because of a perceived scarcity. Stewart Brand offers a telling perspective on this misperception: "In Washington, D.C., there are twenty-three radio stations (licensed and regulated), eleven television stations (licensed and regulated) . . . and two daily newspapers, both of them fully protected by the First Amendment. Which is the scarce medium?"[192]

And then there was the time in 1986 when President Reagan decided that a lot of publicly available information living in electronic data bases should be reclassified as "sensitive" and that access should be restricted.

But mostly we have had pretty easy sailing.

The underlying current in all of this is rather obvious, which is probably why it is not generally perceived. The right of access to information is becoming very much of a political issue, and it is not an issue, as some of the politicos just to the right of John Birch would have us believe, of only economics.

Albert Bressand, a French economist Brand cites, says that a world of information shock is coming and will crest in the 1990s. This will be similar, according to Bressand, to the oil shock of the 1970s and the world banking shock of the 1980s. This will happen—everywhere, all at once—"when the information providers decide to revalue what they produce."[193]

Closely tied with the economic issues encompassing the access to information is the "lowest common denominator" factor. Cable television was supposed to deliver us all from the wasteland of broadcast television by providing a broader spectrum of available programming. What we got instead, with a few notable exceptions, was a steady stream of pablum in the form of broadcast "success" clones. Information services, as well, cater to the lowest common denominator, that point at which there is not so much the most interest as the least friction. This also speaks to the politics of information, as does the economics of information, and we are confronted with the image of a snake eating its tail.

Privacy and Free-Speech Issues and Implications

As networked hypermedia systems begin to come on-line, privacy issues will become of greater concern. In a networked situation, each user will leave telltale "crumb trails," leading into and out of the documents he or she has accessed. New trails will be forged that connect seemingly disparate bodies of information. Who will have access to this trail information? What limits will be placed on its use? What about data security?

One of the promises hypermedia front ends for vast data spaces dangle in front of our noses like a carrot in front of a donkey is the empowering of individuals to design their own search-and-retrieval interfaces. By extension, those hypermedia front ends will enable us to search vast stores of off-site information accessible via systems such as Xanadu.

When 1984 passed with relatively minor whimpers of Big Brotherishness from the fringes of the community-at-large, most felt that issues of governmental invasion of privacy and covert surveillance on the American citizenry were a thing of the past. Most of us filed those paranoic years of the 1960s and early 1970s away in a dusty corner of our gray matter and were thankful to have made it through.

Time to dust off those memories because the current generation of Uncle Edgar's boys are at it again. The FBI has, for at least the past few years, taken to recruiting librarians as junior G-men to keep an eye on "suspicious activity" on the part of the library patrons, specifically, those who use the photocopiers and speak with foreign accents. The FBI, under its Library Awareness Program, insists that crucial national secrets are leaking out of the country and into the hands of The Enemy. The FBI, while offering no substantiation of these claims, says that the program is successful and will be continued.

When pressed, the FBI representatives point to the arrest of a Soviet United Nations employee several years ago for receiving classified information from a foreign exchange student who had been hired to photocopy material from libraries. Most librarians are quick to point out, however, that classified material is not available at any public library they know of, and that the FBI's Library Awareness Program amounts to nothing more than invasion of privacy and First Amendment infringement.

According to Judith Krug, head of the American Library Association (ALA)'s Office for Intellectual Freedom, the FBI has solicited help from at least 14 libraries during 1987 and the first half of 1988, and the ALA has been fighting the issue ever since Columbia University was first visited in 1987 and refused to cooperate. In most states, library records are confidential, although the FBI does not seem to give this fact much regard.

In 1986, the FBI teamed up with the CIA and the Air Force to coerce Mead Corporation into restricting access to its Mead Data Central that publishes the Nexis on-line data base of technical publications. Mead refused, taking the position that all of the Nexis information had been previously published. The government's position, according to Jerry Yung, Mead's vice president of government relations, was that although the material had been previously published and available publicly, "once aggregated with powerful computer software, it could be used against national interests."[194]

While Mead refused the government requests to restrict access to the Nexis data base, the data base that most likely set off the red flag, The National Technical Information Service, was dropped "for business reasons" later that year.

As the information services become more and more interlinked, as will doubtlessly happen since Judge Green's decision finding that the Baby Bells can provide information gateways, the level of data integration available to the average telecommunicator will begin to grow in a geometric fashion. With that will come more and more government irritability, anxiety, and concern. When that access to information is paired with advanced hypermedia engines that are capable of semiautomatic and semi-intelligent information links, the Information Age finally will be under way and the individual suddenly will be capable of performing extremely complex cross-reference searches.

Access to this information is a right not a privilege, as the government would have us believe. What we read and what on-line data bases we search are our own concerns, no one else's. This right must not be compromised in any way and must be defended at any cost.

Similarly, electronic communications are not given the same protection as first class mail is. We continue to suppose that we have freedoms and rights that simply do not exist. Wiretapping, for example, in the past had to be physically carried out. A spook had to be near the person under surveillance to listen in or at least a tape recorder had to be in the immediate vicinity. My friends who helped design the telephone companies' Electronic Switching System (ESS) tell me that this is no longer the case. Now your conversations can be easily eavesdropped on simply by sending the proper signal tones down the telephone wire—from anywhere.

If you think your computer communications are safe from eavesdropping, you are also in for a surprise. All computers, except for those specially modified for use by the—yes, you guessed it—for use by the spooks, emit radio frequency waves that can be quite easily intercepted.

Data encryption is the answer you say? Consider that the United States government's approved encryption standard, Data Encryption Standard (DES), has been shown by researchers as defeatable by the National Security Agency (NSA—spooks to you and me). "The DES system stands impeached. Researchers on both coasts have accused this method of being easily breakable by the National Security Agency, the government's decoding arm; many believe it a fraud perpetrated by the U.S. government to make all 'encoded' transmissions readable by intelligence agencies."[195]

Adding fuel to the paranoia fire, Ted Nelson informs us that a better system was developed at Massachussetts Institute of Technology (MIT) that was subsequently suppressed by the United States government. "Another system of codes has been proposed that supposedly can't be broken by any extant computer in less than millions of years. This is the RSA code, originally proposed by Hellman and Diffie of Stanford, and developed by Rivest, Shamir, and Adelman of MIT. It has several remarkable properties, among them being the ability to exchange unbreakable messages between strangers who have not had a chance to swap code keys; the ability to cosign electronic documents that anyone can read and know you signed; and more. And the U.S. government tried to suppress it."[196]

As if that were not enough, it gets even worse. There is no traditional way of demonstrating the authenticity of an electronic document. There are no typographic elements or watermarks as with paper publishing. Electronic characters are indistinguishable from their counterparts. "But the right sort of encoding—what is called an authentication code—may help us know when documents have been fraudulently replaced. Authentication codes, too, the government is trying to suppress. When you're looking at what purports to be the Mona Lisa on your screen fifty years from now, and she has a mustache, don't say I didn't warn you."[197]

Ted Nelson, in the electronically published hypermedia tome, *Literary Machines,* said it best: "On-line text systems may or may not become universal or replace much of paper publishing. Whichever view you take, the questions are what they are to be like; what things are to be available, and to whom, and under what circumstances; and who may put things in, and who is responsible for their contents, and who may censor them, and who may protest the contents, and what gets thrown away on whose decision; and what is to be their relation to the archiving of our heritage, and how accessible they are to be, and how reliably and accessibly the personal, national, and human heritages are to be preserved. For rolled into such designs and prospects is the whole future of humanity, and, indeed, the future of the past and the future of the future—meaning the kinds of future that become forbidden, or possible."[198]

Do not mistake Nelson's comments as an overstatement. To date, relatively little has been done to address any sort of bill of information rights. Senator Robert Packwood (D-Ore.) sponsored legislation in 1987 to formulate such a bill of rights, but little has been done since. Ted Nelson has perhaps been the most outspoken on the issue, and his proposed Bill of Information Rights is reprinted later in this chapter.

One of Apple Computer's marketing catchphrases for HyperCard is "The Freedom to Associate." This freedom to associate has proved to be a boon to the sudden increased interest in hypermedia systems. It also has brought us heads up against the very concept of freedom of speech. Abbie Hoffman learned the hard way that one cannot cry Fire! in a crowded theater—that there are, in fact, limits to any freedom. Personal freedom in a society is afforded its members only to the extent that it does not interfere with the freedom of others.

These electronic freedoms will be a battleground of the near future. We already have seen how the Reagan administration attempted to block access to information. These are rights that we will have to fight for, as Ted Nelson urges us to think fast. "These problems are real and present, and have been here waiting for us all along. Far on the horizon as they may now appear, soon they will be on us like a tornado. The way to approach these issues, I believe, is not sit in a corner and tremble, like a rabbit in a tiger cage hoping it won't be eaten, but to run between the legs of the beast before it fully wakes up."[199]

Copyright and Intellectual Property Issues and Implications

As hypermedia authors begin to publish their materials, and as others form links to existing materials, our established notions of copyright become burdensome and ineffective. Tied to the issue of copyright, intellectual property issues also must be addressed. This is new territory, and hypermedia authors must inform themselves and actively participate in determining the new rules of the game.

Hypermedia very soon will become a viable alternative for some forms of paper publishing. Surely problems involved with the publishing logistics will crop up and will have to be addressed. Furthermore, differentiations must be formed between public and private publishing.

As mentioned previously, I have been actively engaged in electronic publishing for the past two years, publishing an electronic magazine, *The Arts & Farces Review.*[200] During the 1987 MacWorld Exposition in Boston, the expo at which HyperCard was announced, I attempted an experiment in providing information to my subscribers in the most timely manner possible. At that time the *Review* was distributed via the traditional shareware channels (it has since been removed from shareware distribution and is available only on a subscription basis). The MacWorld/Boston Expo of 1987 was shaping up to the fulcrum point of the widespread use of Macintosh computers and many innovative products were scheduled for release. I felt it was the most appropriate time to test the waters for the distribution of encrypted material via publicly accessible telecommunications networks, specifically General Electric Information Service's GEnie and CompuServe's Micronetted Apple Users Group (MAUG).

I produced four special editions of the publication each of the four days of the exposition and uploaded them in an encrypted format that locked out illegitimate users who did not possess the password to unlock the material. The files were encrypted using Harry Chesley's PackIt III utility and the encryption key was sent, well in advance, to all subscribers. The encrypted files were produced partially in an attempt to say "thanks" to those who were honorable enough to pay for the material.

The response was as surprising as it was disturbing. One negative comment was received via the GEnie network, "I firmly object to you and your so-called company using GEnie as a place to post your useless encrypted garbage text files. . . ."[201]

The response on CompuServe, while more literate, was just as intense:

"It seems to me that if some company wants to pass on material to their paid subscribers, they should open their own SIG."

"Encrypted [entries] seem to violate the 'Forum' philosophy."

"I'm not sure why I'm bothered by the idea of encrypted files in the MAUG data libraries, except that it seems to go against a lot of the feel of the forum. . . ."

"Shareware that's not accessible unless you've paid to get the key to read it is no longer shareware."

"I'm not sure why, but it seems categorically different from the material, say, that a hard disk maker releases. Granted, the hard disk material will only work with one brand of disk, but at least it is open to everyone. If this is really a 'commercial' product with limited release, I am surprised to see it in the [download areas]."

"I am disturbed by the recent appearance of encrypted files in the MAUG data base. I believe that all files should be available to everyone on an equal basis."

"I just wonder what [CompuServe] would say about (1) files taking up valuable space on their disk drives that only a very limited number of people can access, but for which *they* receive no additional revenue; (2) a news publication being distributed through CIS that directly competes with [CompuServe's own publications], which the downloader (apparently) must pay for the right to read. This stuff is definitely *not* shareware, because you can't see it before you pay for it."

And then MAUG system operator, Neil Shapiro, responded: "First, I have told Mary (of MacTalk) and Mike (of A&F) that we will not be accepting encrypted files in the foreseeable future because of many complaints from our members. Now, keep in mind that *no one* ever figured these encrypted files would be a standard—they were 'show issues' being made available to paid-up readers via telecom. I thought it was a pretty acceptable idea at the time. I still do not feel that the idea of encrypted files is completely a bad one. Frankly, I think that the publishers of these types of magazines have a valid feeling that many, many people are downloading their magazines and not sending in the shareware fees. Now, unlike a program, you kinda know what a magazine is going to be like based on past issues of said magazine. So, while having an encrypted program might be asking for blind downloads, it would seem that having encrypted magazines in a *series of nonencrypted issues* gives the downloader a pretty good indication of what he or she will be receiving. After all, when you buy a magazine at the newsstand you do not (at least in New York City) hang out and read the whole magazine before you plunk down your money. Instead you make a 'character judgment' of the magazine based on your experience with back issues, the cover, and the table of contents. In a way, a magazine is sort of encrypted simply by the effort and time it takes to decode it with your eyes and brain. . . ."

Interestingly, but probably not surprisingly, none of the messages I monitored or received opposing the encrypted files were from legitimate subscribers. *Not one.* Secondly, all four encrypted files were clearly labeled as encrypted and completely useless unless you were in possession of the encryption key. Because none of the negative comments came from legitimate subscribers, it was clear to me that the complaints were made only because the correspondent was suddenly confronted with being denied access to something he or she had not paid for.

I generally despise the bottom liners—those who find a sole source of motivation in numbers with dollar signs in front of them—but let's play their game for a minute.

In the first eight months of electronically distributing *The Arts & Farces Review,* I had uploaded well over one and one-half megabytes of original material to the national telecommunications services. I only track the number of accesses on GEnie, and that number was well over 3,500. The average number of accesses for each piece is well over 150. That means that an average of 150 people download each of my pieces from GEnie alone.

Assume that 50 percent of those folks upload the material to either their electronic bulletin board system (BBS) or one where they live (most of our subscriptions come from folks who have downloaded the material from a local BBS). If 100 folks download the material from the local BBSs, our average first-level distribution rate is more than 7,500 for each file. With an average of six files each month, our average number of impressions each month is 45,000. Actually it is much higher than that. This 45,000 monthly impression figure represents only GEnie accesses and first-level redistribution. This does not represent the number of "pass-around" copies, user group distribution, Mac Underground penetration, CompuServe, EchoMac, FidoNet, and so on.

The sad fact was that not even one percent of those first-level distribution folks was subscribing (and the distribution rates were climbing at a steady and constant rate) and the publication was pulled from shareware distribution and made available on a subscription basis only.

One of the underlying research topics undertaken by the Alexandria Institute mentioned in Chapter 3 is the impact of the new communications media, such as hypermedia, on the existing copyright laws. According to Robert Kerr, chief executive officer of the Alexandria Institute, "A copyright system based on the publication, distribution, and compensation for a printed copy of a book may not be a viable model for the protection of intellectual property rights when the 'copy' is a single disc with the full text of 500 books representing more than 1,000 different proprietary interests." As we have seen earlier, Mead Data has addressed this issue in a roundabout way by declaring its copyright on the page breaks contained in its Lexis legal data base. We also have seen how Ithiel de Sola Pool compares hypermedia and other forms of electronic publishing with forms of word-of-mouth communications that have never qualified for copyright protection.

The Alexandria Institute's Kerr proposes a "pay for use" model for electronic publishing copyrights that would enable information providers and publishers to deliver their products to customers for the cost of the media on which it was contained. The information provider would be compensated by an accrual of payments based on a fee structure for the actual use of the information. This fee structure would "reflect the utility of the presentation to the user," according to Kerr. "An electronic copy, for example, obviously carries a higher utility than simply viewing the information on a screen, and would, therefore, command a higher price."

Kerr maintains that such a system would benefit the information provider directly by opening up new avenues of compensation for additional uses of an existing work; allowing price discrimination among types of users; adding incentives to increase the number of users; and allowing for a low-cost point of inventory for publishers. Similarly, libraries would be able to maintain a significantly larger collection at greatly lowered cost, and individuals would enjoy access to a broader knowledge base at a more reasonable cost.

Such a system surely would be met with resistance by both publishers (who would potentially lose duplication control) and libraries themselves, who now generally pay a fixed yearly subscription rate for material delivered on CD-ROM.

On a smaller, individual scale, I favor *Whole Earth Review* editor Kevin Kelly's notion of "share-right," which originally was used in reference to message postings (electronic word-of-mouth communications in the truest sense of the word) on telecommunications networks but that is equally applicable to broader electronic works. An encircled 's,' similar to the copyright symbol (©), would be used to promulgate the notion: "You may reproduce this material if your recipients may also reproduce it."

Hypermedia copyright issues are, in some ways, uncharted territory as far as copyright law goes. Current federal copyright statutes protect only original works of authorship that are contained in a tangible medium of expression. One could argue that hypermedia, and especially the networked hypermedia systems of the near future, are not tangible media.

As far as computer software (including hypermedia tools and documents distributed on disk or in other tangible form) is concerned, the courts have held that very specific aspects of the software are protected by copyright. The underlying source code—the code that actually is written by the programmer—is protected as is the object code, the interpreted or compiled source code that is read by the computer. Information contained in read-only memory chips (ROMs) also is protected as are underlying operating systems used by all computers. Finally, screen formats (generically known as the "look and feel" of an application) also recently have been granted copyright protection.

In the case of hypermedia, most attorneys agree that the underlying structure of a hypermedia document—the connections and links between bits of information—also would be afforded copyright protection, although there is little, if any, precedent in this area.

Using HyperCard as a specific example, the HyperTalk scripts and any external commands and functions (XCMDs and XFCNs) used in a stack would be covered by existing copyright laws, as would the links between the cards within the stack as well as links to other stacks. Many attorneys agree that not only would the source code itself (the actual HyperTalk scripts) be protected but so would the overall "structure, sequence, and organization" of the code itself.[202] Current findings by the courts, and the Whelan case specifically, have resulted in the opinion held by many attorneys that the hypermedia data space itself qualifies for copyright protection. In many cases, the navigation of the data space is the most creative aspect of the hypermedia document and, the attorneys reason, should be afforded the same protections, pointing to the fact that data bases have been protected by copyright for quite some time.

Screen displays also have been protected by copyright in several cases, mostly involving computer games with screens that could be generated by any number of underlying source-code options. The courts have held that screen displays in such instances are afforded separate protection as audiovisual works. A potential double-bind situation could develop here, however, for the United States Copyright Office has maintained that screens may not be copyrighted as audiovisual works if they rely mostly on text to communicate their ideas. Under the current rules, hypermedia screens that contain mostly text are not afforded copyright protection separate from the underlying code that produced them.

This is the point at which the "look and feel" rulings and pending suits (most notably *Apple v. Microsoft and Hewlett-Packard)* come into play and is one of the areas that is most important to the hypermedia author and producer. In 1986, the courts held that screen layouts qualify as eligible for copyright protection against similar, but not necessarily identical, expressions.[203] In this landmark case, the court held that the overall appearance of the screen is subject to protection, not just individual attributes of the screen, although the protection was conveyed to the underlying code of the application, not the audiovisual rules mentioned previously.

Currently, the computer industry is closely watching the developments in a suit brought by Apple Computer against Microsoft and Hewlett-Packard regarding the protections afforded the visual expressions inherent in the Macintosh operating system. Many attorneys argue that if a prediction can be drawn from past cases (although not necessarily precedent-setting cases), Apple will win because the Macintosh screen displays will be determined to be original expressions that can be implemented in other, original, ways.

Apple Computer is arguably right in defending its metaphor—that of a desktop. Although some would say that a desktop is too generic, let's concede the point to Apple, for the time being. Apple, though, assumes that it has a right to exclusive use of certain implements—what it refers to as the Macintosh Interface, items such as windows, elevator bars, thumbs, files represented as icons, etc. And then there are the menus—Apple lays claim to any sort of drop-down, pop-up, spring-out, jump-back, or shut-up menus.

Many continue to argue that what visually and interactively became Macintosh—that is, what makes Macintosh distinctive from the other computers, its interface—came from Xerox's Palo Alto Research Center (PARC). I do not want to argue or belabor that point, except to point out that in actuality, concepts such as mice and windows date all the way back to Doug Engelbart's work at the Stanford Research Institute (SRI). Regardless of where the elements came from, they were combined—no, more appropriately, synergized—by Steve Jobs and his Macintosh development team.

So Apple has a valid claim to the desktop metaphor as implemented in the Macintosh. Apple, however, has no claim whatsoever to any sort of exclusivity on graphics-based interfaces. What happened is that Microsoft got a little too close for comfort to the *complete* desktop metaphor, in Apple's opinion, with its current version of Windows.

Apple chief executive John Sculley claims to have had his metaphorical arm twisted by Microsoft chief executive Bill Gates into granting Microsoft some sort of limited license agreement to use parts of Apple's metaphor in Windows. To hear Sculley tell it, Gates threatened not to update Microsoft's Macintosh software titles if Sculley did not buckle and grant the license. And what a dreadful situation we would all be in if we had not been blessed with the initial, bug-infested release of Microsoft Word V3.0.

But Apple is not really after Microsoft. Or Hewlett-Packard. The Apple legal department has its eye on bigger game. IBM, which currently is said to be an acronym for I'm Building Macintosh, and its Presentation Manager are the real targets. If we assume that I am correct and the target is IBM, what is Apple's motivation? The best they can hope for is to delay IBM for a year or so, or two at the most. And that is the best-case scenario.

In the meantime, Microsoft did not take Apple's suit laying down. It charged, in a cross-complaint, that Apple had violated at least two contracts, acted in bad faith, and damaged Microsoft's relationships with other companies.

On November 22, 1985, an agreement between Apple and Microsoft was signed that begins, "The parties have a long history of cooperation and trust and wish to maintain that mutually beneficial relationship. However, a dispute has arisen concerning the ownership of and possible copyright infringement as to certain visual displays generated by several Microsoft software products."

The 1985 agreement states that Microsoft acknowledges its products are "derivative works of the visual displays generated by Apple's Lisa and Macintosh graphic user interface programs." In that agreement, Apple granted Microsoft a "nonexclusive, worldwide, royalty-free, perpetual, nontransferable license to use these derivative works in present and future programs and to license them to and through third parties for use in their software programs."

The 1985 agreement also makes reference to an Apple patent, United States Patent No. 4,464,652. It also waives any Apple claim of any kind to Windows and calls for Microsoft granting Apple a "nonexclusive, worldwide, royalty-free, perpetual, nontransferable license to use any new visual displays created by Microsoft during a period of five years from the date of this agreement as part of its Microsoft Windows retail software product in software programs and to license them to and through third parties for use in their software programs."

The infamous Word revision clause also is there, in black and white, for the whole world to see: "Microsoft shall revise Microsoft Word which operates on the Apple Macintosh computer by enhancing and improving the program as specified in Exhibit A to this Agreement. Microsoft shall use its best efforts to complete the revision by July 31, 1986."

This is a very important issue for hypermedia developers to watch carefully, as future "look and feel" cases surely will be built on the results of the Apple and Microsoft suit (if it ever gets heard in a court of law; most bets are that the principals will settle).

In some very real ways, Macintosh is pushing the desktop metaphor to a bursting point and the machine now is powerful enough to far surpass any competitor in the interface arena. But to do this, Apple is going to have to use some resources—both money and people—to do the job. And they have plenty of both.

Of greater short-term concern to many hypermedia developers is a claim made in mid-1988 by Paul Heckel and his company, Quickview Systems, revolving around patents awarded for a card-and-rack screen metaphor.[204] Heckel developed, and Quickview subsequently began marketing in 1985, a product for the IBM PC called Zoomracks that employed a card-and-rack screen metaphor front end to a relational data base. Specifically, Heckel claims patent on a "time card rack screen display," manifested in "seeing several lines of a card, several racks side-by-side, and the ability to pull a card."

Heckel is concerned because he sees possible infringement of his intellectual property by HyperCard stackware developers, although he stresses that he is ''not claiming any specific products are infringing'' on his patent. This is a legal maneuver for if he claims someone is specifically infringing his rights, he leaves himself open to an immediate suit. By claiming that stackware developers *may* be infringing on his patents he has ''up to five years to decide whether to sue infringers or not.''

In the spring of 1988, Paul Heckel and Quickview Systems sent many HyperCard stackware developers and publishers a letter, via registered mail, asserting his claim of intellectual property patents for the card-and-rack metaphor, as well as an offer to license his technology in the form of external commands and functions for HyperCard. An advertisement, containing a subset of the information contained in the letter, also appeared in the *MacWEEK* controlled-circulation trade journal: ''As a Stackware developer, you are vulnerable to being an infringer if you are not careful. If you are aware of our patents (and this letter makes you aware) you are potentially liable for **THREE TIMES DAMAGES** plus attorneys' fees for 'egregious infringement.' ''

The hook followed closely on the heels of the threat: ''Quickview's patented technology combined with HyperCard is an unbeatable combination. It offers you exciting opportunities to extend the capabilities of your Stackware programs. An exclusive license in your market area could give your company a long-term competitive advantage.''

During the course of my research for this book I spoke with intellectual-property attorney, Randall Boyer, of Merchant, Gould, Smith, Edel, Welter & Schmidt, P.A., of Minneapolis. I basically wanted to know if Heckel's claim could withstand a challenge and what took precedent: copyright or patent. As a hypermedia producer, these are very real concerns. I did not look forward to the possibility of someone's patent effectively negating my copyright. Boyer's affable but predictably lawyerly response to the precedence question was simply that ''precedence depends on the aspect of the work in question.'' In other words, sometimes yes, sometimes no.

I went on to ask him what bearing, if any, the recent Copyright Office decision to cover screen displays under a single copyright rather than separately had on this matter. Boyer told me that the decision states that ''screen displays are coverable only if they are copyrightable expressions,'' so it begs the screen-display question.

Boyer sees a major push for intellectual-property protection through patents, with some companies going so far as to protect icons, probably as a result of everyone standing around with their hands in their pockets watching Xerox have a wealth of intellectual property slip through their fingers.

One of the main sticking points is that the Patent Office "does not have a large base of prior art in the patent area," according to Boyer. "There's a fair number of patents that are issued that are going to be attacked on the grounds of novelty and prior art," he said in response to my query of whether patents could be rescinded.

Boyer went on to explain that there are two kinds of patents, utility patents and design patents. Utility patents go to functional processes and hold for 17 years from the date of issue. When I asked Heckel which patent he held for Zoomracks, he said that he held a utility patent but not a design patent, although he had never heard it referred to as that.

Heckel told me that the impetus for the registered letter that his company sent to most stackware developers and publishers was that a friend told him that he was going to implement Zoomracks in HyperCard. He also said that he was concerned with the stories that he had heard concerning Apple's plans to implement a card-rack metaphor.

At that point, my conversation with Heckel took a decidedly warped twist off into never-never land. "We've taken Focal Point[205] and implemented it in Zoomracks on the PC and have found significant advantages," said Heckel. I asked him if he planned on marketing the product and he replied, matter of factly, "We've done a prototype and either we or someone else will market the product."

I find this scurrying about locking up metaphors most disturbing. It seems that everyone now is more concerned with locking up rights than with creating great products and information tools. All of this runs contradictory to the macrocosm that is Macintosh and an even smaller macrocosm within it that we know as hypermedia. The hypermedia universe is very new and very small relative to the rest of the world. It is a tool that right-minded individuals can make use of to affect broad and wonderful changes in the world Out There, but not if we are all forced to stew in a prickly sweat waiting for the other intellectual-property foot to drop.

Ted Nelson's Bill of Information Rights

Nelson's Canons
A Bill of Information Rights
By Ted Nelson

It is essential to state these firmly and publicly, because you are going to see a lot of systems in the near future that purport to be the last-word cat's-pajama systems to bring you "all the information you need, anytime, anywhere." Unless you have thought about it you may be snowed by systems which are inherently and deeply limiting. Here are some of the things which I think we will all want. (The salesman for the other system will say they are impossible, or "We don't know how to do that yet," the standard put down. But these things are possible, if we design them in from the bottom up; and there are many different valid approaches which could bring these things into being.)

These are rules, derived from common sense and uncommon concern, about what people can and should have in general screen systems, systems to read from.

1. Easy and Arbitrary Front Ends.

The "front end" of a system—that is, the program that creates the presentations for the user and interacts with him or her—must be clear and simple for people to use and understand.

> **The Ten-Minute Rule:** Any system which cannot be well taught to a layman in *ten minutes,* by a tutor in the presence of a responding setup, is too complicated. This may sound far too stringent; I think not. Rich and powerful systems may be given front ends which are nonetheless ridiculously clear; this is a design problem of the foremost importance.
>
> **Text Must Move:** That is, slide on the screen when the user steps forward or backward within the text he or she is reading. The alternative, to clear the screen and lay out a new presentation, is baffling to the eye and thoroughly disorienting, even with practice.

Many computer people do not yet understand the necessity of this. The problem is that if the screen is cleared, and something new then appears on it, there is no visual way to tell where the new thing came from: Sequence and structure become baffling. Having it slide on the screen allows you to understand where you've been and where you're going; a feeling you also get from turning pages of a book. (Some close substitutes may be possible on some types of screen.)

On front ends supplied for normal users, there must be *no* explicit computer languages requiring input control strings, no visible esoteric symbols. Graphical control structures having clarity and safety, or very clear task-oriented keyboards, are among the prime alternatives.

All operations must be fail-safe.

Arbitrary front ends must be attachable: Since we are talking about reading from text, or text-and-picture complexes, stored on a large data system, the presentational front end must be separable from the data services provided further down in the system, so the user may attach his or her own front-end system, having his or her own style of operation and private conveniences for roving, editing, and other forms of work or play at the screen.

2. Smooth and Rapid Data Access.
The system must be built to make possible fast and arbitrary access to a potentially huge data base, allowing extremely large files (at least into the billions of characters). However, the system should be contrived to allow you to read forward, back, or across links without substantial hesitation. Such access must be implicit, not requiring knowledge of where things are physically stored or what the internal file names may happen to be. File divisions must be invisible to the user in all routine operations (FREEDOM OF ROVING): Boundaries must be invisible in the final presentations, and the user must not need to know about them.

3. Rich Data Facilities.
Arbitrary linkages must be possible between portions of text, or text and pictures; annotation of *anything* must be provided for; collateration should be a standard facility, *between any pair of well-defined objects;* PLACEMARK facilities must be allowed to drop anchor at, or in, anything. These features imply private annotations to publicly accessible materials as a standard automatic service mode.

4. Rich Data Services Based on These Structures.
The user must be allowed multiple rovers (movable placemarks at points of current activity); making possible, especially, multiple windows (to the location of each rover) with displays of collateral links.

The system should also have provision for high-level mooting and the automatic keeping of historical trails.

Then a complex certain very necessary and very powerful facilities based on these things, viz.:

A. Anthological Freedom: The user must be able to combine easily anything he or she finds into an ''anthology,'' a rovable collection of these materials having the structure *he or she* wants. The linkage information for such anthologies must be separately transportable and passable between users.

B. Step-Out Windowing: From a place in such an anthology, the user must be able to step *out* of the anthology and into the previous context of the material. For instance, if the user has just read a quotation, he or she should be able to have the present anthological context dissolve around the quotation (while it stays on the screen), and the original context *reappear* around it. The need of this in scholarship should be obvious.

C. Disanthological Freedom: The user must be able to step out of an anthology in such a way and *not* return if he or she chooses. (This has important implications for what must really be happening in the file structure.) Earlier versions of public documents must be retained, as users will have linked to them. However, where possible, linkages must also be able to survive revisions of one or both objects.

5. Freedom From Spying and Sabatoge.
The assumption must be made at the outset of a wicked and malevolent governmental authority. If such a situation does not develop, well and good; if it does, the system will have a few minimal safeguards built in.

Freedom from being monitored. The use of pseudonyms and dummy accounts by individuals, as well as the omission of certain record-keeping by the system program, are necessary here. File retention under dummy accounts is also required.

Because of the danger of file sabotage, and the private at-home retention by individuals of files that also exist on public systems, it is necessary to have *fiducial systems for telling which version is authentic.* The doctoring of on-line documents, the rewriting of history—cf. both Winston Smith's continuous revision of the encyclopedia in *Nineteen Eighty-Four* and E. Howard Hunt's forging of historical telegrams for "The White House"—is a constant danger. Thus our systems must have a number of complex provisions for verification of falsification, especially the creation of multilevel fiducials (parity systems), and their storage in a variety of places. These fiducials must be localized and separate to small parts of files.[206]

6. Copyright.
Copyright must of course be retained, but a universal flexible rule has to be worked out, permitting material to be transmitted and copied under specific circumstances for the payment of a royalty fee surcharged on top of your other expenses in using the system.

NOTES

[164] Regis McKenna, *The Regis Touch* (Reading, Massachusetts: Addison-Wesley Publishing Company, Inc., 1985).

[165] David Burnham, *The Rise of the Computer State* (New York: Vintage Books, 1984).

[166] Alvin Toffler, *The Third Wave* (New York: Morrow, 1980).

[167] Theodore Roszak, *The Cult of Information* (New York: Pantheon Books, 1986).

[168] John Naisbitt, *Megatrends* (New York: Warner Books, 1982).

[169] Theodore Roszak, *The Cult of Information* (New York: Pantheon Books, 1986).

[170] The Conservative Opportunity Society, formed by Newt Gingrich, Jack Kemp, and others, apparently has disbanded for it no longer occupies its former offices on North Carolina Street in Washington, D.C., and no telephone number is listed in the D.C. telephone directory for the group.

[171] Newt Gingrich, *Window of Opportunity* (New York: TOR Books, 1984).

[172] Theodore Roszak, *The Cult of Information* (New York: Pantheon Books, 1986).

[173] Everett Rogers and Judith Larsen, *Silicon Valley Fever: Growth of High Technology Culture* (New York: Basic Books, 1984).

[174] Theodore Roszak, *The Cult of Information* (New York: Pantheon Books, 1986).

[175] Avron Barr, "AI: Cognition as Computation," *The Study of Information,* ed. Fritz Machlup and Una Mansfield (New York: Wiley, 1983).

[176] Theodore Roszak, *The Cult of Information* (New York: Pantheon Books, 1986).

[177] Britain's Old Poor Law was a collection of various rules and regulations that formulated policy for dealing with the sick, indigent, aged, insane, and handicapped.

[178] Ithiel de Sola Pool, *Technologies of Freedom: On Free Speech in an Electronic Age* (Cambridge, Massachusetts: Harvard University Press, 1983).

[179] Theodore Roszak, *The Cult of Information* (New York: Pantheon Books, 1986).

[180] Ibid.

[181] John Naisbitt, *Megatrends* (New York: Warner Books, 1982).

[182] David Burnham, *The Rise of the Computer State* (New York: Vintage Books, 1984).

[183] Ibid.

[184] David Burnham, *The Rise of the Computer State* (New York: Vintage Books, 1984).

[185] Parallel processing is covered in greater detail in Chapter 5: Future Hypermedia.

[186] John Naisbitt, *Megatrends* (New York: Warner Books, 1982).

[187] Theodore Roszak, *The Cult of Information* (New York: Pantheon Books, 1986).

[188] Stewart Brand, *The Media Lab Inventing the Future at MIT* (New York: Viking Penguin, Inc., 1987).

[189] Ibid.

[190] Ithiel de Sola Pool, *Technologies of Freedom: On Free Speech in an Electronic Age* (Cambridge, Massachusetts: Harvard University Press, 1983).

[191] Stewart Brand, *The Media Lab Inventing the Future at MIT* (New York: Viking Penguin, Inc., 1987).

[192] Ibid.

[193] Ibid.

[194] Ann Hagedorn, ''FBI Woos Librarians to Spy on 'Commie' Readers,'' *The Wall Street Journal,* May 19, 1988.

[195] Theodor Nelson, *Literary Machines,* elect. ed. (Bellevue, Washington: OWL International, Inc., 1987).

[196] Ibid.

[197] Ibid.

[198] Ibid.

[199] Ibid.

[200] *The Arts & Farces Review* is available for $75 per year from Arts & Farces Video & Information Services, 2285 Stewart Avenue, Suite 1315, St. Paul, MN 55116; (612) 698-0741.

[201] Electronic correspondence received from a GEnie account-holder.

[202] *Whelan, Inc. v. Jaslow Dental Laboratory, Inc.*, 797 F.2d 1222 (3d Cir. 1986).

[203] *Broderbund Software, Inc. v. Unison World, Inc.*, 648 F. Supp. 499 (N.D. Cal. 1986).

[204] Patents 4,486,857 and 4,736,308 belong to Paul Heckel and his company, Quickview Systems. Heckel sent a registered letter to many HyperCard developers in the spring of 1988 offering a licensing agreement for his patented card-and-rack screen metaphor.

[205] Focal Point is a HyperCard stackware product by Danny Goodman that is published by the TENpoint0 division of Mediagenic, 3885 Bohannon Drive, Menlo Park, CA 94025.

[206]These are now called ''authentication systems''; very sophisticated ones exist, and the government is trying to suppress them.

FUTURE HYPERMEDIA

CHAPTER 5

- *Xerox's Palo Alto Research Center (PARC)*
- *MIT's Media Lab*
- *Conclusion*

Hypermedia, electronic publishing, and networked hypermedia promise to have the greatest impact on society in the past 500 years. Five hundred years ago we learned to read; now we are on the verge of learning to add intelligence to what we read in the forms of the linkages, references, and parallels that we draw in the material we absorb. Central to this paradigm shift are the communications skills that we have collectively developed and nurtured.

In a short 30 years we have managed to wrest control of computing technology from the hands of those who told us it was too valuable and too complicated for anything other than specialized uses and to place it in the hands of individuals who are interested in augmenting their intellect with the use of these tools. Those who are interested in meta-tools—tools used to create other tools—no longer are perceived as being eons outside of the mainstream of our society.

Howard Rheingold, in his excellent *Tools For Thought,* identifies three generations of computer explorers that he credits with sharing a "vision of *personal* computing in which computers would be used to enhance the most creative aspects of human intelligence—for everybody, not just the technocognoscenti."[207] The first generation, active decades (and in some cases centuries) ago, are identified by Rheingold as the *patriarchs,* those that laid the rudimentary foundation for the next generation to build upon. The second generation, referred to by Rheingold as the *pioneers,* were the creators of what we now acknowledge as the personal computer technology. Many of the pioneers, such as Doug Engelbart, are alive and well, and still active in the computer industry. The third, and current, generation are the *infonauts,* those who are exploring the nether regions of the groundwork laid by the patriarchs and pioneers. The Ted Nelson's and Alan Kay's are the figureheads of this generation.

The infonauts are more concerned with pushing the envelope of the technology and exploring its inherent processes than they are with creating marketable products. They are fully aware that "when information processing grows into knowledge processing, the true personal computer will reach beyond hardware and connect with a vaster source of power than that of electronic microcircuitry—the power of human minds working in concert."[208]

Although there are surely any number of small pockets of infonauts throughout the known universe, traditionally they have gravitated to one of two places: Xerox's Palo Alto Research Center (PARC) on the West Coast and the Massachusetts Institute of Technology's Media Lab on the East Coast. There is evidence that this gravitation is currently in flux, with a general decentralization taking place.

Xerox's Palo Alto Research Center (PARC)

Xerox PARC is most widely known for its Alto personal computer, the *first* personal computer. Much of the work at PARC in general and on the Alto specifically was later successfully commercialized at Apple by Steve Jobs and the Macintosh development team. The Alto was unique in its use of Ethernet (a network structure that enabled groups of Altos to be connected), windows, a high-resolution display screen, and the mouse.

PARC also is known for the work of Douglas Engelbart on his augmentation of the human intellect that is covered in Chapter 1, History and Underlying Concepts. Doug Engelbart enjoys the peculiar position of having a foot in two of the three generations Rheingold speaks of. The early stages of his augmentation work, while at Stanford Research Institute and later at PARC, firmly qualify him as one of Rheingold's *pioneers*. His augmentation work continues, with the formation in late 1988 of the Bootstrap Institute, placing him in the *infonaut* generation as well.

The Bootstrap Institute was formed as a nonprofit computing think tank located in Palo Alto, California. Engelbart envisions the Institute as a clearinghouse and meeting ground for vendors and end-users to explore the further reaches of computer technologies. The Bootstrap Institute, which was begun with a $100,000 seed-money donation from an anonymous personal-computer entrepreneur, will focus on Engelbart's theories of the human-computer interaction that he termed augmentation of the intellect.

Xerox PARC continues to explore hypermedia in earnest and has made several significant contributions in the past few years.

MIT's Media Lab

The Media Lab, under the direction of Nicholas Negroponte, at the Massachusetts Institute of Technology, is deeply embroiled in the study of various forms of electronic-communications technologies and how they can be used to enable humans to communicate better. By definition, this would include hypermedia research, and indeed it does.

Perhaps the most unique aspect of the Media Lab is that, unlike more traditional research facilities that tend to shun corporate and government sponsorship, MIT and the Media Lab welcome—even expect—it. Where other university research facilities insist that professors not moonlight by working outside the university, the Media Lab encourages professors to spend up to 20 percent of their time in the pursuit of profitable interests, including the formation of start-up companies.

Nicholas Negroponte has used a set of three rings to illustrate the intersecting focus of the Media Lab since 1978. The three rings represent the confluence of three medias and their attendant industries: the broadcast and motion picture industry, the print and publishing industry, and the computer industry. We recognize this as hypermedia. The three rings, which also are what Negroponte refers to as the Media Lab's marketing symbol, are shown in *Figure 5.1.*

The Media Lab is chartered to explore the territory of this coming together of three medias and industries that a few short years ago were seen as quite distinct. According to Negroponte, "All communication technologies are suffering a joint metamorphosis, which can only be understood properly if treated as a single subject, and only advanced properly if treated as a single craft. The way to figure out what needs to be done is through exploring the human sensory and cognitive system and the ways that humans most naturally interact."[209]

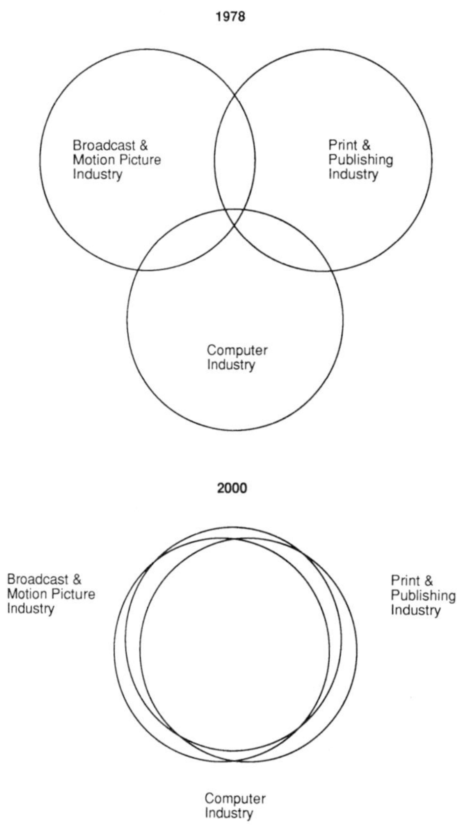

● ***Figure 5.1*** *Nicholas Negroponte's marketing symbol for the Media Lab.*

The Media Lab is subdivided into 11 rough categories of research, all of which promise to have a significant impact on future hypermedia systems. In brief, they are:

- Electronic Publishing, mostly funded by IBM, explores the future of electronic books and custom-originated electronic newspapers and magazines.
- The Speech group gets most of its funding from the Defense Advanced Research Projects Agency (DARPA) and Japan's Nippon Telephone and Telegraph. It is most involved in speech synthesis and recognition tools.
- The Advanced Television Research Program receives most of its funding from broadcasters and manufacturers of broadcast television equipment and focuses its research on the development and acceptance of more advanced technical standards for the broadcast medium.
- The Movies of the Future group receives most of its backing from the motion picture industry and is concerned with the creation of what it calls "paperback movies," full-length feature motion pictures distributed on compact discs.
- The Visual Language Workshop is funded mostly by IBM and Polaroid and is concentrating on the area of human-machine interfaces and visual design.
- The Spatial Imaging group works mostly with grants from General Motors and DARPA to explore the potential of holography.
- The Computers and Entertainment group is most widely known for Alan Kay's Vivarium project that is funded by Apple Computer, Inc. The group also is heavily involved in the area of artificial intelligence, under the auspices of Marvin Minsky.
- Funded by two Japanese conglomerates, NHK and Bandai, the Animation and Computer Graphics group is convinced it can develop a real-time computer animation system by imitating underlying patterns found in various aspects of life itself.
- The Computer Music group is exploring the realms of music cognition and receives most of its funding from the Science Development Foundation.
- The School of the Future, headed by Seymour Papert (the primary architect of the LOGO computer language) and actually in practice at the Hennigan School is funded largely by IBM, LEGO, Apple, the National Science Foundation, and the MacArthur Foundation. Its charter is to explore the possible uses for computers in education.

- The Human-Machine Interface group is funded mostly by the National Science Foundation, DARPA, and Hughes. It is actively developing the interfaces that we will use in the future, including machines that can read the user's lips and eyes.

The Instant Newspaper

The Media Lab's Electronic Publishing group is hard at work on developing a delivery system for a personalized newspaper. Such a development, called NewsPeek in the nomenclature of the Media Lab, would provide an electronic hypermedia document that would contain pieces from various newspapers, electronic news sources, and the broadcast media. It would be delivered to the user each day and would contain only topics of interest to the individual based on artificial-intelligence techniques.

Such a system would allow virtually instantaneous information delivery on a specialized basis to the user. Most of the news that we read in this morning's newspaper was written as much as 20 hours before. We need the information faster than it is currently available.

The specialized nature of the news received via NewsPeek would be as important as the speed with which we receive it. Anthony Smith, in *Goodbye Gutenberg,* states that "Only about ten percent of the total information collected every day in the newspaper's newsroom and features desk (all of which is held on-line, i.e., in continuous direct communication with a computer) is actually used in the paper, and yet, according to most surveys, the reader only reads ten percent of what has gone into the paper. It seems, therefore, that the whole agony of distribution is undergone in order to feed each reader just one percent of the material that has been so expensively collected."[210]

The form and content of the NewsPeek personal newspaper would have to be what Negroponte refers to as a "highly evolved scanning device." He points to the middle column of the front page of the *Wall Street Journal* as an example of such a scanning device because of its familiarity and accessibility.

Central to the success of such a mechanism is the concept of what the Media Lab staffers refer to as "broadcatch." Broadcatch is a form of customizable selectivity that is specific to both source and content. If we recognize, as Stewart Brand points out, that the buttons on a car radio are the closest example of broadcatch we currently have available to us, we can begin to grasp the concept by recognizing that the car radio buttons are customizable as to source, but not content.

Also central to the notion of a personalized news retrieval system—and to a more generic networked hypermedia, for that matter—that is immediately available on demand is the notion of an adequate transportation system. The most recognizable transportation mechanism is the telecommunications network that we already have in place.

Pundits are always quick to tell us that progress comes at a price, and in the case of telecommunications there may be a grain of truth to this. In May of 1988, Pacific Bell, one of the Regional Bell Operating Companies (RBOCs or "Baby Bells"), ceased working on Project Victoria.

Project Victoria was an innovative telecommunications experiment that provided homes and businesses with a 9,600-baud data line, four slower-speed data lines, and two voice lines through the use of a remote multiplexer. Pacific Bell supposedly invested more than $25 million in the project that it summarily canceled after the Federal Communications Commission (FCC) deemed that the remote multiplexer was "customer-premise equipment" rather than part of the telephone network. The 1983 AT&T breakup specifically prohibits the Baby Bells from manufacturing customer-premise equipment.

Such an information transportation system would be more than adequate for services such as NewsPeek, but it remains to be seen when such a transport system will be in place.

Alan Kay's Vivarium Project

Apple Computer, Inc., provides most of the $2 million annual budget for Alan Kay's Vivarium, which is conducted under the auspices of the Media Lab. Carried out in Los Angeles, Vivarium is best described as an artificial ecology—a vibrant aquarium. Kay credits former Atari compatriot Ann Marion with coining the term as he describes one of their Atari projects as developing "intelligent autonomous Warner cartoon characters. You'd send Bugs Bunny and Elmer Fudd into the forest, and they would play out a cartoon as a result of their personalities."[211] Kay goes on to state that Marion came up with the notion of a Vivarium as being "something that would be interesting because of its ecological and social communication in an environment."[212]

Consequently, Marion developed a computer aquarium in which a fish would stalk another fish and eat it of its own volition. After the Atari research group dispersed, Kay revived the project as a more generalized Vivarium at Apple.

Alan Kay currently presides over the real-world Vivarium that inhabits part of the Open School in Los Angeles. The students are charged with the assignment of creating "life," which behaves, learns, and evolves on its own. The underlying concept is that school-aged children can learn a great deal about the world around them by creating their own world.

Vivarium, as plausible as it sounds, needs future-generation forms of animation, robotics, and computer interfaces in order to be successful. According to Kay, "The hardest thing in design is to get that first good image of the thing, and to get it in a way that is least prejudiced by what you already know. Everything else is relatively easy, because once you have the image, the image tells you what to do. Doing animals is a nice control on the child's sense of quality, whereas doing robots you could get away with almost anything and say that's what a robot does."[213]

The Vivarium Project, while currently pure research, promises to offer tremendous insight into the realm of interfaces and animation, among a host of other things, which will prove of immense importance to hypermedia producers in the near-term future.

Alan Kay envisions software programs, Agents, that observe—and more importantly, learn from—a user's individual learning and working style. The agents, when called on by the user, suggest efficient ways of working. For example, if the user calls the Dow Jones News Retrieval Service on a twice-daily basis with his or her computer and modem to retrieve the current stock price of a group of five stocks, the agent, after a "learning" period, would suggest to the user that he or she let the agent carry out the stock-price retrieval while the user went on to more productive work. Kay's agent concept, which grew directly out of his Vivarium "pure research" work, plays a vital role in the future of hypermedia and promises to change the way many of us work.

Alan Kay's Dynabook

Prior to his Vivarium work at Atari, Apple, and MIT's Media Lab, Alan Kay promoted the notion of a computer small enough to be carried around comfortably—the Dynabook. While at Xerox PARC, Kay envisioned the Dynabook to be powerful enough to do virtually anything the user desired while remaining small enough to be completely portable, as one carries around a book.

Dynabook, as Alan Kay envisioned it in the early 1970s, was capable of handling several MBytes of text and used a graphics interface and development environment called "Paintbrush." Paintbrush would enable children to create programs by making pictures and animating them. Dynabook also would be capable of linking up to other Dynabooks and any library in the world via a simple telephone connection. Finally, it would be made available for under $500 and would be provided to every schoolchild out of textbook budgets.

Dynabook, as a complete concept, remains several years in the future, although the graphics interface and programming environment has become widely available as the Smalltalk development language.

John Sculley's Knowledge Navigator

Closely related to and building on the concepts of Alan Kay's agents and Dynabook, hypermedia, advanced telecommunications, interprocess communications, and Vannevar Bush's Memex, Knowledge Navigator, created by Apple's chief executive John Sculley, aims to guide Apple in the creation of a marketable product that embodies these concepts in a commercially viable manner.

Outlined in his book, *Odyssey,* and featured in Apple-produced videos, including ''Knowledge Navigator,'' ''Project 2000,'' ''HyperCard 1992,'' and ''The Grey Flannel Navigator,'' is Sculley's concept of a device that allows us to access to vast stores of information. Conceived as a two-pound, flat-screen, full-color computer the size of a notebook, the Knowledge Navigator is capable of voice recognition and wireless communication to information sources anywhere in the world.

Apple's Advanced Technologies and External Research groups now are working on the foundation for such a device by focusing on four main areas: New Interactive Media, Collaborative Computing, Global Transparent Connectivity, and User Tailorability.

Apple's explorations in New Interactive Media will likely result in such advancements as full motion video animation to support various simulations, as well as video telecommunications and hypermedia production. The group is actively working on such things as voice annotations for documents, as well as speech recognition and synthesis.

The notion of collaborative computing is not new. People have been using electronic mail and fax machines to link geographically dispersed work groups. Products already exist, such as Partner[214] and Timbuktu[215], that allow interactive collaborative computing on a one-to-one basis. Apple hopes to expand this to on-line conferencing that incorporates both audio and live video, as well as simultaneous document modifications within work groups.

Global Transparent Connectivity is a mouthful that represents not only the physical connectivity to networks and services, but the actual navigation of the information contained within them. Apple's vision of Global

Transparent Connectivity is a mouthful that represents not only the physical connectivity to networks and services, but the actual navigation of the information contained within them. Apple's vision of Global Transparent Connectivity includes custom navigation paths and breakthroughs in information presentation.

User Tailorability addresses concepts such as macros and script languages that already exist, as well as future developments such as the agent process described previously and in the next section.

Interapplication Communication

If, as I suppose, Macintosh was the second paradigm shift in personal computing, and hypermedia promises to be the third, Apple Computer, Inc., again set the wheels for the shift in motion during the last week of April, 1988, at its developer conference held in San Jose, California. Apple, for the first time that I am aware of, shared its general technology directions with developers and the press without requiring nondisclosure agreements.

The most significant Apple announcement at the developers conference, and the one that will grease the wheels of the next paradigm shift potentially as much as HyperCard itself, is the intention of Apple to provide something called interapplication communications (IAC).

Scheduled for release in a future System Software release, interapplication communications will allow applications to communicate with each other on a level that we have barely been able to imagine to date. Think of the benefits of, while working on your department's budget for the next quarter, being able to tell the bank of applications you normally use for these things to increase the fourth quarter's budget by ten percent. Automatically, and without intervention on your part, the system is intelligent enough to leave your entry point in, perhaps, Excel, and update your budget information in your 4th Dimension data base, your tax software, other related Excel worksheets and charts, and all your correspondence that originates in Word relevant to the fourth-quarter budget. Each application then is free to respond to the updated data in its unique way.

As another example, consider that one of your clients has moved and you have just received the new address—without a ZIP code. Like most knowledge workers, you keep that client's address information in at least five different places. The interapplication communications aspect of the new System Software would enable you to enter the data in only one application and then "tell" it to update the other places where the client's address is kept. It also would look up the ZIP code in the related data-base file.

Coupled with Alan Kay's concept of agents, which would add intelligence to the interapplication communications process, the impact on hypermedia and other areas will be immense. Ponder yet another example. You are a smart business person and you realize that information and access to that information helps you maintain an edge. You further realize that the best way to currently access the information you need is via the telecommunications networks, but your experience is like being in a darkroom filled with rack after rack after rack of file cards and a small single-beam flashlight. The only thing you can see is what the flashlight is pointed at—the frontmost card where your light happens to fall. An intelligent software agent, coupled with an adequate search-and-retrieval engine front end to a vast hypermedia repository and interapplication communications would pinpoint your information navigation task. Automatically.

A software agent would observe the way you navigate on-line, what your interests are, which services you call for what information, and so on. Initially you would communicate your priorities to the agent by highlighting important terms within paragraphs. The agent would attempt to key the important words in that passage and would pop up a dialog, asking which ones you wish to pursue in further research.

As you continued to go about your on-line research and ruminations, your ever-present agent would be there with you, looking over your shoulder. From time to time it would present you with more dialogs. For example, "you seem to be interested in Alan Kay, the computer scientist, but not much interested in Alan Kay, the owner of the local Pontiac dealership; should I flag this concept now?" Suddenly you are dealing with a semi-intelligent helper that can make your work significantly more productive. And suddenly you are not dealing with word pairings or phrases any longer, but their underlying concepts.

Just a step or two beyond interapplication communications is the concept of interprocess communications (IPC). Also on the near horizon, interprocess communications would enable two applications to communicate with each other across networks. To again use the telecommunications example, your local agent could request a remote agent living on the host computer to carry out your bidding for you in your (and your local agent's) absence.

Conclusion

Paradigm shifts, by nature, generally are not very comfortable and the hypermedia paradigm shift in the midst of which we find ourselves is no exception. Hypermedia promises to be the first new communications medium with an affordable entrance fee. Access to the Xanadu system, for example, is expected to be quite reasonably priced and available to a greater number of the general population than any previous medium. We are past the pioneer stage and quite a ways into the early-adapter period, that time in which significant numbers of people become interested in and adapt to a new technology.

It is apparent that there is no turning back, and it is imperative that we understand the problems confronting us as we all become infonauts. We must take appropriate action to ensure that this new medium with the greatest potential since television is available to anyone who desires access to it in an equitable manner. Never before in the history of our society has the promise of access to information looked so achievable. We collectively share the burden of responsibility of making the most of this new medium; we are charged with making it better—with not allowing it to degrade to the level of broadcast television; we must aim higher than the lowest common denominator. For the first time, the tools with which to do so are at our disposal or will be shortly. For the first time we will collectively have access to a medium that does not bind us to unwavering consumerism; for the first time consumers will have access to the production tools of the medium from the start.

For information providers and publishers the future looks very bright, indeed. For the first time in a long time information providers will be held in an esteem other than tolerance and may even begin to get paid for their endeavors. Also for the first time in a long time, the gatekeeper mentality has reached critical mass, and there is much evidence to indicate that the attitude will no longer be tolerated.

Things look quite positive for the gatekeepers as well. As more and more people become interested in and begin to demand access to information, the gatekeepers will see their coffers grow. The only difference is that there will have to be a more equitable distribution of the pie.

For the information consumer, things could not look better. The level of information keeps growing, but so does its accessibility and level of quality. Already there are vastly improved information navigators and managers, such as the products covered in these pages. Tools and techniques are already in place that will empower the information consumer to become an information provider. Within a few short years they will be remembered with a fondness as the seeds that started it all. Ken Kesey was right: "You can count how many seeds are in the apple, but not how many apples are in the seed."

N O T E S

[207] Howard Rheingold, *Tools for Thought* (New York: Simon & Schuster, Inc., Computer Book Division, 1985).

[208] Ibid.

[209] Stewart Brand, *The Media Lab Inventing the Future at MIT* (New York: Viking Penguin, Inc., 1987).

[210] Anthony Smith, *Goodbye Gutenberg: The Newspaper Revolution of the 1980s* (New York: Oxford, 1980).

[211] Stewart Brand, *The Media Lab Inventing the Future at MIT* (New York: Viking Penguin, Inc., 1987).

[212] Ibid.

[213] Ibid.

[214] Partner was developed by Scott Armitage and is available from Arts & Farces, 2285 Stewart Avenue, Suite 1315, St. Paul, MN 55116; (612) 698-0741.

[215] Timbuktu is available from Farallon Computing, 2150 Kittredge Street, Berkeley, CA 94704; (415) 849-2331.

BIBLIOGRAPHY

APPENDIX A

Ambron, Sueann, and Hooper, Kristina, eds. *Interactive Multimedia: Visions of Multimedia for Developers, Educators, & Information Providers.* Redmond, Washington: Microsoft Press, 1988.

Anderson, John R. *Cognitive Psychology and Its Implications.* New York: W. H. Freeman and Company, 1980.

Backer, D., and Gano, S. ''Dynamically Alterable Videodisc Displays.'' *Proc. Graphics Interface 82,* Toronto, May 1982.

Bandura, A. *Social Learning Theory.* Englewood Cliffs, New Jersey: Prentice-Hall, 1977.

Bar, Avron. ''AI: Cognition as Computation.'' *The Study of Information,* eds., Fritz Machlup and Una Mansfield. New York, New York: Wiley, 1983.

Barney, Clifford. ''The Prophet from Xanadu.'' *PC World,* vol. 1, no. 3 (undated, ca. June 1983).

Beeman, W., et al. ''Hypertext and Pluralism: From Lineal to Non-Lineal Thinking.'' *Hypertext '87 Papers.* Chapel Hill, North Carolina: November 1987.

Bell, Daniel. *The Coming of Post-Industrial Society.* New York, New York: Basic Books, 1973.

Bender, W. ''Imaging and Interactivity.'' *Proc. Fifteenth Joint Conference on Image Technology.* Tokyo: November 26, 1984.

Borning, A., and Weyer, S. ''A Prototype Electronic Encyclopedia.'' *ACM Trans. Office Information Systems,* vol. 3, no. 1., January 1985.

Brand, Stewart. *The Media Lab: Inventing the Future at MIT.* New York, New York: Viking Penguin, Inc., 1987.

Bruner, Jerome. *On Knowing: Essays for the Left Hand.* Cambridge, Massachusetts: Harvard University Press, 1962.

Burnham, David. *The Rise of the Computer State.* New York, New York: Vintage Books, 1984.

Byers, T. J. ''Built by Association.'' *PC World,* April 1987.

Daniels, Jerry, and Mara, Mary Jane. *Applied HyperCard: Developing and Marketing Superior Stackware.* New York, New York: Brady Books, 1988.

Davis, Stanley M. *Future Perfect.* Reading, Massachusetts: Addison-Wesley Publishing Company, Inc., 1987.

Drexler, Eric K. *Engines of Creation: Challenges and Choices of the Last Technological Revolution.* Anchor/Doubleday, 1986.

Engelbart, Douglas C. ''A Conceptual Framework for the Augmentation of Man's Intellect.'' *Vistas in Information Handling,* eds., Howerton and Weeks. Washington, D.C.: Spartan Books, 1963.

Engelbart, Douglas C. ''A Research Center for Augmenting Human Intellect.'' *Proc. FJCC,* vol. 33, no. 1. Montvale, New Jersey: AFIPS Press, Fall 1968.

Engelbart, Douglas C. ''Authorship Provisions in AUGMENT.'' *Proc. COMPCON Conference,* San Francisco, February 27–March 1, 1984.

Engelbart, Douglas C. ''Collaborative Support Provisions in AUGMENT.'' *Proc. COMPCON Conference,* San Francisco, February 27–March 1, 1984.

Engelbart, Douglas C. ''Coordinated Information Services for a Discipline- or Mission-Oriented Community.'' *Proc. Second Annual Computer Communications Conference,* San Jose, California, January 24, 1972.

Engelbart, Douglas C. ''Evolving the Organization of the Future: A Point of View.'' *Proc. Stanford International Symposium on Office Automation,* eds., Robert Landau, James Bair, and Jeannie Siegman. Norwood, New Jersey: Ablex Publications, March 23–25, 1980.

Engelbart, Douglas C. ''The Augmented Knowledge Workshop.'' *Proc. ACM Conference on the History of Personal Workstations,* Palo Alto, California, January 9–10, 1986.

Engelbart, Douglas C. ''Toward High-Performance Knowledge Workers.'' *Proc. AFIPS Office Automation Conference,* San Francisco, April 5–7, 1982.

Engelbart, Douglas C. ''Toward Integrated, Evolutionary Office Automation Systems.'' *Proc. Joint Engineering Management Conference,* Denver Colorado, October 16–18, 1978.

Engelbart, Douglas C. ''Workstation History and the Augmented Knowledge Workshop.'' *Proc. ACM Conference on the History of Personal Workstations,* Palo Alto, California, January 9–10, 1986.

Engelbart, Douglas C.; Watson, Richard W.; and Norton, James C. ''The Augmented Knowledge Workshop.'' *Proc. NCC 73,* 1973.

Ferguson, Marilyn. *The Aquarian Conspiracy: Personal and Social Transformation in the 1980s.* Los Angeles: Tarcher, 1980.

Gingrich, Newt. *Window of Opportunity.* New York, New York: TOR Books, 1984.

Goldberg, A. *Smalltalk-80: The Interactive Programming Environment.* Reading, Massachusetts: Addison-Wesley Publishing Company, Inc., 1984.

Goodman, Danny. *HyperCard Developer's Guide.* New York, New York: Bantam, 1988.

Goodman, Danny. *The Complete HyperCard Handbook.* New York, New York: Bantam, 1987.

Halasz, F., and Trigg, R. "Notecards in a Nutshell." *Proc. ACM/SIGCHI Conference on Human Factors in Computing Systems '87,* Toronto, April 1987.

Hawken, Paul. *The Next Economy.* New York: Holt, Rinehart & Winston, 1983.

Heckel, Paul. *The Elements of Friendly Software Design.* New York, New York: Warner Books, 1982.

Illich, Ivan. *Tools for Conviviality.* New York: Harper and Row, 1973.

Irby, Charles H. "Display Techniques for Interactive Text Manipulation." *Proc. NCC 74,* 1974.

Johnson-Laird, P.H. *Mental Models: Towards a Cognitive Science of Language, Inference, and Consciousness.* Cambridge, Massachusetts: Harvard University Press, 1983.

Kobayashi, Koji. *Computers and Communications.* Cambridge, Massachusetts: MIT Press, 1986.

Krueger, Myron. *Artificial Reality.* Reading, Massachusetts: Addison-Wesley Publishing Company, Inc., 1985.

Lambert, Steve, and Ropiequet, Suzanne, eds. *CD ROM: The New Papyrus.* Redmond, Washington: Microsoft Press, 1986.

Landow, G. " 'Context 32,' Using Hypermedia to Teach English Literature." *Proc. IBM AEP Conference,* 1987.

Levine, Howard, and Rheingold, Howard. *The Cognitive Connection: Thought and Language in Man and Machine.* New York, New York: Prentice Hall Press, 1987.

Licklider, J. C. R.; Taylor, Robert; and Herbert, E. "The Computer as a Communication Device." *International Science and Technology,* April 1978.

McKenna, Regis. *The Regis Touch.* Reading, Massachusetts: Addison-Wesley Publishing Company, Inc., 1985.

McLuhan, Marshall. *Understanding Media: The Extensions of Man.* New York, New York: McGraw-Hill, 1965.

Meyrowitz, Norman, et al. "The Intermedia System: Requirements." *IRIS Report.* Providence, Rhode Island: Institute for Research in Information and Scholarship, September 1985.

Meyrowitz, Norman. "Intermedia: The Architecture and Construction of an Object-Oriented Hypermedia System and Applications Framework." *Proc. OOPSLA '86,* Portland, Oregon, September 1986.

Minsky, Marvin. *The Society of Mind.* New York: Simon & Schuster, 1986.

Naisbitt, John. *Megatrends.* New York, New York: Warner Books, 1982.

Negroponte, Nicholas. *The Architecture Machine.* Cambridge, Massachusetts: MIT Press, 1970.

Negroponte, Nicholas. *Soft Architecture Machines.* Cambridge, Massachusetts: MIT Press, 1975.

Nelson, Ted. "A Conceptual Framework for Man-Machine Everything." *Proc. National Joint Computer Conference,* 1973.

Nelson, Ted. "A Dream for Irving Snerd." *Creative Computing,* ca. July 1977.

Nelson, Ted. "A File Structure for the Complex, the Changing and the Indeterminate." *Proc. Association for Computing Machinery,* 1965.

Nelson, Ted. "A New Home for the Mind." *Datamation,* March 1982.

Nelson, Ted. "A Vision of the Future." *Publishers Weekly,* 23 November 1986.

Nelson, Ted. "As We Will Think." *Proc. Online 72 Conference,* Brunel University, Uxbridge, England.

Nelson, Ted. "Barnum-Tronics." *Swarthmore College Alumni Bulletin,* December 1970.

Nelson, Ted. *Computer Lib/Dream Machines,* rev. ed. Redmond, Washington: Tempus Books of Microsoft Press, 1987.

Nelson, Ted. "Computopia and Cybercrud." *Computers in Instruction,* ed., Levien. The Rand Corporation, 1974.

Nelson, Ted. ''Computopia Now!'' *Digital Deli,* ed., Steve Ditlea. San Francisco: Workman Publishing, 1984, pp. 349–51.

Nelson, Ted. ''Data Realms and Magic Windows.'' *Proc. ACPA-5,* Meeting of the Association of Computer Programmers and Analysts, 1975.

Nelson, Ted. ''Electronic Publishing and Electronic Literature.'' *Information Technology in Health Science Education,* ed., DeLand. Plenum Press, 1978.

Nelson, Ted. ''Getting It Out of Our System.'' *Critique of Information Retrieval,* ed., Schechter. Thompson Books, 1967.

Nelson, Ted. ''Hypertext Notes.'' Ten brief essays on hypertext forms, ca. 1966. Manuscript.

Nelson, Ted. ''Interactive Systems and the Design of Virtuality.'' *Creative Computing,* November and December 1980.

Nelson, Ted. ''Las Vegas Confrontation Sit-Out: A CAI Radical's View from Solitary.'' *SIGCUE Newsletter,* 1971.

Nelson, Ted. *Literary Machines,* electronic ed. Bellevue, Washington: OWL International, Inc., 1987.

Nelson, Ted. ''New Media and Creativity Systems.'' Graphical brochure intended to expound computer graphics and related concepts, ca. 1966.

Nelson, Ted. ''No More Teacher's Dirty Looks.'' *Computer Decisions,* September 1970.

Nelson, Ted. ''Replacing the Printed Word.'' *Proc. IFIP 80,* ed., S. H. Lavington. *Information Processing 80.* North-Holland Publishing Co., 1980, pp. 1013–23.

Nelson, Ted. ''Stretchtext.'' Unpublished paper on stretchable hypertext form, 1966. Photocopy.

Nelson, Ted. ''Suggestion for an On-Line Braille Display.'' *Proc. Society for Information Display,* Fall 1965.

Nelson, Ted. ''The Hypertext.'' *Proc. World Documentation Federation,* 1965.

Nelson, Ted. ''The Magicians, the Snark and the Camel.'' *Creative Computing,* December 1981.

Nelson, Ted. ''The Tyranny of the File.'' *Datamation,* 15 December 1986.

Nelson, Ted; Carmody, Steven; et al. ''A Hypertext Editing System for the 360.'' *Pertinent Concepts in Computer Graphics,* eds., Faiman and Nievergelt. University of Illinois Press, 1969.

Nelson, Ted; DeFanti, Tom; and Sandin, Dave. ''Computer Graphics as a Way of Life.'' *Proc. Siggraph Conference,* 1974.

Norman, Donald A., and Draper, Stephen W., eds. *User Centered Design: New Perspectives on Human-Computer Interaction.* Hillsdale, New Jersey: Lawrence Erlbaum Associates.

Onosko, Timothy. ''Let There Be Light.'' *Creative Computing,* September 1985.

Papert, Seymour. *Mindstorms: Children, Computers, and Powerful Ideas.* New York: Basic Books, 1982.

Pool, Ithiel de Sola. *Technologies of Freedom: On Free Speech in an Electronic Age.* Cambridge, Massachusetts: Harvard Press, 1983.

Rheingold, Howard. *Tools for Thought: The People and Ideas behind the Next Computer Revolution.* New York: Simon and Schuster, 1985.

Rogers, Everett, and Larsen, Judith. *Silicon Valley Fever: Growth of High Technology Culture.* New York, New York: Basic Books, 1984.

Ropiequet, Suzanne, ed. *CD ROM: Optical Publishing.* Redmond, Washington: Microsoft Press, 1987.

Roszak, Theodore. *The Cult of Information.* New York, New York: Pantheon Books, 1986.

Schneiderman, Ben. *Designing the User Interface.* Reading, Massachusetts: Addison-Wesley Publishing Company, Inc.

Shannon, Claude. ''A Mathematical Theory of Information.'' *Bell System Technical Journal,* Volume 27, 1948.

Schneiderman, Ben. ''User Interface Design for the Hyperteis Electronic Encyclopedia.'' *Hypertext '87 Papers,* Chapel Hill, North Carolina, November 1987.

Smith, Anthony. *Goodbye Gutenberg: The Newspaper Revolution of the 1980s.* New York, New York: Oxford, 1980.

Smith, D. C.; Irby, C.; Kimball, R.; and Verplank, B. ''Designing the Star User Interface.'' *Byte,* April 1982.

Toffler, Alvin. *The Third Wave.* New York, New York: Morrow, 1980.

Trigg, R.; Suchman, L.; and Halasz, F. ''Supporting Collaboration in Notecards.'' *Proc. Conference on Computer-Supported Cooperative Work '86,* Austin, Texas, December 1986.

van Dam, A.; Feiner, S.; and Nagy, S. ''An Experimental System for Creating and Presenting Interactive Graphical Documents.'' *Trans. Graphics,* vol. 1, no. 1, 1982.

Yankelovich, N.; Cody, D.; and Landow, G. "The Creation of a Hypermedia Corpus for English Literature." *SIGCUE Bulletin,* vol. 19, Spring/Summer 1987.

Yankelovich, N.; Haan, B.; Meyrowitz, N.; and Drucker, S. "Intermedia: The Concept and the Construction of a Seamless Information Environment." *IEEE Computer,* January 1988.

Yankelovich, N.; Meyrowitz, N.; and van Dam, A. "Reading and Writing the Electronic Book." *IEEE Computer,* vol. 18, no. 10, October 1985.

APPENDIX B

- *Hypermedia Press Contacts*
- *Macintosh Hypermedia Software Publishers*
- *Hardware Manufacturers and Service Providers*

Hypermedia Press Contacts

The following contacts are writers in the Macintosh community who cover Macintosh-specific hypermedia for various publications. Some are free-lancers and may be contacted directly; others are staff writers for the publications, in which case it is usually best to contact the publication directly.

Arts & Farces Review
Michael Fraase
2285 Stewart Avenue, Suite 1315, St. Paul, MN 55116
612/698-0741

Byte Magazine
Ezra Shapiro
One Phoenix Mill Lane, Peterborough, NH 03458
603/924-9281

CompuServe Micronetted Apple User's Group (MAUG)
Neil Shapiro
P.O. Box 520, Bethpage, NY 11714
516/735-6924

HyperLink
David Brader
P.O. Box 7723, Eugene, OR 97401
503/484-5157

InfoWorld
Michael Miller
1060 Marsh Road, Suite C-200, Menlo Park, CA 94025
415/328-4602

MacUser
Michael Swaine
110 Marsh Drive, Suite 250, Foster City, CA 99404
415/570-5110

MacWEEK
Eric Alderman, Steve Michel
525 Brannan Street, Suite 308, San Francisco, CA 94107
415/882-7370

MacWorld
Danny Goodman
501 Second Street, San Francisco, CA 94107
415/546-7722

Macintosh Hypermedia Software Publishers

The following are companies and individuals within the Macintosh community that specialize in publishing hypermedia software.

Apple Computer, Inc.
20525 Mariani Avenue, Cupertino, CA 95014
408/996-1010

Applied Imagination
John Pritchard
64 Morton Street, Suite 1-B, New York, NY 10014
212/645-7199

Arts & Farces Video & Information Services
Michael Fraase
2285 Stewart Avenue, Suite 1315, St. Paul, MN 55116
612/698-0741

Autodesk, Inc.
2320 Marinship Way, Sausalito, CA 94965
415/332-2344

BMUG, Inc.
Steve Costa
1442A Walnut #62, Berkeley, CA 94709
415/549-2684

Brainpower
24009 Ventura Blvd., Suite 250, Calabasas, CA 91302
818/884-6911

Bright Star Technology, Inc.
1003 111th Avenue NE, Bellevue, WA 98004
206/451-3697

Computer Solutions, Inc.
Steve Vetter
1261 North Court, New Brighton, MN 55112
612/631-3682

Eastgate Systems, Inc.
Mark Bernstein
P.O. Box 1307, Cambridge, MA 02238
617/782-9044

First Reference, Inc.
516 Fifth Avenue, Suite 706, New York, NY 10036
212/730-8211

Heizer Software
1941 Oak Park Blvd., Suite 30, Pleasant Hill, CA 94523
415/943-7667

Hyperpress Publishing
P.O. Box 8243, Foster City, CA 94404
415/345-4620

Ideaform
Michael Porter
P.O. Box 1540, Fairfield, IA 52556
515/472-7256

KnowledgeSet
4920 El Camino Real, Los Altos, CA 94022
415/968-9888

Manor of Micro, Inc.
6827 Black Duck Circle, Lino Lakes, MN 55014

Microlytics, Inc.
300 Main Street, Suite 801, East Rochester, NY 14445
716/377-0130

Micromaps
P.O. Box 757, Lambertville, NJ 08530
609/397-1611

New West Software
5462 Oceanus, Suite B, Huntington Beach, CA 92649
714/898-1039

Nine-to-Five Software
P.O. Box 915, Greenwood, IN 46142
317/887-2154

Nordic Software, Inc.
3939 North 48th Street, Lincoln, NE 68504
800/228-0417

OWL International, Inc.
14218 NE 21st Street, Bellevue, WA 98007
206/747-3203

Prolog Software
P.O. Box 1446, Henderson, TX 75653
214/657-7394

Softworks, Inc.
P.O. Box 2285, Huntington, CT 06484
203/926-1116

STAX, Inc.
Bob LeVitus
8008 Shoal Creek Blvd., Austin, TX 78758
512/467-4550

Symmetry Corp.
761 East University Drive, Mesa, AZ 85203
602/844-2199

TENpointO
3885 Bohannon Drive
Menlo Park, CA 94025
415/329-0800

Voyager Company
2139 Manning, Los Angeles, CA 90025
213/475-3524

Xanadu Operating Co.
550 California Avenue, Suite 101, Palo Alto, CA 94306
415/856-4112

Xerox Special Information Systems
P.O. Box 5608, Pasadena, CA 91107
818/351-2351

Xiphias
Peter Black
13464 Washington Blvd., Marina del Rey, CA 90292
213/821-0074

Hardware Manufacturers and Service Providers

The following companies manufacture hardware related to Macintosh hypermedia or provide services to the hypermedia production community.

Apple Computer, Inc.
20525 Mariani Avenue, Cupertino, CA 95014
408/996-1010

Arc Laser Optical Technology (ALOT)
10 Victor Square, Suite 600, Scotts Valley, CA 95066
408/438-7400

Discovery Systems
7001 Discovery Blvd., Dublin, OH 43017
614/761-2000

Giga Cell Systems
P.O. Box 4088, Santa Clara, CA 95054
408/727-1049

Grolier Electronic Publishing
Sherman Turnpike, Danbury, CT 06816
203/797-3500

Meridian Data, Inc.
4450 Capitola Road, Suite 101, Capitola, CA 95010
408/476-5858

NEC
4942 West Rosecrans Avenue, Hawthorne, CA 90250
213/978-8363

Optical Media International
485 Alberto Way, Los Gatos, CA 95032
408/395-4332

SilverPlatter Information, Inc.
37 Walnut Street, Wellesley Hills, MA 02181
617/239-0306

Telebit Corporation
1345 Shorebird Way, Mountain View, CA 94043
415/969-3800

GLOSSARY

APPENDIX C

Access software
See **Search-and-retrieval software.**

Access time
The time span from search command to display of optical text on the screen.

Analog
An infinitely variable characteristic or signal, such as time, temperature, or movie video, as opposed to a discretely variable digital characteristic or signal, such as a pulse, digitized image, or animated video.

Apple key
See **Command key.**

Application software
Software programs designed to perform specific tasks, such as search and retrieval of optical text, data-base management, or word processing.

background button
A button that belongs to a background; it appears on, and its actions are the same for, all cards with the same background. Contrast with **card button.**

background field
A field that belongs to a background; its size, position, and text attributes remain constant on all cards associated with that particular background, but its text changes from card to card. Contrast with **card field.**

background picture
A picture that belongs to a background; it applies to a series of cards. You see the background picture by choosing background from the Edit menu. Contrast with **card picture.**

background
A type of HyperCard object; a basic template that is shared by a number of cards. The background is composed of the **background picture, background fields,** and **background buttons.**

Baud
The number of bits per second transmitted over a communications connection. As for example, at 1200 baud, data is transmitted at the rate of 150 typed characters per second. See **Bit** and **Byte.**

bibliographic data base
A collection of bibliographic material in the form of bibliographic references to original books, articles, or other literature.

Bit
Binary digit. The smallest unit of computer data, represented by 1 (on) or 0 (off). See **Baud** and **Byte.**

Boolean operators
These AND, OR, and AND NOT connectors comprise a class of key word-search commands enabling one to search for combinations or exclusions of certain specified words or phrases. They are used by more experienced searchers to achieve a higher degree of search selectivity.

Browse tool
The tool you use to click buttons and to set the insertion point in fields.

browse
To wander through HyperCard's stacks.

Button tool
The tool you use to create, change, and select buttons.

button
A HyperCard object; an action object or "hot spot" on the screen. For example, clicking a button with the Browse tool can take you to the next card. See also **background button, card button.**

Byte
A sequence of bits generally eight bits long. One byte represents one typed character. See **Baud** and **Bit.**

card button
A button that belongs to a card; it appears on, and its actions apply to, a single card. Contrast with **background button.**

card field
A field that belongs to a card; its size, position, text attributes, and contents are limited to the card on which the field is created. Contrast with **background field.**

card picture
A picture that belongs to and that applies only to a specific card. Contrast with **background picture.**

card
A type of HyperCard object; HyperCard's basic unit of information.

CAV
Constant Angular Velocity. On CAV discs, data is recorded on concentric tracks. This format is used to store analog signals (movies) on 12-inch videodiscs.

CD (Compact Disc)
This is the standard 12-cm. (4.72-inch) plastic disc created by Philips and Sony to store digital information in microscopic pits that can be read by a laser beam. This disc, originally designed to store high-fidelity music (standardized as the Red Book Standard), now is also becoming widely used to store optical text (CD-ROM) in the new field of electronic publishing.

CD-I (Compact Disc-Interactive)
This is a standard compact disc containing prerecorded digital video, audio, and optical text data. Also known as the Green Book Standard. The data cannot be erased or modified. This type of disc was expected to be used extensively in home consumer applications when it became available in 1988. Standards have been established by Philips and Sony so that CD-I players also will play CD-ROM discs as well as CD-I discs.

CD-ROM (Compact Disc-Read Only Memory)
This is the same disc as the audio compact disc except that it contains optical information instead of audio information. Also known as the Yellow Book Standard. Extremely large volumes of up to 552 megabytes of optical text are compressed onto small compact discs that can be machine-searched to instantly locate and retrieve any desired information on demand. ''Read Only Memory'' means that the recorded data cannot be erased or altered. This format is ideally suited for storage/access of large reference-information data bases.

CD-ROM disc player
A standard type of laser disc player used to play CD-ROM discs. It is connected to a personal computer by a controller card attached to an expansion slot in the computer. Disc-player mechanicals are of the low load type and are virtually maintenance-free. Discs do not become worn because the player-reading mechanism does not make contact with the discs.

CD-ROM operating system
See **Disk operating system.**

chunk
A piece of the character string representing a value. Valid chunks are characters, words, items, and lines.

Circuit board
See **Controller card.**

CLV
Constant Linear Velocity. On CLV discs, data is recorded on one long spiral track. This format is used to store digital optical text on CD-ROM discs, on a spiral track approximately three miles long.

Command key
The key at the lower-left side of the keyboard that has a propeller-shaped symbol. On some keyboards this key also has an Apple symbol and might be called the *Apple key.*

command
A response to a particular message; a command is a built-in message handler residing in HyperCard. See also **external command.**

Compression
This refers to techniques used to store information in less than the normal amount of space, generally by removing redundancy of characters, spaces and gaps. This is becoming increasingly important in CD-ROM publishing because of the enormous amounts of memory required to store digitized images. All compressed information must be expanded by a reverse operation called decompression.

constant
A named value that never changes. For example, the constant empty stands for the null string, a value that also can be represented by the literal expression " ".

container
A place where you can store a value. Containers are: **fields,** the **Message box,** the **selection,** and **variables.**

control structure
A block of HyperTalk statements defined with key words that enables you to control the order or the conditions under which it executes.

Controller card (Circuit board)
An interface device connecting a CD-ROM player to one of the expansion slots in a personal computer. It controls the flow of information between the computer and the disc player. Controller cards are normally provided along with the CD-ROM players.

current (adj.)
The card, background, or stack you are using now. For example, the current card is the one you can see on your screen.

data preparation
This is the first stage in the production of CD-ROM discs. It includes converting the data into machine-readable format, building the files and file directories, and transferring the data to magnetic tape. This is then followed by premastering to master tape, mastering to master CD-ROM disc, and disc replication.

Data-base management system
A software program designed to create and to organize a data base, to store information to the data base, and to retrieve information from the data base.

Data base
A relatively large and complete collection of stored, machine-readable information of the same information category.

Device driver
A small software program needed for a computer to communicate with any external device, such as a CD-ROM player or printer. This is normally supplied on a floppy diskette along with the CD-ROM player, and also may be incorporated into the software supplied along with some types of CD-ROM disc products.

Digital
A discretely variable signal or characteristic, such as a pulse, digitized image, or animated video, as opposed to an infinitely variable analog signal or characteristic, such as time, temperature, or movie video.

Digitizer
A device used to transform two-dimensional textual or graphic information into digital format. See **Scanner.**

Digitizing
The process of transforming two dimensional textual or graphic information into digital format. See **Scanner.**

Disc drive
Another name for disc player. See **CD-ROM disc player.**

Disk drive
A computer device used to read from, and write to, floppy diskettes and hard disks.

Disk operating system (DOS)
A software program that instructs a computer how to transfer information to and from peripheral input/output devices. MS-DOS, the predominant standard personal computer operating system, must be extended or amplified to operate as a CD-ROM operating system. CD-ROM operating systems include TMS's LaserDOS, Microsoft's MS-DOS with CD-ROM extensions, Digital Equipment Corp.'s Uni-File, and Reference Technology's STA/File. The trend is toward CD-ROM operating systems that are compatible with the proposed High Sierra Group CD-ROM standards.

dynamic path
A series of extra objects inserted into the path through which a message passes when its **static path** does not include the current card, current background, and current stack.

electronic publishing
The storage and distribution of information in a machine-readable electronic format made accessible to users for viewing on screen, printing, or downloading to storage. The major forms of electronic publishing now include CD-ROM discs and on-line information services. Several other electronic publishing media, such as videotext (transmission via television programming to TV sets), have not yet become commercially successful. Future electronic publishing media may include new developments, such as transmission via satellite to mass-storage devices.

Erasable
In the production of CD-ROM, audio CD, and CD-I discs, lasers physically burn small pits into the discs to represent bits of data. The data is then read by lasers scanning the track and identifying the pits. This procedure produces a permanent record that cannot be erased or altered. Several companies are working on erasable products but none are yet commercially available.

Error correction
During CD-ROM premastering, an error correction code is added to each physical block of data (2048 bytes) to ensure detection of any erroneous data.

Expansion slots
Slotlike openings in a personal computer into which controller cards (circuit boards), such as CD-ROM disc player controller cards, can be plugged to add functions to the original equipment. For example, the IBM PC/XT/AT and compatibles contain both long slots for 13-1/8-inch-long cards (Philips CD-ROM players) and short slots for 4-3/8-inch-long cards (Hitachi CD-ROM players).

expression
A description of how to get a value; a **source of value** or complex expression built from sources and operators.

external command
A command written by a programmer to extend HyperCard's built-in command set, attached to a stack or in HyperCard.

factor
A single element of value in an expression. See also **value.**

Field tool
The tool you use to create, change, and select fields.

field
A **container** in which you type regular (as opposed to Paint) text. Also, the tool you use to create a field. HyperCard has two kinds of fields—**card fields** and **background fields.**

formal parameters
See **parameter variables.**

Full-text data base
A data base containing the full original text of the subject information.

function call
The use of a function name in a HyperTalk statement or in the Message box, invoking either a function handler or a built-in function.

function handler
A handler that executes in response to a function call matching its name.

function
A named value that HyperCard calculates each time it is used. The way in which the value is calculated is defined internally for HyperTalk's built-in functions, and you can define your own functions with function handlers.

General tool
Any HyperCard tool that isn't a Paint tool. The General tools are Browse, Button, and Field.

Gigabyte
1,000 megabytes.

global properties
The properties that determine aspects of the overall HyperCard environment. For example, user level is a global property that determines the current **user level** setting.

global variable
A variable that is valid for all handlers in which it is declared with the global keyword. Contrast with **local variable.**

Graphics
Information that is not character-related, such as maps, charts, graphs, and all photographs and pictorial representations. In order to be storable in a data base, graphics must be digitized using a scanner. This produces a series of dots that can be handled by a computer but requires large amounts of storage space unless compressed. See **Compression.**

Green book standard
See **CD-I** (Compact Disc-Interactive).

handler
A block of HyperTalk statements contained in the script of an object that executes in response to a message or a function call matching the handler's name. HyperTalk has **message handlers** and **function handlers.**

hierarchy
See **object hierarchy.**

High Sierra Group Standard
This is the informal name of the draft NISO Standard ANS Z39.60-198X, "Proposed American National Standard for Information Sciences—Volume and File Structure of CD-ROM for Information Interchange" (see **NISO).** The trend is definitely toward CD-ROM products that are compatible with this standard.

Home card
The first card in the Home stack; it generally is used as a pictorial index to stacks. Choose Home from the Go menu to get to Home (or press Command-H). You also can type go home in the Message box or include it as a statement in a handler.

HyperTalk
HyperCard's built-in script language for HyperCard users.

identifier
A character string of any length, beginning with an alphabetic character, containing any alphanumeric character and, optionally, the underscore character. Identifiers are used for **variable** and **handler** names.

Index
The indexing of a CD-ROM disc is similar to that of a printed book except in degree. The subject index at the rear of many printed reference texts

includes the primary locations of the more important book subjects. A CD-ROM disc, by comparison, contains indexes that locate each and every word appearing on the disc (excepting only "noise" words such as "the," "an," "to," etc.).

Interactive media
An information storage/access format, such as the CD-ROM format, capable of delivering user-requested information in a sequence specified by the user. This represents a significant advancement over the linear format that delivers information in only one sequence starting at the beginning and continuing to the end, such as audiotape cassettes or records.

Interface
A link between two systems, such as the controller card connecting a CD-ROM player to a personal computer. See **Controller card.**

Jukebox
A disc-playing system, similar to the well-known record jukebox, that can hold more than one disc for access one at a time. Prototype models now exist and commercial models are expected to appear soon. This is one of the two most likely types of multiple-disc CD-ROM player systems expected to predominate in university and public libraries. The other is the multiplayer system. See **Multiplayer.**

keyboard equivalent key
A key you press together with the Command key to issue a menu command.

Key-word combination
A selective combination of key words located by advanced key word–searching techniques. See **Boolean operators** and **Proximity connectors.**

Key-word searching
The process of electronically searching a data base on a CD-ROM or other optical disc or on-line information service for all locations of any specified key words or key-word combinations within the data base.

Key word
Any word in an electronic data base that is indexed to allow its location(s) in the data base to be identified on-screen at the user's command. On CD-ROM discs, more than 99 percent of all words are key words.

key word
Any one of the 14 words that have a predefined meaning in HyperTalk. Examples of key words are on, if, do, and repeat.

Laser (Light amplification by stimulated emission of radar)
A device that processes a beam of light through a special crystal to produce an extremely narrow coherent beam of vastly increased power. Stronger-level laser beams are used to record information onto CD-ROM discs by burning microscopic pits into the surfaces of the discs. Weaker-level laser beams are then used to read the discs.

Laser card
A plastic card about the size of a credit card containing two to ten megabytes of nonerasable machine-readable information.

layer
The order of a button or field relative to other buttons or fields on the same card or background. The object created most recently is ordinarily the topmost object (that is on the front layer).

literal
An expression denoted by double quotation marks at either end of a character string; its value is the string itself.

local variable
A variable that is valid only within the handler in which it is used (local variables need not be declared). Contrast with **global variable.**

Machine-readable information
This is digital information electronically stored in a computer or mass-storage device that can be key word–searched and manipulated by means of appropriate software programs.

Mass-storage device
A device that can hold vast amounts of machine-readable information for electronic access on demand, such as a CD-ROM disc.

Mastering
The process of producing an original recording on tape or disc. The stages in producing CD-ROM discs consist of data preparation, premastering to master tape, mastering to master CD-ROM disc, and disc replication.

Megabyte
A term for 1,048,576 characters of information, or approximately one million bytes. The storage capacity of a CD-ROM disc is 552 megabytes.

Message box
A **container** that you use to send messages to objects or to evaluate expressions.

message handler
A handler that executes in response to a message matching its name.

message
A character string you send to an object from a **script** or the **Message box,** or which HyperCard sends in response to an event. Some examples of HyperTalk messages are mouseUp, Go, and push card.

MS-DOS
A disk-operating system distributed by Microsoft. See **Disk operating system.**

Multiplayer
A disc-playing system consisting of an eight (the most popular number) CD-ROM player unit assembly that can be connected to and controlled by a single personal computer. The user can choose to access any or all of the eight CD-ROM discs at the same time. The first models now are commercially available. This is one of the two most likely types of multiple-disc CD-ROM player systems expected to predominate in university and public libraries. The other is the jukebox system. See **Jukebox.**

NISO
Establishes U.S. national standards for libraries, information sciences, and publishing, including CD-ROM (see **High Sierra Group Standard).** National Information Standards Organization, National Bureau of Standards, Gaithersburg, MD, (301) 975-2814.

Notepad
This is an electronic work and storage space with word-processing capabilities incorporated into certain published CD-ROM discs. This enables one to type in ideas or comments in combination with information extracted from the data base to produce letters, reports, or memos for printing or storage.

number
A character string consisting of any combination of numerals zero through nine, optionally including one period (.) representing a decimal value. A number can be preceded by a hyphen or a minus sign to represent a negative value.

object descriptor
Designation used to refer to an object. An object descriptor is formed by combining the name of the type of object with a specific name, number, or ID number. For example, background button three is an object descriptor.

object hierarchy
The ordering of HyperCard objects that determines the path through which **messages** pass.

object properties
The properties that determine how HyperCard objects look and act. For example, the location property of a button determines where it appears on the screen.

object
An element of the HyperCard environment that sends and receives messages. There are five kinds of HyperCard objects: **buttons, fields, cards, backgrounds,** and **stacks.**

on-line help
Assistance you can get from an application program while it is running. In this user's guide, on-line help refers to HyperCard's disk-based Help system.

Operating system
See **Disk operating system.**

operator
A HyperTalk language element that you use in an expression to manipulate or calculate **values.**

Optical disc
An information storage device that has been recorded using lasers and is read using lasers. This includes both analog video/audio information discs (movies and interactive video) and digital audio/graphics/textual information discs (CD-ROM, CD-I, WORM, laser cards).

Optical publishing
See **electronic publishing.**

Optical scanner
See **Scanner.**

Overhead
The amount of storage space required by the index of a full-text data base, normally 40 to 50 percent of the storage space required for the information contained in the data base.

Paint text
Text you type using the Paint Text tool. Paint text can appear anywhere, while **regular text** must appear in a field created with the Field tool. When you finalize Paint text by clicking, it becomes part of a picture.

Paint tool
Any HyperCard tool you use to make pictures. Tools include Lasso, Brush, Spray, Eraser, Paint Text, and many others.

painting properties
The properties that control aspects of HyperCard's painting environment, which is invoked when you choose a Paint tool. For example, the brush property determines the shape of the Brush tool.

palette
The name for a **tear-off menu** when it has been torn off. A palette remains visible on the screen so you can use it without having to pull down the menu. HyperCard has two palettes—Tools and Patterns.

parameter variables
Local variables in a handler that receive the values of parameters passed with the message or function call initiating the handler's execution.

parameters
Values passed to a handler by a message or function call. Any expressions after the first word in a message are evaluated to yield the parameters; the parameters to a function call are enclosed in parentheses or, if there is only one, it can follow "of."

picture
Any graphic or part of a graphic created with a Paint tool or imported from an external file, which is part of a card or background.

point
In printing, the measurement of the height of a text character; one point is about 1/72 of an inch. When you select a font, you also can select a point size, such as 10-point, 12-point, and so on. Also, a location on the screen described by two integers, separated by a comma, representing horizontal and vertical offsets, measured in pixels from the top-left corner of the card window or (in the case of the card window itself) of the screen.

power key
One of a number of keys on the Macintosh keyboard you can press to initiate a menu action when a Paint tool is active. Power keys are enabled when you choose Power keys from the Options menu or you check Power keys in the User Preferences card in the Home stack.

Premastered tape
A magnetic master tape ready for recording on an optical master disc.

Premastering
The process by which information is prepared for mastering on optical discs. This includes formatting the data, inverting the files for indexing, and other technical tasks. The stages in producing CD-ROM discs consist of data preparation, premastering to master tape, mastering to master CD-ROM disc, and disc replication.

Prefix operator
This is a useful key word–searching feature incorporated into certain published CD-ROM discs to locate all words with common beginnings but different endings.

properties
The defining characteristics of any HyperCard object and of HyperCard's environment. See also **global properties, object properties, painting properties,** and **window properties.**

Proximity connectors
These W/n, PRE/n, and NOT W/n connectors comprise a class of key-word search commands that enable one to search for certain specified words or phrases occurring within/not-within a specified number of words. They are used by more experienced searchers to achieve a higher degree of search selectivity.

Recent
In Hypercard, a special dialog box that holds pictorial representations of the last 42 unique cards viewed. Choose Recent from the Go menu to get the dialog box. Also, as in recent card, an adjective describing the card you were on immediately prior to the current card.

recursion
The continued repeating of an operation or group of operations. Recursion occurs when a handler calls itself.

Red book standard
See **CD (Compact Disc).**

regular text
Text you type inside a field. You use the Browse tool to set an insertion point in a field and then type. Regular text is editable and searchable, while **Paint text** is not.

Replication
The process of mass producing copies of CD-ROM discs.

Resolution
A measure of the density of dots per unit of area of a digitized image. More dots per unit area means higher resolution and a better picture.

ROM (Read Only Memory)
The type of memory or storage device for prerecorded permanent information that cannot be erased or altered.

Scanner
Scans and digitizes two-dimensional information consisting of pictures, graphics or text into a stream of bits. Also called **Optical scanner.** Scanners are incorporated into several different types of devices such as WORM drives.

script
A series of handlers written in **HyperTalk** and associated with a particular object.

Search-and-retrieval software
This is a software program enabling one to use the CD-ROM discs supplied by a particular publisher. Most publishers claim their software to be superior and it does not appear likely that one universal standard search-and-retrieval software program will evolve. This is not a serious problem, however, inasmuch as all CD-ROM discs produced in accordance with the proposed High Sierra Standard can be played on the same standard disc players controlled by the same computers.

Search hit
The product of a successful key-word search; that is, each location of the key word or key-word combination is retrieved and displayed on the screen.

search path
The route the computer must follow to retrieve a file you ask for.

selection
A container that holds the currently selected area of text. Note that text found by the find command is not selected. See also **container.**

Sideways search
This is a useful key word–searching feature incorporated into certain published CD-ROM discs. The user can initiate a secondary, or "sideways," search from within the text of the data base and return to the same point when sideways searching has been completed.

source of value
HyperTalk's most basic expressions; the language elements from which values can be derived: **constants, containers, functions, literals,** and **properties.**

stack
A type of HyperCard object that is a collection of cards; a HyperCard document. See also **card.**

static path
The message-passing route defined by an object's own hierarchy. For example, the static path followed by a message sent to (but not handled by) a button would include the card to which the button belongs, the background associated with that card, and the stack containing them. Contrast with **dynamic path.**

system file
Software your computer uses to perform its basic operations.

system message
Messages sent to an object by HyperCard in response to an event, such as a mouse click or the creation or deletion of an object.

target
The object that first receives a message.

tear-off menu
A menu that you can convert to a **palette** by dragging the pointer beyond the menu's edge. HyperCard has two tear-off menus—Tools and Patterns.

text field
See **field.**

text property
A quality or attribute of a character's appearance. Properties include style, font, and size.

tool
An implement you use to do work. HyperCard has tools for browsing through cards and stacks, creating text fields, editing text, making buttons, and creating and editing pictures.

user level
The property of HyperCard ranging from one to five, usually chosen on the User Preferences card in the Home stack, that lets you use HyperCard's tools and abilities. The five user levels are: Browsing, Typing, Painting, Authoring, and Scripting.

value
The information on which HyperCard operates. All HyperCard values can be treated as strings of characters.

variable
A named container that can hold a value consisting of a character string of any length. HyperCard has **local variables** and **global variables.** See also **container.**

videodisc
This is a 12-inch diameter laser disc used for years for recording analog video and audio, mostly movies. This disc now is being used successfully for interactive video, primarily for training and educational purposes. This disc also is now being used to a limited extent for recording digital information in both the eight-inch and 12-inch diameter sizes.

window properties
The properties that determine how the Message box and the Tool and Pattern palettes are displayed. For example, the visible property determines whether or not the specified window is displayed on the screen.

WORM (Write Once Read Many)
This is a laser disc system for custom data-base creation. The user begins with a blank disc and scans or writes in any information desired, such as employee medical records, and so on. This system uses a 5.25-inch diameter disc and a different disc player and so is not compatible with CD-ROM. WORM systems now are commercially available.

Yellow book standard
See **CD-ROM.**

A LOOK FORWARD TO THE COMPANION VOLUME

APPENDIX D

Afterword

The work you hold in your hands will serve largely as a reference and a foundation for your explorations into Macintosh hypermedia. The book was written in a style I am not much accustomed to and was quite dry, formal, and even pedantic in places. It had to be. The available hypermedia information is mostly limited to the proceedings of esoteric computer conferences and the work of Ted Nelson. This work, hopefully, has begun to bridge the gap between the dryness of the conference proceedings and Nelson's illuminated, but sometimes off-the-wall, ramblings.

I continually find myself drawn to R. Buckminster Fuller's concept of synergetics[216]—the study of patterns and cooperations of elements within systems. Central to the notion of synergetics is the phenomenon of state change, that point reached when the cooperating elements of a system begin to behave differently, signifying a new mode or condition. Jerry Daniels and Mary Jane Mara have pointed out the relevance of synergetics to HyperCard stackware development and marketing.[217] The state change soon to be reached in hypermedia promises to result in a paradigm shift; our traditional ways of perceiving and working with data, information, and knowledge has rapidly begun to change.

This book serves to lay the groundwork for a second, companion volume, *Macintosh Hypermedia Volume II,* to be available concurrently from Scott, Foresman and Company. Where the first volume covered the energy event and the phase transition of the synergetic process, Volume II will address the order parameter event and actual state change leading to the information paradigm shift. Where *Macintosh Hypermedia* was mostly a history and philosophy book intended to have long-term appeal as a reference source, the second volume will have a more approachable, "hands-on" tone. It will focus on the "real-world" uses and applications for hypermedia and will refer the reader back to this volume for more information on the theoretical and historical aspects of hypermedia.

The second half of the hypermedia equation (the software is the first half) lies in the availability of appropriate development, storage, and distribution media and hardware tools. *Macintosh Hypermedia Volume II* will investigate the available and almost-available hypermedia delivery vehicles.

NOTES

[216] R. Buckminster Fuller and E. J. Applewhite, *Explorations in the Geometry of Thinking: Synergetics* (New York: MacMillan Publishing, 1975).

[217] Jerry Daniels and Mary Jane Mara, *Applied HyperCard: Developing and Marketing Superior Stackware* (New York: Brady Books, 1988).

INDEX